Durgacharan Rakshit was born in 1854, at Khantura, Gobordanga, in the district of Nadia (West Bengal). It is said that his ancestors had migrated from Saptagram in Hooghly district. Later the Rakshit family set up a large business of ghee and sugar in Kolkata, in Burabazar. Durgacharan was sent to a Sanskrit school in Varanasi. He completed the unfinished work of Bipin Behari Chakraborti, *The History of Khantura* and *Kushdeep* in 1901. After this, he toured across India and wrote his famous travelogue *Bharat Pradakshin*, in 1903. He also wrote *The Relation of Tambuli Community* (1901), *Tambuli Merchant* (1901), *The Vaishyas of Bengal* (1903). In 1906 he handed over his business to his sons and moved permanently to Varanasi. There he established a school for girls, Durgacharan Girls' School. He was one of the pioneers of the Bangiyo Sahitya Samaj. Durgacharan passed away in 1938.

Dr Sarbani Putatunda was a teacher at East Calcutta Girls College. She is a Shakespeare scholar and has several academic papers to her credit which have been published in both national and international journals. She has also authored, translated and edited several books. After her superannuation, she is simultaneously working for the welfare of rural communities in West Bengal and continuing with her passion of writing.

JOURNEYS ACROSS INDIA

Durgacharan Rakshit

Translated by
Sarbani Putatunda

SPEAKING TIGER

SPEAKING TIGER BOOKS LLP
125A, Ground Floor, Shahpur Jat, near Asiad Village,
New Delhi 110049

First published by Speaking Tiger Books 2024

All illustrations courtesy Subhasish Das,
except when mentioned otherwise

ISBN: 978-93-5447-628-0
eISBN: 978-93-5447-630-3

10 9 8 7 6 5 4 3 2 1

Typeset by SÜRYA, New Delhi
Printed at Impressions Printing & Packaging Ltd., Noida

CONTENTS

WEST

SOUTH

'Without affection no sight will appear worth seeing'

It is well known that Bangalis (including this one) are inordinately fond of travelling. Witness the mass exodus from cities and towns during Durga Puja and other holidays. We are equally fond of travelogues, which have been a popular genre for a very long time. I am a great fan of travelogues myself, especially when they provide insights into the history and culture of a region.

It was delightful, therefore, to come across a travel book written more than a hundred years ago. Durgacharan Rakshit, born in 1854, was a scholarly and spiritual man. His great grandsons give us some idea of his life in the Foreword and Introduction to this book. You could say that Rakshit was the average educated, middle-class householder of the time, except for two things. He decided to travel the length and breadth of India, quite literally; more remarkably, he observed keenly and chronicled his travels in accounts that were published in periodicals of the time. These accounts were then compiled into a book, *Bharat Pradakshin*, that received a great deal of critical acclaim.

As an aside, I remember fondly that a group of us were able to do our very own Pradakshina more than three decades ago. We filmed a TV series, travelling from Gomukh to Ganga Sagar. That project showed me that travel is much more than a hobby. It can transform the way you view life.

The current generation of Durgacharan's extended family

must be commended for reviving interest in their ancestor's work by embarking on an English translation of his journals. This was no easy task, as the translator, Sarbani Putatunda's Preface will tell you. Prose Bangla was still in its formative stage when the book was written. To decipher and translate it required a great deal of fortitude and research.

Bharat Pradakshin or *Journeys Across India* will take you to places where standard history books seldom go—to the life and times of ordinary people and extraordinary places more than a century ago.

Dhritiman Chaterji
Kolkata/Goa
2024

Foreword

My appreciation of this noble effort to bring to light a long-lost significant work of my great grandfather Sri Durgacharan Rakshit.

Commenting on the work by me shall be superfluous for a number of reasons. Firstly, when the original work was being published part by part in various Bengali periodicals, there were ample observations, comments and appreciations in the form of reviews which appeared in those and other periodicals of the time. Moreover, the respected translator has touched upon every aspect of his work in the preface. Lastly, given my limited experience in literary appreciation, my eligibility is in question. What I would venture here is to introduce Sri Durgacharan Rakshit, the person, to the readers.

Durgacharan Rakshit was born of Srimati Nabinmani Rakshit and Sri Umesh Chandra Rakshit on 9 October 1854 (24 Ashwin 1261 in the Bengali calendar). That was the year Umesh chandra started Durga Puja in his home in Khantura, West Bengal. Hence, the newborn was named Durgacharan.

From his early childhood, Durgacharan was very gentle and quiet in nature. Playfully he used to imitate puja rituals and loved to worship idols of Lord Shiva made by himself with clay. He started learning Sanskrit at the age of eleven. His Sanskrit teacher, Sri Bamandev Bhattacharya resided in his student's residence. Durgacharan did not merely take lessons from him, but kept him company throughout the day. This imparted an exposure to religious literature and spiritual discourse and practices. As a result, he developed into an ethical man with spiritual inclinations. Patience and restraint were his natural traits. He engaged himself in every work with deep concentration. Durgacharan avoided comforts and undertook penance to prepare himself for any adversity that may come his way. He strictly followed a regular routine in his daily life and did not allow this routine to be disturbed even on special occasions or celebrations. It is said that all his noble deeds are not fully revealed to us as he was deeply introverted, and never craved for appreciation from any quarter*.

His spiritual inclination made him disinterested in marriage and he intended to devote his life to sadhana by becoming a sanyasi. However, his parents did not agree and he was compelled to marry and begin a family life. He also looked after his father's business and set an example on how to run a successful business without deceit and unscrupulous practices. In spite of such compromise and deviations from his inner spiritual urge, Durgacharan continued to pursue the study of philosophy and spiritual discourses. Apart from Bengali and Sanskrit, he also became well-versed in English. He authored several books in Bengali. Among them, *Tambul Banik* needs special mention as it is an anthropological study that encapsulates and reflects upon the socio-economic history of the Tambuli merchants till that period.

He worked incessantly for the spread of education, and to honour his desire to promote women's education, his eldest son established Durgacharan Girls' School in Varanasi in 1924. After the introduction of Secondary Education in the country, it was renamed Durgacharan Girls' Inter-college. It is on the verge of celebrating its centenary in 2024.

I have gathered from my elders that several pandits of Varanasi were regular visitors who came to him for discussion on the shastras. In his later years, when his vision was impaired,

---

* Referred in *Jeeban Prasanga: Kushdweep Kahini* by Bipin Bihari Chakraborty.

he arranged to listen to topics of his choice through appointed readers. His liberal bent of mind becomes apparent from his unpublished writings as he reflects on the changes that are bound to take place in religion and society with the passage of time. He frankly and openly practised self-introspection to constantly develop as a better mortal. Sri Durgacharan Rakshit passed away on 21 February 1938 (8 Falgun 1344).

I am thankful to every person who has contributed to this wonderful work of translation. It is hard to realize the tremendous efforts that must have gone in to bring out the true nuances of the age-old Bengali narrative in English. I thank every person who conceived the idea, who took the responsibility to translate, who provided insights and information, who printed, edited, and published *Journeys Across India*. I hope the work will enrich many interested readers.

Atonu Rakshit
2024

Introduction

About Durgacharan Rakshit

Durgacharan Rakshit (DCR) is my maternal great grandfather, born in 1854, near Calcutta. The ancestors of his father, Umesh Chandra Rakshit, had migrated from their roots in Saptagram in the wake of the Bagri attacks (the Maratha Expeditions 1741-51) which had led to widespread economic losses besides instilling a sense of deep fear in the people of Bengal.

As a young child of seven years, he was sent to Kashi (Varanasi) to learn Sanskrit, guided by an enlightened scholar, Bipin Behari Chakroborty. His curiosity about life, in the universal sense, probably got triggered during this phase. Later he even completed some of the unfinished writings of his *mastermoshai*.

At some point after returning from Varanasi, DCR joined the family business started by his father in 1848 in Calcutta. 'Shree Ghee' celebrated 175 years in 2023; it is a brand which continues to flourish and is currently managed by the seventh generation.

The rare establishment of an industrial venture by a Bengali *bhadrolok* was appreciated by several luminaries. The head of the Ramakrishna Mission at Belur, Rabindranath Tagore at Shantiniketan, Subhash Chandra Bose, Jagdish Chandra Bose are just some of these giants who strode around the time of DCR.

DCR's curiosity as a Seeker must have led him to undertake his journeys across India. The first line of his travelogue: *A storm arose at the confluence of River Ganga and Bay of Bengal. The sailors let down the sail and I went to the top deck of the ship to view the terrifying beauty of nature* is probably sufficient to harness the attention of a reader. His first stop was on the banks of River Mahanadi in Orissa, then called Udro.

It is said that his journeys happened in four parts and were spread over eighteen years, during which he travelled to the East, North, West and South. A good guess about the exact years of the travels would be ranging between 1875-1900. He used various modes of transport like ships, steamers, rafts, boats, ox carts, *ghoragari* (horse-drawn carriages), *palki*, steam trains and even elephant-drawn carriages! And, of course, he must have walked a lot too. It is also significant to mention that considering camera was introduced in India only in 1855, he had put together almost twenty beautifully poignant half-tone pictures. What camera did he use, and how did he ferry it across the subcontinent are questions for which there are no certain answers.

I was intrigued to read the travelogue ever since my Chotomama gave me a faded photocopy while we sat around our Calcutta home grieving the passing of my Ma, in September 2002. It was lying with me, till Sarbani appeared at our Ranikhet home to reconnect with childhood school friends in 2019, and took up the challenge to translate the document—so that we could all read it!

The travelogue soon became an obsession as Sarbani emailed the first chapter. It was apparent that the journal, while brilliantly describing every blade of grass across the Indian subcontinent, also revealed the depths of our ancestor's mind. It was almost like reading his soul as he wrote his thoughts about the ecological diversity of the land and her people, temple architecture, religion, literature, governance, music, food and culture so very vividly. But ultimately, it is a treatise about the country in the late nineteenth century. It is also unique that not a word on politics finds space in his voluminous diaries. But then such were the times, when people could hold views and yet not necessarily agitate others, like in modern times.

DCR is said to have left Calcutta after handing over the reins of the family business in 1906 at the age of fifty-two, to more or less live in Kashi. It could be safely assumed he had sufficient time to dedicate himself to his thoughts and writings, besides initiating significant charitable and social activities. He pioneered the Bangiyo Sahitya Samaj which promoted literature. He also established the Durgacharan Girls' School, which is celebrating its centenary in 2024. DCR passed on in 1938, at the age of eighty-four in Kashi. He left behind a rich legacy of thoughts and actions which we are now attempting to 'document' for posterity.

Reading the book today, we see how he sees, feels, smells as he traverses the wide open country with a unique mix of ecosystems and people. For him this journey meant everything, as it was the first time he had left home as a young man. He documented everything, from the physical to the metaphysical! Sometimes much too much of the latter, but then DCR seems to have been a scholar, as well as an eminently successful businessman-philosopher.

DCR's diaries are somewhat like Walt Whitman's *Song of Myself*. Though it describes in minute details life and times in India almost 200 years ago, the main focus is always on the spirituality of nature and the relevance of universal reality. It is certainly an important piece of literature regarding the depths of our roots.

Our family is indeed grateful for the kindness of people from the world of books who have been responsible for bringing forth this book in its present form. Firstly, Sarbani Putatunda who had to replace her jaw many times while translating the old Bangla language; Neeta Gupta, who encouraged me and also introduced the translation to Ravi Singh of Speaking Tiger, who in turn immediately thought about a much wider readership than just our extended family. Finally, thanks to Sudeshna

Shome Ghosh, who edited it so that it could be published under the flag of Speaking Tiger.

Very little is known of DCR and we hope more of those who know of him will tell us some nuggets about his life. However, this much is known that he read a lot, wrote a lot and of course, he travelled. This book is a testimony to his wandering days. And, quite a few of us have that particular genetic heritage thriving in us!

Finally, the last word on DCR is best pronounced by the man himself in the final paragraph of *Journeys Across India*:

My first journey across the country had begun with a sea voyage...the conclusion too involved another sea voyage. Now I started feeling cold. In southern India we did not need to take out our warm clothes. On the left we could see the land. This is the confluence of Gangasagar—the land of Kapil Muni. He had propounded the theories of modern logic; he was also the founder of Tantra. No wonder he is considered to be the confluence of the Vaishnavas and the Nayikas. This is the right place for the liberation of our ancestors. Today is Makar Sankranti. After many days it was sheer bliss to be back in my motherland.

Kalyan Paul
Ranikhet
Makar Sankranti 2024

Translator's Introduction

Even though we do not know much about the personal achievements of the author, we can well surmise from his writings, that he was an outstanding scholar. Had it been a mere travelogue, the book would not have seen three editions within a span of few years. He went round the country, observed every bit of it and presented a graphic picture of India. Whether it be the natural beauty, the people, the social customs, the religious trends, or even linguistic aspects of the local tongue, his knowledge seems to be all pervasive. This is really a remarkable feature of the book.

For instance, when he talks about a local language, he measures it in terms of the Old Germanic tongue which the Aryans had brought with them. How far they were similar or how much they deviated, etc. Clearly, he was a multi-dimensional scholar knowledgeable in various fields of learning. Another aspect of the book is an in-depth study of Indian philosophy. Since he was well conversant both in Bengali and Sanskrit, it was easy for him to talk about Vedas, Upanishads, Advaita philosophy at one go. But as a translator it was an uphill task for me to go into the nuances of these distinctions and record them authentically.

He was a great thinker, a man who had an insight into the details of everything he undertook. The book, as the title indicates, is his personal experiences, which he gathered while touring the nooks and corners of our country. While translating, what impressed me most was his insight. He visited a place, even though as a tourist, yet he took in everything he came across. He saw the people, studied their customs like an anthropologist, paid great attention to their language like a linguist and finally reflected upon everything he saw. Sociology, anthropology, linguistics, and philosophy all combined in one.

When my good friend Mr Kalyan Paul approached me with a request to translate this voluminous work, I was very happy to comply. But as I proceeded, I knew that I had unknowingly undertaken a herculean task. First of all, because of its volume, and second was its language. My friends who are masters in Bengali language were aghast at the difficulty in penetrating each word, leave aside each sentence. Some words were not to be traced even in the dictionaries. The reason for such impenetrability they pointed out was simple—the language Mr Rakshit was using was at its formative stage—just emerging on its own capacity as prosaic Bengali. Prior to him possibly no one else had dared to compile such a travelogue in pure Bangla. On many occasions I found words which were straightaway derived from its mother language Sanskrit. So, the reader can well imagine the immensity of labour I had to put in to understand what each word actually wanted to convey.

For instance, the very opening chapter of the book is titled Udro. Now no dictionary offered me the exact meaning of the word Udro. So, I appealed to a good friend of mine Dr Mitali Bhattacharjee to explicate the meaning of Udro. Scratching her head for some time she said, 'Well Udro is the ancient Bangla for Orissa.' And then when I went back to the chapter, I knew she was absolutely right. Such incidents took place frequently and I must confess, Mitali's immense love for me and infinite patience helped me overcome such unexpected hurdles. Mitali herself, being an authority of Bangla and linguistics, may have found pleasure in dealing with such linguistic intricacies. I do not dare to question her further on this matter, though.

What also amazed me was that one, despite its tough exterior and formidable language, this book was reprinted thrice even in contemporary times. Two, the book's old-world flavor. There are places mentioned in the book which are not to be found now. Many temples and buildings were there during his time but are not there now. Even our history does not mention anything about these places. Were they lost? Or was it due to our indifference towards preserving our heritage that these buildings were destroyed? I have no clue. Three, his comparative approach. Wherever he went, Mr Rakshit studied the place thoroughly and kept comparing it with other parts of the country. This is indeed a novel finding. We are told that comparative study is a recent development, and it is altogether a different field of study. Yet, here was a man who had unknowingly undertaken a research work of comparison.

Finally, after a year's labour, I must admit candidly that *Bharat Pradakshin* has really taken me to places which I would never ever visit even in my wildest dreams. I hope the reader will share my astonishment while going through the book.

Reviews from the Previous Editions

Prabashi (1905): The author of the present book has shown his adeptness in minute observation while travelling and that has made his record highly interesting. The book both educates and entertains us. There is no unnecessary poetic description but is full of interesting information. For all practical purpose the book provides us an insight into the variety of culture, attires, social customs, castes, races, and societies existing in our country.

Nabyabharat (1905): A part of this book was published in *Nabyabharat* and gave the readers an inkling to the author's interesting and simple writing style. One comes to know many things from reading the book. Language is lucid and it is expected that the book will be appreciated by all.

Kushdah (1914): Even though a travelogue, the book in itself is a scholarly study on various subjects. The scholar has discussed many subjects and it is not necessary that the readers agree with his opinions, but the way he has risen above orthodoxy of existing society and made objective reflections is really commendable. Reading the book is not only a pleasurable experience but is intellectually enriching. Orthodox people will not be offended by his observations, it is true, but will be enriched intellectually.

Janmabhoomi (1913): Essays like Andhra, Kalidipalli, Sea etc. were previously written in *Janmabhoomi*. The readers of *Janmabhoomi* were thus previously familiar with Durga

Charan Babu's wonderful narration. The book gives a graphic description of all important places of our country along with the specialties of each region, language, culture, religion, attire, and everything. That travelling and visiting places can be both enlightening and educative, is made amply clear in the book.

Suprabhat (1915): Written in simple and lucid language the descriptions are really very attractive.

The Amrita-Bazar Patrika (1912): Topographical accounts are generally interesting, but the accounts given in these pages have a relish of its own, while the simple style of its author has added a peculiar charm to the work. Besides the descriptions of the places the author had to travel, he touched on many other points, such as historical, religious, social and even philosophical, treating these subjects with a wide knowledge. It is to be admitted that the learned author appears to have tried his best to enrich this work with various information, and he has been successful in his aim to a very great extent.

The Bengalee (1912): Babu Durga Charan Rakshit, it appears to us from a perusal of his book, was not only a keen observer of his surrounding wherever he went; he studied objects, animate or inanimate, with the eye of a critic.

East

Orissa

(Udro)

A storm arose at Ganga Sagar, where River Ganga flows into the Bay of Bengal. The sailors let down the sail and I went to the top deck of the ship to view the terrifying beauty of nature. The ship was rolling fiercely, and I felt a churning inside me. So, I went to my cabin and lay down. After some time, I started vomiting and my body went limp. A person came and said, 'Move your hand from the pathway.' Unable to move, I suggested, 'Move it yourself.' It was impossible for me to even lift my hand. Till now, I had only read poetic descriptions of the sea but today I saw what the sea actually was. In the morning the sea had been so beautiful and quiet.

The sparkling sunrays reflecting on the fast-flowing blue waters created a magnificent sight. Like a poet had once said, it was as if 'someone had whisked and poured ambrosia/ upon the blue physique of Lord Krishna.' But I couldn't enjoy the beauty for long when the confluence of three rivers opened up a new vista for me. We had already reached the shore and I mounted a cow-driven cart. There is a temple at Padampur, built by Dabisha. He had worshipped Lord Shankar, asking him not to bless him with a male heir because he knew his heir would boast and claim the ownership of the temple.

Crossing the long sandy bank of Mahanadi and travelling down the midpoint of the city of Cuttack, I reached the inn where I was going to stay. In the city still stands the great wall[1]

1. Around a fort about which he talks next

constructed by Markat Keshari, to protect it against floods and enemies. The outer part of the fort is dilapidated and almost in ruins. Yet, I found British soldiers still guarding it diligently. While loitering around, I came across a village inhabited by weavers from Telangana.

Orissa is situated between Bengal and Telangana. The people of Orissa resemble the Bengalis in their habits and customs. Maybe the rulers of Utkal[2] were south Indians. Even the rulers of the Sen dynasty of Bengal had clear connections with Karnataka. In fact, it was through Cuttack that the Dravidians reached Bengal. The custom of the brahmins to be clean shaven with a small tuft of hair on the scalp (which incidentally is never cut) is probably an indication of their Dravidian link.

I followed a different path altogether instead of the pilgrim spot for which I had come all the way. It was getting dark, and I was sure that I had taken the correct path. Yet, I couldn't arrive at my destination. Clearly, I had lost my sense of direction. To worsen the situation, the wind was harsh, and I kept brushing against branches of trees and creepers in the dark. There were very few people around who were interested to talk to me and provide any assistance. I had money with me, hence I, too, did not dare to be overtly friendly with anyone and tell them about my destination. Finally, out of desperation, I thought of trusting some men and asking them the right path. The men I approached happened to be two fishermen, who helped me reach the inn where my servant was waiting for me with my luggage. I knew I would never meet these fishermen again, yet, out of sheer gratitude and affection I enquired their names and addresses.

Next morning, I commenced my journey from the city named Mokam. By two o'clock in the afternoon, I reached a mango orchard where I espied several temples. It reminded me

2. Orissa—an old form of address

of Varanasi, and I was ecstatic. I bathed in the Bindu Sarovar and then accompanied by Bikhari Mahapatra, my tour guide, I went to see the Koti (crore) Lingeshwar temple. Bhubaneswar resembles Kedareshwar of Varanasi but is situated at a higher altitude. I returned to my shelter and feasted on Karmavai dhoop[3], which the temple priest (panda) had provided. But both the vegetable curry and the sweets were horrible in taste. The panda wanted to share the food from my plate since that is the custom here. I have observed a similar practice in case of the prasad[4] served at the Jagannath temple of Puri. Likewise, in Telangana too, while consuming the rice prasad served at the Venkatram temple, one does not observe any caste barriers. In the Dravidian temples of Vishnu at Kanchi, Srirangam, and also at the Meenakshi temple situated at Mathurapuri, rice balls made by brahmins are sold to people. To completely ignore the prevailing caste system, however, is a specialty of Puri. Hence, to consider the system as an impact of Buddhism is not totally incorrect. Just as the remnant of a river exists in the form of one or two tributaries, similarly a few old customs still prevail in some societies and the above practice is a manifestation of an ancient custom.

In order to avoid the heat, I did not go round Bhubaneswar, rather preferred to enter a temple. The architecture of the Bhubaneswar temple is similar to the four-hundred-year-old Kardameshwar temple situated at Panchkroshi, a place one comes across while visiting Varanasi. But this temple appears to be taller and larger than most temples of northwestern India. However, compared to the temples of south India, it is not that big. It is built of soft stones. The part of the temple where food is served to the gods is constructed of such soft stones that one mistakes it to be made of clay. Consequently, a large part of the structure has been destroyed and is now held together in

3. Prasad or food that has been offered to God—here Lingeshwar possibly

4. Food offerings to the deity

the form of lumps. The temple was constructed in 1212, by King Lalatendu Keshari. Adjacent to the temple, on several balconies stand large black-coloured stone deities. The deities are exquisite to look at. Some of them are so beautiful and artistic that they look like living beings. The engraved dresses of the deities are similar to what the ancient people used to wear. There are numerous sculpted figures of gods and demons on the walls. Some of them are not only repulsive but also bear clear marks of tantric influence. Tantric practices had travelled from Kamrup (in Assam) to the Himalayas and had thereby merged with Buddhism. The figures of Mahakal, brought from Bhutan and displayed at Bhot Bagan in Calcutta, are also very fearsome to look at.

In the morning I set out for Neelachal[5] from Bhubaneswar. We had to travel through a forest where we came across people carrying stones for building houses. There were few wood cutters too, carrying wood to the nearby city. After walking for about four miles, we reached the beautiful ashram[6] of Shyamdas Babaji, at the foothills of a hilly range. Canopies of trees and creepers surrounding the ashram made the place exquisite to look at. We had our bath and were refreshed enough to climb the hill. Either because of its low height or because of the dwelling of the Khandav race there, the range is known as Khandagiri. It is divided into two parts, Udaigiri and Astagiri. We mounted Udaigiri first. After climbing a few steps, we came across a terrace, and adjacent to it stood a room. The room, the terrace and even the pillars, were all scooped out of the rocks. Traversing several other similar rooms and galleries we finally reached the last room which took our breath away.

A large two-floor high chamber stood in front of us, all carved out from the rocks. Last evening the beautiful temple of Bhubaneswar had marveled me, but today I found this

5. Ancient name for Puri

6. Hermitage

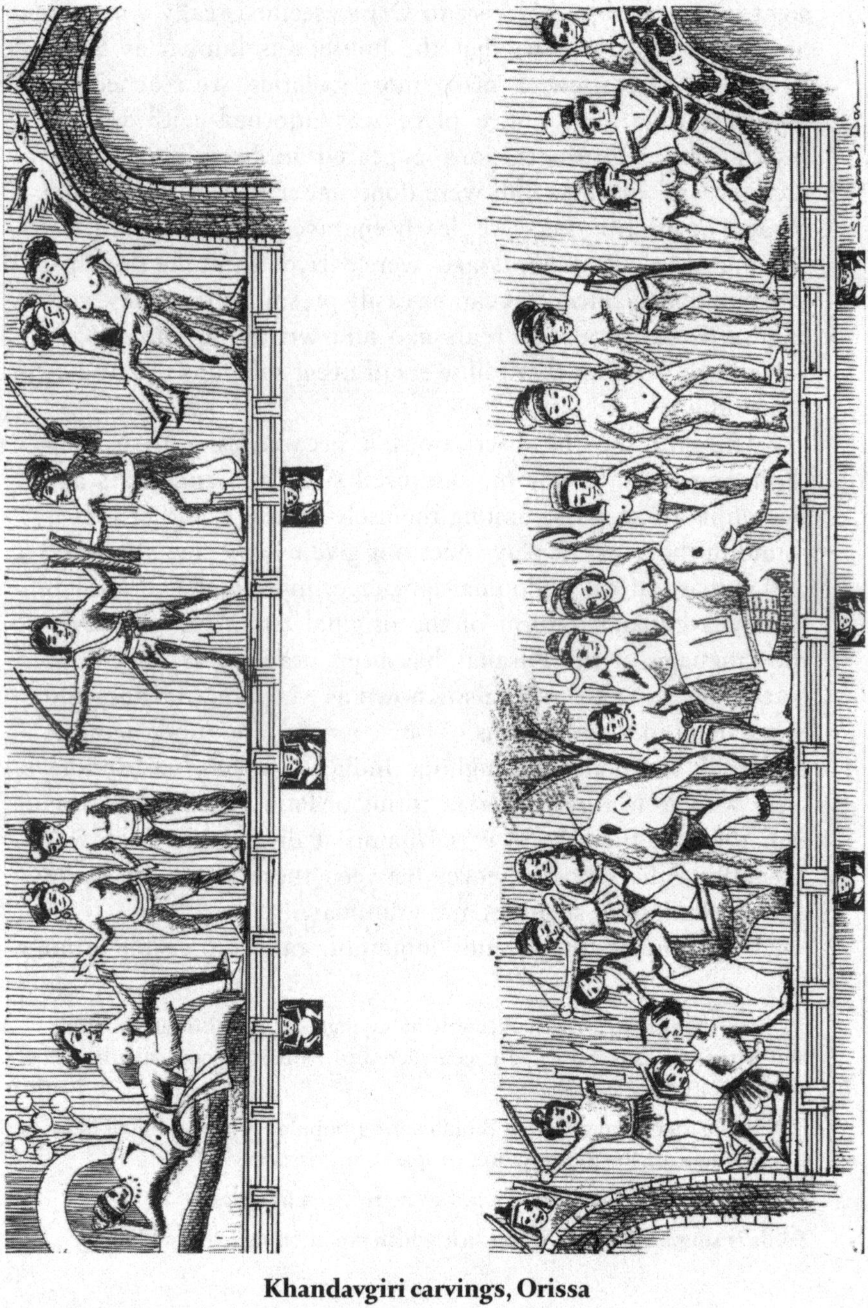

Khandavgiri carvings, Orissa

sight incomparable. My visit to Orissa seemed really worth it. Shyamdas informed me that the house was known as Ranihansapur. After viewing many more galleries, we reached the Elephant cave. The entire place was adorned with various inscriptions. The inscriptions appeared to be a part of the architectural carvings and were done under the orders of King Viraj. The inscriptions were clearly engraved under the influence of King Ashoka as the messages were derived from the Buddhist Dhammapada[7]. Hence, it can be easily presumed that they were engraved two thousand years ago and written in Pali[8]. (King Priyadarshi[9] desires that followers of other religions too, to live peacefully.)

After reading the inscriptions it became clear to us that the language in it was the one used two thousand years ago by people to converse among themselves. The Prakrit[10] that is found in the Sanskrit plays does not give us any clue about the authenticity of the colloquial language. In fact, that Prakrit is merely a corrupted form of the original Aryan tongue. Even the language of the Puranas has been branded as Prakrit by certain sages. Prakrit was also known as Marathi, Magadhi and Shoursheni in some regions of our country. The other name of Magadhi was Pali. Throughout India, Ashoka's inscriptions were written in three different forms of Pali. The first one was Punjabi Pali, the second was Ujjain(i) Pali and the third was Magadhi Pali. The differences between these forms are slight and are mainly of spellings and grammar.

Even though the Dhauli mountain range is visible from

7. The Dhammapad is a collection of sayings of Lord Buddha in verse and is most widely read and is considered to be best in popularizing the teachings of Lord Buddha

8. It is the sacred language of Buddhism—a popular version Middle Indo-Aryan language for the common people to understand

9. That was how King Asoka used to be referred at times

10. It is simplified form of Sanskrit which common people could use

Khandagiri, the inscriptions found in Dhauli were written in Ujjain(i) Pali while the inscriptions of Khandagiri were written in Magadh(i) Pali. Dhauli is within Orissa while from Khandagiri begins the borders of Kalinga.

After viewing a few more caves we proceeded to Astagiri. On entering the large Satkura cave, we found several engraved figures of Buddha in meditative pose. Shakya Muni[11] was the last of the series of Buddha. All those incarnations who came before him, are also worshipped here along with the progeny of Maya Devi[12]. But I failed to identify the figures of each Buddha. On the first floor of the building there is a newly constructed Jain temple, built by a Jain Sramana. A festival is held here every year during Maghi Purnima[13]. The priest indicated a place and said that it was an original shrine. Place three stone slabs one upon the other, within a night it will turn into a shrine. I pointed out similar other stone slabs here and there placed by different people to him and enquired why they haven't turned into a shrine.

After descending Astagiri, we visited Akash Ganga[14] and Radha Kunda. Because the deep dungeon of the hill is filled solely by rainwater, the place is called Akash Ganga[15]. After my meal I asked my servant to carry my finely woven mat and his rough one to Rani-hansapur, where I spent the night in a room where the kings and queens used to revel. Almost immediately my guide slept off.

It is really impossible to describe the construction of these ancient buildings. And even if one tries to, there is every possibility to commit some error. The house that has been

---

11. Another name for Lord Gautama Buddha

12. Mother of Lord Gautama Buddha

13. During full moon in the month of January

14. There is another Akash Ganga in the state of Bihar—Gaya

15. The pure water, like the water of River Ganga that descends from the sky, hence the name; Akash means sky

carved out of this hill looks indeed like a house, but the pillars are different. The entrance is in the eastern side with a large portico in the middle. There are three upper floors constructed on the three sides, to the west, north and south, with balconies, while there is no construction at the top of the eastern part. Maybe there was a large portal on the eastern side. On the left and right-hand sides of the portal stand two rooms extending towards north and south. The doors of these two rooms are situated on the rear side, adjacent to two temples. Figures of armed guards are carved there[16]. Almost at the end of the portico on the western side are the servants' rooms. The portico also includes two small (almost three arm's length) roofless rooms on two sides. I failed to understand their utilities since modern houses do not have rooms like these on the porticos. There are large vacant areas after these rooms both on the north and southern sides. On the western side there are several rooms which have bay windows but no balconies. There are rooms on the first floor on the western and the northern sides with large buildings in front. The southern part, however, does not have any room on the first floor. The pillars of the rooms situated on the first floor of the western side have almost been destroyed, even though the roof has remained intact. My guide informed me that the pillars were deliberately destroyed by the British, five or six years ago.

All the external parts of both the pillars and buildings of Rani-hansapur are decorated with wonderful carvings of flowers, creepers and men and women. I found a funny engraving of a poet carving out his poem with a battle-axe. The more I looked at it the more I laughed to myself. There was also the engraving of a herd of mad elephants fighting a group of beautiful girls. An elephant was attacking them with raised trunk, while a lady was countering it by hurling a garland of flowers. Another lady was dragging her away, to flee

16. Probably indicating that the rooms were meant for security personnel

from there. Yet another lady was attacking the elephant with a stemmed lotus flower, while another group was fighting it empty-handed. Some of them were in front while some were at the back. There was however, only one brave man among the group of ladies who had a stick in his hand.

The engravings gave us a fair idea about the type of dresses men and women wore in those ancient times. The man wore a loincloth by tucking it tightly between his legs while his waist was covered with a piece of cloth. The upper part of his body was bare. His long hair was tied with a piece of cloth. He had a clean-shaven face and wore ornaments like a chain, earrings, and a thick bangle. The girls, however, true to their nature were adorned with various ornaments, bangles, earrings, necklace, anklets etc. Though slightly different, the girls too wore clothes which were tucked in at their waists. Their long hair was tied in plaits of various styles. A shield was engraved there and an umbrella which had a long tassel hanging from its handle. The man was bare-footed. Only the door keepers in these engravings wore leg covers which went up to their knees. It might have been due to Greek influence.

If you have a prefixed idea about something, it's easy for you to find examples to substantiate it. You can find arguments both for and against it. But in order to ascertain a truth and validate it, you have to be both skeptical and objective in your approach. Without proper logical arguments and deductions, it is really not fair to come to a definite conclusion. Ferguson had a preconceived notion that all Indian architecture was basically derived from Greek architecture. However, Mr Rajendralal Mitra very deftly refuted all his (Ferguson) arguments.

We returned in the afternoon after paying a little money to the nagging priests of Kapileshwar. Next day we reached Harekrushnapur. The roaring of the ebb and flow of the sea which was audible even at such a distance put us to sleep that night.

The sight of Puri made me languid. This is my first time

travelling outside home. A disinterested egoist person cannot make friends easily. And if he ever does make acquaintances, the relationship doesn't last long. It's only now I have come to realize the necessity of human companionship. I felt like communicating with any Bengali, whenever I came across one! One day an unknown person came up to me and said, 'Mahananda babu was enquiring about you. Since I keep visiting the market, his mother asked me whether I have come across you. And this is what she said, "Maybe he has left the place by now or else he would have come here again. But he appeared really sad without a companion".' The words struck a delicate chord in my heart and for a moment I felt the love of a mother's heart.

Expectedly one ought to enjoy visiting new places. But to really enjoy travelling, one should have a coloured glass to view the world around him. Without it the world will not appear novel at all. I prefer terming the view through a coloured glass as affection. Without affection no sight will appear worth seeing. And because of the absence of this affection our everyday world doesn't strike us as something unique. But in a new place if you have the required mindset, you will enjoy even the trivialities as something unusual. Unfortunately, I have lost the coloured glass, and hence been deprived of the pleasures of sightseeing.

In order to interact with the sea, it is necessary to visit its shore every day. Accordingly, every day, following the tracks of the crabs escaping into the sea, I got into the water. And when the sky touched the coastland, I ran back towards the shore. A few waves then approached me to wash my feet and make me laugh. On the seashore in a sandy house lived a Bengali poet Nabinchandra Sen. When I met him, I begged him to recite a few lines from (his noted work) *Palashir Juddhya*[17], particularly

17. Translated as *The Battle of Palassay*, a noted patriotic poetic work in Bengali which won the wrath of the British imperialists at that point of time. It was composed by Nabinchandra Sen, considered to be one of Bengal's great poets, prior to Rabindranath Tagore.

the lines uttered by Mohanlal in the poem. The poet informed me that he belonged to East Bengal[18], and accordingly started reciting the following lines:

Where goest thou, look back O thousand radiant rays.
Look back for once O Sun.
O God if you set,
A melancholic dark night will descend upon Bharat (India).
In such a melancholic state,
Don't leave Bharat, O Sun.
What sight was it that had made you rise in Bengal?
Now what is the sight that is compelling you to set?
Completing only half of your revolution,
How is it possible to restore the fate of half the world?

The poet continued reciting the lines with a glowing face and both the audience and the poet appeared deeply immersed in the beauty of the poem. 'Bhudev babu had shed tears on hearing these lines,' said the author. Enjoying the sublimity of a poetic work is one of the two important fruits our material world offers us. I met Nabinchandra Sen again while attending a marriage party. He appeared radiant, like the sun, oozing out poetry by his sheer presence. He kept reciting lines from poems in different languages. After that Annapurna from Ganjam began her performance with a Sanskrit sloka and then went on to sing a song in her native dialect. She was accompanied by different instrumentalists who played the sarangi, tabla, cymbals and bagpipes. But when one of the instrumentalists started singing, we were extremely annoyed. After the performance, the host invited us to take the prasad that was being served to the guests. But because I was not inclined to participate in social functions here, I thought of opting out of dinner, where caste rules were

18. At present Bangladesh. In undivided India that part of the land was known as East Bengal. The people dwelling there spoke Bengali in a different dialect. Hence, it was necessary to inform the author about his native land

not being observed.[19]

The groom set out on a palanquin to get married. There was a large tray full of betel leaves placed before him and two dancing girls held the two sides of the palanquin. This may have been a custom they had adopted from their neighboring Andhra Pradesh. A few people also have sword players displaying their skills before the groom, while he travels in a palanquin.

I met the poet once again when I visited the Puri's Jagannath temple for the Lord's bathing ritual. He was wearing a red-coloured flower garland round his head and when he saw me, he pointed to a building and said, 'this is the freedom pavilion'. But readers don't confuse it with Dinabondhu's *Freedom Pavilion.*[20]

The idols of Lord Jagannath, Balarama and Subhadra along with the Sudarshan Chakra were taken out in a procession. Both the Sudarshan Chakra and Subhadra were carried by men on top of their heads while Lord Jagannath and Balarama had to walk their ways. A cord was tied to their waists and dragged in front while a person followed them from behind thereby maintaining a balance. A margosa tree (*Azadirachta indica*, also known as neem tree) dressed as a human figure was being carried by him, and it appeared to me like a person dancing with the crowd. This journey is known as the Pandava Vijay (victory of the Pandavas). People in places were tearing off the covering of the margosa tree. At another place people were worshipping the lord with lighted lamps. A person carrying an earthen pot filled with lighted coconut husks was walking in front. The din of cymbals, drums, bugles, and the loud cheers of the crowd reverberated all around the sacred place. It clearly heralded the affluence of the Chatra and Udani festivals.

Fifty priests and attendants led the procession. A person

19. Clearly the author was quite caste conscious, like many others of the time

20. A noted work in Bengali literature

flaunting two pieces of cane was whipping the air around him. When I asked him what he was trying to do, he replied that it was his way of serving the lord. The dais where the lord was taken for his bath was covered at the top. Inside the temple a draw well was created, filled the previous day with hundred and eight pitchers of water. This site was known as the greatest pilgrimage. Today it was worshipped elaborately with sixteen offerings. The head priest was present there and his status was clearly established by his immaculate white headgear and white dress. The common people of Orissa do not use headgears. The head priest represents the king and conducts all religious festivals such as this one. It was he who first poured water drawn from the well upon Lord Jagannath and immediately there arose the deafening noise of hailing the lord by the devotees. They then offered flowers to the deity. Then the other priests followed suit and bathed the lord. The temple singers fanned the deity and sang devotional songs in praise of the lord.

Following the Dravidian architectural style, the temple of Lord Jagannath is surrounded by a boundary made of two large stones. The stones are 450 arm's length, and the width is 436 arm's length. The Srirangam temple of Tiruchirappalli is situated after seven gateways. The specialty of the temple of Orissa is its pyramid-like structure at the top, with a wide and circular courtyard. The topmost part of the temples of Varanasi are similarly circular in appearance but they are not as high as this one. It was clear that architecturally temples keep varying from one region to another. But there is some similarity between the Dravidian structure of the dining space and the dining space of Lord Jagannath's temple. Like the Meenakshi Temple of Madurai, the main entry gate of this temple is situated on the eastern side. Near it stands the lotus ground (Padma Kshetra) brought from Konark, and the Sun Pillar. After entering the main gateway, one comes across the deity of Patitpavan consecrated by Sri Chaitanya, and then one has to climb twenty steps. On the north stands the bathing space of

Lord Jagannath, to the left of which is a small pond and the Kashi Visweshara's temple. In the huge kitchen there is the oven where food is being cooked in earthen vessels. Large vessels stand at the bottom while smaller vessels are placed at the top cooking rice and vegetables simultaneously for Lord Jagannath. At Ananda bazar customers taste the food and buy it as prasad. Inside the second enclosure there are numerous temples of Nrisingha, Surya, Shiva, Parvati, Lakshmi and others. In order to provide different services, different rooms made of stones, are assigned such as—panthi, bhetmandap, chun-kuta dwar etc. At the center of the courtyard there is a large temple for different deities, moulded from crushed stones. The deities are anointed with sandalwood paste. The temple is 100 arm's long, 45 arm's-length wide and 126 arm's-length in height.

The temple is divided into four parts—the sanctum sanctorum, the middle part, the Jagmohan or the hall, and the dining space. There is a jewelled stand called Ratna Singhasan made of black stone inside the sanctum sanctorum on which stands the idol of Lord Jagannath. There stands an obscene figure in front of the temple which really puts people to shame. Six hundred and ninety-two years ago, the temple was constructed by the valiant king Gajapati Anaga Bhim, ruler of Gaur, Karnataka and Utkal. He was from Karnataka. His ancestors came from Karnataka and established their kingdom in Orissa. And because their kingdom extended to Tamluk (part of Bengal) they were also called the kings of Bengal.

After cooking my meal and eating it in the afternoon, I lay down on the stony floor of the Jagmohan. So many sinners visit the deity daily confessing their sins and surrendering themselves to the lord by way of unburdening their minds. A person stood in front of the idol of Garuda, and glancing towards the sanctum sanctorum called out to the lord in Oriya and narrated his sufferings. The loud sonorous voice of the priest and other temple servers boomed all around. Some were busy talking to the visitors. The kitchen employees with covered mouths were busily carrying large containers of prasad through a secret passage that was specifically meant for the purpose. It is said that even if there are millions of people here lined up to get prasad in the temple, there will never be a dearth of it! Out of the various food offerings throughout the day, are the ballabhog[21], the khichuri dhoop, sandhya dhoop, and barashingar dhoop.[22] The offerings during the second part of the day seem to be more sumptuous.

Both in and around the city of Puri, when people arrange feasts or banquets, they send food items to the temple to acquire the required amount of prasad for their guests. No other temple of the country has a system of offering such a huge amount of food to the deity. From that standpoint, Sri Kshetra (Puri) appears unique. Even the Padmanabha temple of Travancore appears rather small compared to this arrangement at Lord Jagannath's temple of Puri. Under the immense banyan tree here, childless women spread the ends of their saris and sit expectantly, waiting for some fruits to drop, which they will then consume.

The entire temple premise consists of several entry points or gates. On the northern part is the Antara gateway. Entering there, one comes across a confinement room named Vaikuntha[23]. It is situated on the first floor. Nearby, stands an almost rotting figure of the deity carved out from the trunk of a margosa tree. Lord Jagannath had to assume new forms twice, during the Muslim invasions. During the invasion of Raktabahu, Lord Jagannath had gone underground. And Kalapahar, a Muslim, had forced Raju, a brahmin, to light a pyre and cremate Him.

Just as the architecture of Lord Jagannath's temple indicates south Indian influence, likewise certain customs observed in

21. Food that is offered

22. Names of the food offerings in different parts of the day. Dhoop here refers to prasad

23. Supposed to be heaven

worshipping the deity seem to be derived from south India as well. For instance, the Devadasis or the temple dancers of Puri have their counterparts in the south Indian temples where they are called Kanchani. They take part in singing and dancing when festivals are held at the temple. The Chandan Yatra[24] of Lord Jagannath is actually a south Indian temple festival. Just like in south Indian temples where a small replica of the deity undertakes this journey, here in Jagannath temple too, small replicas of the deities undertake the journey. The replicas are named as follows—Madan Mohan, Ramakrishna, Nrisingha and Dol Govinda. Subhadra is represented by a golden figure called Sree and a silver figure called Bhudevi. Even though Subhadra is known to be the sister of Lord Jagannath in Indian mythology, here Sree and Bhudevi are two forms of Goddess Lakshmi. Hence, here Subhadra seems to have assumed the form of Lord Jagannath's wife. In the month of Baishakh[25] every year on the third day after the new moon, the replica idols are taken on a chariot to a lake called Narendra Sarovar. There the replicas reside either in a house or in a boat for twenty days surrounded by water on all sides. A high chariot called Telepakkam is used for a similar purpose in the Shaivite and Vaishnava temples of Andhra, Karnataka, and other Dravidian states. Hence, it is not necessary for us to either visit Fa Hsien's Khotan or Lord Buddha's Teeth Festival to see a chariot being driven to a water body. The south Indian chariots resemble the decorated portals of the garden house of Vrindavan Seth or gopurams[26]. The chariots are decorated with the engravings of gods and goddesses along with several obscene figures.

It will, therefore, be unfair to suggest that the figureheads of Lord Jagannath, Subhadra and Balarama have been derived

---

24. A journey undertaken after anointing the deity with sandalwood paste etc

25. the first month in a year, according to Bengali calendar—some time in mid April

26. Ornamental city gates

from Buddhism even though there are several temples of Lord Shiva and Lord Vishnu which clearly manifest an influence of Buddhism. But what is so strange about it? Buddhism is not an alien religion for us Indians. Now because it is being followed by those living in Tibet, we tend to brand it as an alien religion. Added to it, since the philosophy of Buddha is termed as Buddhism and not mere philosophy, this misconception has magnified significantly. It has grown to such monstrous extent that we are surprised to note the inclusion of Lord Buddha's name among the ten Vishnu avatars!

We can categorize our gods into three parts: the Vedic gods, the Mythic gods, and the Village gods. Lord Jagannath, Subhadra and Balarama belong to the mythic category. But my assumption is all of them have actually been derived from the old village gods of Kalinga. The surrounding villages with clear marks of South Indian influence, which has helped me to formulate this idea.

Manar-Swami and his mother Pachumma: Under the banyan tree is a half-finished small room. Inside it stands a stone idol with her face smeared with vermilion and dress smeared with turmeric. She is Pachumma, worshipped for preventing diseases. Her priest belongs to the lower caste. Clay figures of horse, elephant and ferocious looking demons are offered to Manar-Swami standing outside the room. Both Manar-Swami and Pachumma are basically supernatural spirits or demi-gods. But none of them accept animal sacrifices. However, demons like Bal, Sen, Dahod and Mrityu accept animal sacrifices. Both Marima and Putlima too, accept animal sacrifices. There are few wooden idols of other gods as well.

Lord Jagannath and his sister Subhadra: It is said that Vidyapati was sent by Indra to Bosu-Shabar's[27] house, and had a vision of Bosu-Shabar worshipping Lord Neelmadhav[28] under

27. Shabar is actually a hill tribe thriving on hunting.

28. Possibly Lord Jagannath

a banyan tree. Bosu-Shabar's son Dwaityapati continued the tradition. But later his successors split Dwaityapati's name into two parts and assumed two different titles, Dwaitya and Pati. They too continued the tradition of serving Lord Jagannath down the ages. The clan originating from Dwaitya, still familiar as Shabar, is assigned the task of beautifying the idol of Lord Jagannath. The clan originating from Pati, elevated to the status of brahmin, worship the lord while being beautified. The name Shabar had originated from the word Shoyar and they are considered to be brahmins originating from Bal Bhadra. They are assigned to look after the utensils of the large kitchen of Lord Jagannath. A junior Shoyar cooks, while a senior Shoyar is assigned the task of making sweets and carrying the food to be offered to the lord.

The ancient sculpture of the deity may have been rather frightful in appearance. On seeing a stone sculpture of a human skull near Titicaca lake at Tiahuanaco (now Tiwanaku), a child had once enquired 'Father, is it the face of Lord Jagannath'. Even in the Dravidian land when one comes across the monstrous figure of a demon resembling a tiger, one is reminded of Lord Jagannath, godhead of Kalinga. The secret name of Lord Jagannath is Dadhivaman.

The Bhosle dynasty from Nagpur had procured the ownership of the temple of Lord Jagannath from the British imperialists. And then in order to prevent the process of conversion by the Christian missionaries, the temple was handed over to the King of Kurdah. Recently, 'the living Vishnu' royalty of the said family has been exiled for life on charges of homicide.

The annual expenditure of the temple is about 32,000 rupees. The items required for constructing the chariot of Lord Jagannath is supplied by the head of Purushottam Math. And Math enjoys the benefit of owning a zamindari for the purpose. Once, to view the festival of Nabakalebaur[29] both the head

29. Reinstalling the newly carved idol of Lord Jagannath—in other words Lord Jagannath assuming new form

and a host of members of Papariya Math had come to Calcutta to visit Puri. All the religious Maths of India have a branch here. In Puri both the pandas[30] and the heads of the Maths are considered to be first-grade citizens.

Due to the fear of the ongoing epidemic of cholera I did not dare to view the idol placed inside the chariot. The memory of my sea sickness further prevented me to make any attempt either. Rather I preferred travelling from Dolopmandapsahi to Ranigunj towards Cuttack on a cow cart and viewing the different chariots—Garuda[31] Dhwaja[32], Padma[33] Dhwaja and Langal[34] Dhwaja, which were being constructed. In Cuttack we crossed Virupa and ventured into a new road. The interplay of clouds atop the Varuni Hill of the Nilgiris range was exquisite. On reaching the bank of River Karshaja, we had to wait for a long time for the boat to take us across. It was really a trial of patience for us. The distance between Puri and Calcutta is a little more than 300 miles and Baleshwar lies just in the middle.

River Subarnarekha flows down the north of Utkal[35]. But men residing slightly south of the river do not sport long hair. The residents of Jaleshwar trim their hair like the Bengali people. Some however have retained their tuft of hair on the scalp. The ladies of Danton wear bangles like the Bengalis do. Some even wear bangles made of conch shells like married Bengali ladies. It seems they have given up wearing similar looking brass bangles. This makeover of the ladies pleased me immensely. Had I not travelled by land I would not view all these subtle changes. That Orissa was fast following the footsteps of Bengal was apparent here. And I would have missed it had I voyaged on sea.

---

30. Priests and other associate workers of an Indian temple
31. Mythical Prince of birds on whom Lord Vishnu rides
32. Flag or banner—the chariot bearing the flag of Garura
33. Lotus flower
34. Plough
35. Another name for Orissa

The residents of Danton call themselves citizens of the middle land. In their primary schools Oriya is taught in first half and Bengali in the second half. The Oriya script is very similar to Telugu script, rather round in shape. And both Oriya and Telugu are written by piercing iron needles in palm leaves. But certain Oriya letters bear marked resemblance both to the Bengali alphabet and few other Devanagari scripts including Pali. Since Orissa is adjacent to Andhra Pradesh the ladies do not apply vermilion[36] on their hair partings, like their counterparts in Bengal. And their way of wearing a sari too is similar to the ladies of Andhra Pradesh. From Baleshwar onwards their dress sense is clearly influenced by the dress sense of Bengali ladies. On reaching Bilwachati, about two miles from Danton, I found their getup was entirely like the women of Bengal. Their language, however, is still Oriya with sporadic inclusion of a few Bengali words. On reaching Makrampur, about ten miles from Danton the language is Bengali with inclusion of a few Oriya loan words every now and then.

36. This is a custom followed by married women in many parts of the country

Varanasi

(Agnishtom[37] Yajna[38])

The Soma yajna that was begun by Sri Bala Shastri in the Bengali year 1286[39] on the quay of the royal temple was ongoing when we reached Varanasi. I was so elated that I immediately changed into new clothes and went to attend it. I had for long wished to view this yajna and now my wish was being fulfilled. The yajna had already begun and was going to continue for a little more than a week. Since I had missed the ceremonial beginning, I asked someone about it.

Looking at the priests sitting before the yajna fire, I was transported to an ancient world. The entire scenario—the houses, the mandap[40], the chariot and the lives of people came to me in a flash. It was as if ancient sages were sitting before me and singing songs from the *Sama Veda*[41]. And when the priests were leveling the ground to construct a podium for the yajna, I felt that they too were men from the ancient Vedic ages. It was as if they had not reached the Iron Age and there still didn't exist the job distribution based on caste system. The one who was conducting the yajna was playing multiple roles—of a builder and a carpenter. Aryan civilization was still a little child and had not yet reached adulthood.

The head priest, Sri Bala Shastri, and his wife were constantly present at the site. And interestingly the lady did not cover her head. She just had a red-coloured net covering the front portion

---

37. Sacrifice to the fire

38. A Vedic sacrifice

39. It was in 1880 approximately; the date mentioned in the text belongs to the Bengali almanac

40. Pavilion

41. Normally the Sama Veda contained the rituals of a yajna

of her scalp. It was clear from the sight that women were not barred from attending such functions in the ancient Vedic age.

Sri Bala Shastri was an old man, but his wife was much younger to him. She was his second wife. She was chanting the mantras assigned to her, and it was clear to me that she understood every word she uttered. Where the mantras specifically mentioned something about giving birth to a male heir she started laughing along with the priest. Off and on she drank some milk and chewed some pomegranate seeds. Even the priest ate intermittently, which, too, is a normal practice.

The manner in which the priests were feeding the fire astonished me. A hole was made in the upper part of a thick wooden stick, where a gimlet was placed. A matchstick was placed above it and tied to a string. The middle part of the wooden stick controlled the string to light the matchstick as and when required. The lit-up matchstick then ignited the fire. A few goats were brought in for sacrifice after the rituals. They were not only taken away to a secret place, but their mouths too were stuffed with betel nuts to prevent them from screaming. But what actually transpired there I really can't say because after prolonged absence when the priest returned from the goat shed, he had a stick which had the flesh of the animal stuck to it. He applied ghee to it and then put it in the fire for roasting. After being roasted, the flesh was offered as a part of the sacrifice. Both the head priest and his wife tasted a tiny morsel of the offered flesh. A Dravidian brahmin would be considered an outcaste if he consumed flesh, but in this Vedic ritual, consuming a tiny morsel is perhaps permissible.

The king paid a visit to the sacrificial site the day the fruit of soma was being offered. It looked somewhat like the drumstick. A few Maharashtrians residing here in Varanasi cultivate soma plants in flowerpots. But these soma plants do not bear leaves. It is said in the Vedas that soma plants grow well on mountain tops. Maybe because of that, when cultivated in the plains they are devoid of leaves. Or maybe these are not original soma plants, merely replicas! Offering the extract from the soma plant seems to be the most important feature of this yajna. The largest pavilion constructed at the yajna site was used for offering it.

Many more priests arrived that day to conduct the elaborate ceremony. At first, they all encircled the large pyre and started offering soma rasa to the fire from wooden tumblers they held in their hands. Then intermittently they kept drinking the soma rasa from the same wooden tumbler. In case of other sacrifices (which incidentally were not as elaborate) the priests consumed the offerings only after the conclusion of the ceremony. But in case of the soma rasa the priests could not waste even a single moment. They kept consuming it even while performing the sacrificial rituals. Clearly, they could not wait any longer. And what is more, they straightaway drank it from the very same[42] sacred tumbler they were using for the yajna! Clearly, the sages of the ancient Vedic age were confirmed drunkards.

The king, amidst the beating of a drum, offered clothes, a plate full of silver coins and a certificate of appreciation. Even though the head priest was performing the sacrifice and was not supposed to talk in any other language other than Sanskrit, he asked the coin bearer in Hindi the whereabouts of the king! Bala Shastri is undoubtedly a great scholar and is well versed in the Vedas and grammar. He was a professor at the Royal College of Varanasi. However, on the insistence of the king, he left the job and assumed the caste of Agnihotri to conduct this yajna. Only an Agnihotri brahmin can conduct a yajna. Any king can arrange a yajna in Varanasi but cannot conduct it himself. Only an Agnihotri brahmin can conduct it for him.

Before the dawn of learning it was believed that nature was as inconsistent as human behaviour. Just as in the material

42. Using any utensil, which is specified for the gods is generally considered to be sacrilegious. Hence the author has specifically mentioned this aberration.

Manikarnika Ghat at Kashi, Varanasi

world things happened as a consequence of human activities, likewise, all the unusual happenings of nature occurred because of the activities of some unknown person(s). The power of fire was visible to them. But when the sun rose, they got the requisite bright light, and at night the moon gave them essential light. These were two separate entities, visiting the world, and disappearing when they desired. The sky at times got covered with clouds and the wind with its mighty power at times blew wildly, unsettling them. All those who controlled these natural agents were undoubtedly very powerful creatures. And if they desired, they could harm human beings as well. So, it was evident that they could also provide human beings whatever they needed to survive since human beings had very little power to survive either self-sufficiently or independently. It was therefore best to seek the assistance of all the natural agents like the sun, the moon, the fire, and the wind to survive on earth. No wonder the ancient sages of the Vedic age prayed through yajnas to these natural agents as a gesture of appeasement. With growing affluence this ritual of yajna developed immensely. Then to make their appeal effective through yajnas, they composed elaborate poetic shlokas. It needs immense poetic talent to compose shlokas for each and every item existing on earth. And in order to appreciate the inherent talent of the poet, each shloka begins with the name of the composer and instructs the reader how and in what rhythmic pattern the shloka has to be read out. By undertaking an analysis of the shlokas, one gets the pleasure of understanding, if not everything, but a large part of the societal structure of the ancient world. The shlokas help us visualize the ancient world of the Aryans. The language of the shlokas is so simple and vivid that it is necessary to utter them thrice for emphasis.

Even though gold (not in the form of coins) was used in the ancient Vedic age, it was not easily available. Things were valued in terms of gold but in lieu of it either a cow or a ram was offered. It has been mentioned in the Agnishtom yajna that the host conducting it would have to go to the seller of a soma creeper to buy the plant and after evaluating it in terms of gold either pay him through a cow or a ram. The cows of the ancient world were not roped round their necks but had shackles on their legs. The ancient Aryans were terribly scared of robbers. Added to it they did not have a king.

Now, goats are sacrificed during Agnishtom yajna, but in the ancient world, cows used to be sacrificed. And if the cow happened to be pregnant, those performing the yajna had to do a penance. The penance was an additional yajna where after opening the stomach of the animal the flesh of the fetus was offered to the sacrificial fire.

Suradhani

(River Ganga)

Varanasi: In the land between the two rivers Varna and Asi is situated the present city of Kashi. This ancient city previously stood on the left of River Varna, where Sarnath is now situated. Gautam Buddha first preached his sermons here. His objective was to attain nirvana through one's own realization and spiritual knowledge. With time there grew a strong belief that if ever one could breathe one's last here in Kashi, the person would be liberated from the cycle of rebirth.

By this time human habitation had already developed on the southern bank of River Varna. During the Puranic age, the temple of Pashupati had come up, following which human residences developed. Consequently, 'Kashi khanda' was added to the already extant *Skanda Purana*. People from various parts of the world would flock to Kashi to breathe their last. A few decided to renounce the material world here and not to remain only in Kashi itself. A person who is capable of fulfilling his need for food and lodging does not generally accept anybody else's munificence, even if it's a mere invitation for a meal or a token gift. To curb all material cravings of the world becomes his primary objective in life.

On the north of Dufferin Bridge, at the point of River Varna's confluence, stands the hermitage of Mataji. Kalikrishna Tagore of Calcutta spent enough money to build this ashram with magnificent pillars. When our boat reached the embankment of the hermitage, we found Mataji busy inspecting the construction work that was going on. Seeing strangers like us she left the place with a very pleasant expression on her face. We disembarked from the boat and entered the hermitage to find Mataji sitting under a tree with rosary in her hand and adorned in a namabali (a special type of cloth with the name of Lord Krishna printed all over). She was aged and dressed in the style of a Hindu widow and had a pleasant demeanour. Her words indicated her humble nature. 'Yoga has now been commercialized,' said Mataji. 'Colonel Olcott has done this favour to us. Previously when we used to talk about yoga our English educated countrymen were not ready to pay any attention to it. Now they are serious about it and also about our scriptures.'

Mataji is known as Munmun Bai. She is the daughter of a Gujarati Nagar brahmin. She has spent her entire life here in Varanasi. She had learnt yoga from her father. The present hermitage was established by a Peshwa sannyasi. Mataji's father was initiated by him and finally he too became a sannyasi. But Mataji being a woman was prevented from becoming a sannyasin. For that reason, she has had to preserve his loincloth in a container and placed it beside his picture.

The hermitage has been constructed following certain yogic rules. It has three small cubicles in the basement. A yogi first practices pranayama in the first cubicle and then when he learns to control his breath, he closes the door of the first cubicle and enters the second cubicle. When he progresses further, he enters the third cubicle for carrying on his spiritual activities. According to the science of physiology, human blood circulates round the body and accumulates many undesirable gaseous elements like carbon dioxide, carbonic acid etc. which increases if not let out. Pranayama helps one to let out these unwanted elements from the body and inhale oxygen for the better working of the blood. If you withhold your breath (kumbhak), the undesirable carbonic acid cannot be released. Hence, it is mandatory for a yogi not to indulge in a lifestyle which might increase the carbonic acid level. While holding his breath during kumbhak, the yogi should not have a problem of unnecessary carbonic acid accumulating in his blood to harm him. But in case a person remains unconscious for a long time while performing kumbhak, he might turn weak and emaciated but will not die. There are a few animals who sleep for six months a year. It has been observed often that severely sick people may remain unconscious even for a period of three months at a stretch, without consuming food. A yogi can bring about that state through his yoga. But that does not mean they acquire extraordinary power merely by practicing such yogic traits. It is just that by practicing them they gain the power to control both their physical conditions and mental instincts. A theosophist had once said that Mataji in reality was a Tibetan Lama, who at present has assumed the guise of a woman here.

Ghazipur: Almost 36 miles from Mataji's ashram is the ashram of Pavhari Baba[43]. Twenty-eight miles from the ashram is Samna village where lived Narayan Das Tiwari in his grandfather Ramanandji's house, Dev Kutir. After a few years of study, Narayan Das left his home and undertook a long pilgrimage. He went to Rameswaram, Dwarka and several other place for five to six years and learnt yoga. When he returned, he found his grandfather had died. He covered the house with straw

43. He (1798-1898) was an ascetic and saint from a Hindu brahmin family. He belonged to the Ramanuja school of Shri sect.

and constructed a mud cave within. There he practiced yoga for long and came to be known as Pavhari Baba. At present Lakshman, a contractor, has constructed a wall around Dev Kutir and set up few tall brick houses adjacent to it. Baba does not meet visitors. People address him through the closed door of his room, he answers them and sends letters. At night when his assistants leave various items required to conduct his puja, and fruits for consumption, he opens the door and collects them. At times when he decides to make a public appearance, followers gather, and the police has to control the growing crowd.

Parauli is a village near Gorakhpur. There is a Math there of another Pavhari Bairagi. The disciples of this Math assume this title. Recently this Pavhari undertook a long pilgrimage with a large retinue of his disciples. He too thrives on fruits. On the other bank of Ganga there is a place called Indrapur. Long ago, a silk trader had been struck by lightning while rowing across the river. Fifty years later a sick man dreamt of the incident and constructed a temple there and thereby was cured of his illness. The place is now sanctified by the people worshipping there. The deity is known as Bijlia Baba. On the fields nearby cereals like barley are grown. And except mid-spring, white roses bloom merrily throughout the year.

From the bank of River Ganga, Ghazipur looks almost like Varanasi. The language of the people too is the same. There is a high hill where stands a fort belonging to King Gadhi, who ruled over Rameshwar, Chitnath and Kirki Ghat. There is also a white-coloured house of a British Aghori there. The distance of the place from Calcutta is by rail (cord line) 445 miles, by road 431 miles, and by river 784 miles.

Buxar: The place is important because of certain mythological happenings that occurred near it. Important incidents mentioned in the *Ramayana*, like the destruction of Taraka the demon, Vishwamitra's hermitage, the revival of Ahalya from stone to human form, took place near Buxar. There is a temple of the ascetics near Ramlekha buoy. According to archeologists, the stories of the *Ramayana* hardly have any historical basis. The cult figure of Rama was drawn from the Vedic figure of Lord Indra.

A mud fortress was constructed by Prince Dayad Singh of Jagadishpur here at Buxar. The place is close to Bhojpur. Everyone here is familiar with the local saying 'the utensil is either yours or mine'. The story behind it is like this: A robber approaches a person who is cooking in an utensil and asks him 'Whose utensil is it?' If the person replies, 'The utensil is mine', then the robber throws away the cooked material and takes away the utensil by force. In case the person replies 'it is yours' the robber gives him the time to consume the food and then allows him to retain the container. Even though things are not that bad right now, the region lying between Calcutta and Varanasi by river is full of pirates. At night the sailors kept a watch over our boat and never anchored it.

Baliya is close by, where dwelt the sage Bhrigu. There is a temple dedicated to him and inside it is a stone lotus with the sacred Gayatri mantra carved out. Sage Bhrigu meditated upon it and got moksha. Beside it, his footprints have been sculpted and placed. A sacred text narrates the history of this place, Durdur-Mahatma. The soil of the place is so hard and solid that the stairs on the banks of River Ganga are built just by digging and shaping them. No external adhesive is needed to hold them in shape. A steamer operates from here (Baliya) carrying goods to Buxar. We walked up the bank and saw two sugar mills.

Four miles away to the west of the city of Chhapra, River Sarayu has merged with River Ganga. We spent the night at Telka Ghat. In the morning the fog was so thick that we could not see anything beyond a few feet. But because we were bent on touring, we climbed up the bank and found that beyond the fog, at a distance, a troop of ladies were carrying bundles of green peas. Their partings were dabbed with deep vermillion marks while their dresses too were red in hue. Even though their language had not changed, their dress was in the Bihari style. The language spoken here is very different from the language people use in Patna. It is quite possible that it was the Muslims of Ayodhya who had travelled down the northern bank of Sarayu and carried with them the western style Hindi to a land of people speaking eastern style Hindi. The language people use in Bihar is neither Bhojpuri nor midland Hindi.

Patna: The confluence of River Sone and River Ganga is in the city of Danapur. During summer when the river is dry, the Bengal Northwestern Railway Company lays rail tracks across the river to send goods-carrying rail wagons to the ships waiting in the Ganga. The ancient Pataliputra city lies submerged in the bed of the Ganga. Here the river is about six miles wide. But when a river becomes too wide silt deposits occur in its middle. The huge silt deposit near Patna has split the Ganga into two streams which finally merge at a distance.

From afar, while travelling down the Ganga, Patna appeared to us as an affluent city. We went to visit the Patna Devi Temple. There is a small temple standing inside a large building and the interior of the temple is filled with mud. The priest told us that this is one among the fifty-two peeths (sacred place where body parts of Goddess Sati fell). Here a piece of the goddess's garment seemed to have dropped, hence the place is called Patna, derived from the word 'pat' or clothing. But where has the dynasty of rulers vanished? Vanished into oblivion. Here the houses are not constructed of stones, but of carved wood. The scarcity of stone is so glaring that even the Shiva lingam in one temple is placed upon a wooden disc-shaped platform called Gauri pattya.

The place where River Sone meets the Ganga, the water is enclosed, and redirected through a canal. And the force with which the water emerges through a small outlet, is a sight to behold. The rebounding water droplets glitter brilliantly and when the sun rays fall upon them an image of a rainbow is created.

We left Bankipur at eleven-thirty in the morning and soon crossed the Gandaki river. The Gandaki merges with the Ganga of Varanasi. The place however is very dangerous, since the fast-flowing Gandaki is constantly loosening the earth on its banks on the northern side and engulfing the surrounding land with a roaring sound. Our sailor however remarked that the river is yet to attain its full form. Every year during the full moon, the river acquires terrible strength and the boats journeying across its reverse tide face tremendous hardship.

We reached the sacred Harihar Kshetra (Sonepur) and viewed the deity of Hari Harnath. It is basically a copper Shiva lingam and right in front of the lingam stands the idol of Lord Vishnu. In ancient times, here stood the hermitage of Sage Pulaha. As the story goes, Sage Durvasa had once reached the court of Lord Indra in heaven and requested the Gandharvas, Haha and Huhu, to sing. Since they did not comply, Durvasa cursed them, and they were born on earth as an elephant and a tortoise. After some time, the elephant came to drink water here and the tortoise met him and loudly they called Harihar. Then Lord Vishnu and Lord Shiva came to their rescue, and they regained their former Gandharva status. Since then, the place has become a sacred site for pilgrimage. There is purana mentioning the importance of the place called *Hariharkshetra Mahatma*. In all likelihood, the work is a recent one and is the contribution of the local priests or pandas. They however claim that it is a part of *Linga Purana*.

The adjacent fairground comprises of shops and houses built of cloth. And many respectable and aristocratic people visit the fair. This fair is a major source of attraction for the affluent people of Patna, Chhapra and other nearby places. Some stay in tents, some stay in their own boats, celebrating the occasion through singing, dancing, and gambling. But the sight before the Hari Harnath temple is very different—scores of people performing ablutions and standing in long queues in wet clothes, carrying holy water in containers to pour upon the deity.

There are multiple shops displaying wares both indigenous and imported. From Varanasi stone-carved figures of temples have been brought, from Gaya stone crucibles and bowls have been brought here to sell to the local people. Ivory ornaments and tidbits have been brought here from Punjab. Other than these we saw brass and copper utensils, desks, cars, palanquins, lamp shades, cots, various musical instruments, and numerous other items which were on sale. It was tiring to view all the sections in details. Then we went to see the elephant market. Various types of elephants were on sale; all the animals stood patiently for the customers to arrive. Elephants from Assam and Nepal are brought here. Similarly, we found a horse mart. There were about 4000 horses up for sale. We were not able to see the entire market as it was too large for viewing. There was the ox market too, comprising of about 4000 oxen. We could not see that. Neither could we visit the livestock section of the fair where sheep, donkey, and dogs were being sold. There was the bird market as well. Interestingly, in a garden nearby stood courtesans waiting for customers. The Hindu courtesans of Danapur have mostly adopted Islam since caste distinction does not exist in Islam. And the doors of Hindu religion is permanently shut for them.

Fatuah: We began our journey on boat from the confluence of Ganga and Pun Puna river. It was early morning. As the morning advanced, the tide rose, and our boat increased its speed. In order to control its movement, the boat threw down the anchor. The boats named Ujania, Melhogni and Salina, which keep plying up and down tediously, rowing against the tide, were now seen flying at great speed. Our boatsmen, finding a little respite, started conversing with the other boatsmen travelling down the same route. Everyone kept asking them why they were plying so slowly, little realizing that unlike their cargo boats, ours was a passenger vessel. Most of these boats ply with cargoes like salt, rice and husks, going from east to west and back again.

My doctor had warned me about the efficacy of the medicine I was taking. 'If the medicine is not working why are you taking it? It is harmful to consume a medicine that does not work.' It was according to his advice that I had undertaken this journey by boat. Going to Deogarh by bus is more tedious than going by a boat. Our body is automatically exercised by a boat journey. The day we travel a lot by boat, our appetite increases.

We had to procure milk. And like other food, milk too could be got from the fair. The small shops of the villages could only supply tobacco in small quantities. All the ingredients we needed for our meals were stored in the boat. At present the boat was our home. All the items we needed to make ourselves feel at home were to be found in the boat. The wind being favourable, we started our journey. We saw clouds collecting in the north-western sky followed by lightning. The clouds darkened the water. The boatsmen looked worried about an impending storm. They started rowing fast towards the bank. But all efforts proved futile as the storm overtook us and it started raining. The boatsmen failed to reach the bank because of the strong wind. The boat full of passengers and all the heavy weight finally made it even though our boatsmen, instead of striving further just gave up, saying, 'Let Lord Narayan do what he wills.'

I asked one of them, 'Now what will happen?'

'We will not be able to reach the bank,' he said.

Our boat instead of reaching the destined bank now kept flowing towards an unknown destination, as directed by the strong wind of the storm. The chief boatsman merely kept indicating the direction. Finally, we reached a sandy bank and the chief boatsman ordered to anchor the boat. The wind subsided but the clouds remained dark and ominous. This small sandy island was to be our resting place for the day. After some time, we saw a huge steamboat full of cargo, completely ignoring the storm and the cloud plying towards Patna at a leisurely pace.

Rarh: The moment our boat reached the bank, a flower seller came to worship the river with his garland of flowers, the milkman came forward with his offering of curd, and the beggar too made his appearance. Previously the Chumma fakirs of the region used to trouble the new arrivals and hence no boatsman wanted to anchor his boat in the region. The boatsmen had to pay whatever these fakirs demanded. One even asked to pierce the newcomer's body with a knife and offer his blood to the fakir. And the poor man had to comply.

Morning dawned and the morning bathers started appearing one by one. Some shunned pronouncing the names of both Sita and Ram while some avoided mentioning the name of Radha and Krishna. These behaviours entertained us amply for quite some time. In the fog-covered ambience, a strange sound surprised us. On enquiry we came to know that there was a troupe of swans in the lonely shore. And the sound was being produced by them. They always live in groups. A flying shoal of cranes drew a beautiful picture in the sky. The land was full of greenery and the sight was soothing. There stood a few tall trees amidst this greenery. At a place we saw several herons and donkeys strolling about. Gradually we approached human habitations. Across stood the state railways for commuting and a steam ferry service. There is a place called Ramdiri where 200 mounds of milk are produced every day. Khutia being relatively barren, the cows were being ferried across to graze grass. A hilly river, brown in colour, emerged from Suryagarh and sunk itself into the Ganga. Consequently, the colour of the water there took a different hue.

Munger: The place where we had anchored our large boat last year could not be found, and hence we had to anchor elsewhere. The water level had sunk almost seven arms length below the expected height. The heavy downpour of monsoon had inundated the place with loads of mud, converting it into a shallow watery area. We had not seen such interplay of the river either at Varanasi or Kanpur. Ganga had turned into a fiercely flowing river from Patna. Previously River Sone was not assisted by either Sarayu or Gandak rivers. But now Ganga seemed to have assumed multiple forms—in some place it had turned three-fold wild, while at another place it had become two-fold wild. In addition, flesh-eating crocodiles appeared from the river and mud dunes that could capsize boats. When boats approach these mud dunes, an avalanche of mud slides over them and the river simply whisks them away. The Ganga has a quaint way of working—breaking the loose muddy banks everywhere it diverts its course, washing away houses and trees in its pathway. Where the river existed earlier there are human habitations now, and the previous habitations have now been submerged deep into the water of the river. Our boatsmen, fearing the onslaught of mud during the night, did not anchor our boat near any muddy area.

The fort built by the nawab of Bengal Mir Kasim in the middle of a water body has now turned into a dilapidated structure, covered by grasses, and converted into a worshipping place for the British. There is a buoy named Kastaharini (reliever of suffering). Nearby is the Moudgalya Ashram. The Pir Hill renowned in the area is visible from a distance of approximately sixteen miles while voyaging across the river. Near this is Sita Kund. It is said that seventy years ago from Ram Navami (birth of Lord Rama) till the full moon in the month of July-August, the water of the Kund used to remain cool and no vapours would rise from it. Since then, it would only remain cool for an hour or two. However, two years back, the water had once remained cool for a month and a half. The priests of the region are of the opinion that this anomalous behaviour of the water will deter pilgrims from visiting the place. To them the sanctity of the place had almost vanished. The water from Sita Kund is not hot enough to cook rice in it though it does act as a medicinal mixture for curing liver diseases.

There is a small hill resembling Mangala or Vikram Chandi.

There is a temple in the middle of it. It is famous as a Tantric holy place and is known as Madhyadesh Mahamaya. Hundred years ago, a spiritually enlightened sage known as Ramgiri used to live here.

Here, the flavour of Bengali is observed in the local language. Instead of 'bh' they use 'sh'. Instead of 'bhavati' they use 'asti'. Prakrit 'hoi' has turned 'hoy' and Prakrit 'achhi' has turned in Bengali as 'achi', using the alphabet 'ch' (as in children). For example, Western Hindi—nahi hai, Purvi or Bhojpuri Hindi—noi khoi and Midland Hindi—na chay. And since the region is inhabited by people speaking both Hindustani and Bengali, the nomenclature has become midland. Hindi is best spoken by people of Delhi. The language there sounded so pleasant to me that I feel like going back to it once again just to hear it.

Jahangira: Since our vessels were heavy, we could not take the main course of the river straight away. So we travelled to the confluence of Bagmati and then went on to reach the Ganga. Six to eight miles away lay a village. On the bank was the grazing ground of buffaloes. At places herds of buffaloes were found half immersed in the water. A herdsman here owns about twenty to thirty cows.

There are two submerged rocks lying inside the Ganga near Sultangunj. On one side there was a stretch of silt deposit where a mosque had come up. Muslims offer their namaz there. But on one of the mountains engraved figures of Hindu gods and goddesses are to be found. While at the top of another mountain a temple of Lord Shiva stands tall along with the residence of the head priest and engravings of Hindu gods. There are also interesting figures of Shesh-shai, Shiva, Parvati and a half-carved temple. Pilgrims have named the place after Sage Janhu and it is called Janhu Kshetra. Along with the figures of Lord Shiva by the Shaivites, there are a few engravings of Buddha as well. Recently the Saraugiras (a religious clan) are worshiping Shesh-shai as Parasnath. A few pillars and idols have been brought here from outside and the deity of Gaurinath has been added to this place of worship. Deva Griha is about 60 miles from here. Pilgrims on their way to Baidyanath come to Jahangira to collect the holy water of Ganga and carry it on their shoulders. Accordingly, a market selling pots and bottles have come up here. Hundreds of people come here in groups and carry the holy water on their shoulders. Resounding cries of 'Bolo bom' fill the air as they make their way in groups. On their way back the refrain is 'lord take our offerings and fill up our pots and bottles with material wealth'.

While journeying down the river we saw a village called Dudhel (milk). This clearly indicates the abundance of milk and its creamy extracts of ghee and butter the place offers.

Bhagalpur: We know about Karna the giver, and it is said that his fort is situated here. The fort is at Champa city. In the story of Behula there is a reference to this Champa city. But at present in the fort there stands the sole deity of Lord Shiva, the wish fulfiller, and he is worshipped regularly. It is said that when a wish is fulfilled hundred buckets of water are poured upon the Shiva lingam. Words written on a memorial of Cleveland[44] here made me very happy. The words were: 'Without bloodshed or the terrors of authority, employing only the means of conciliation, confidence, and benevolence, he attempted and accomplished the entire subjection of the lawless and savage inhabitants of the Jungle Terry (forest frontier) of Rajmahal who had long infested the neighbouring lands by their predatory incursions, inspired them with a taste for the arts of civilized life, and attached them to the British Govt. by a conquest over their minds, the most permanent as the most rational mode of dominion.'

Bhagalpur is a big city. While travelling around its fringes

---

44. Augustus Cleveland (1754 to 1784) was an East India Company administrator in the Province of Bengal, and a Collector of Revenues and Judge in the districts of Bhagalpur and others

one gets coated by a fine layer of dust. Steamboats are employed to carry people. There is a hermitage at Kahole—a nearby village. One has to cross two huge rocks submerged in the river and reach the steps leading to the temple of Boteswarnath. Some distance away one can see the horizon where the mountain range merges with the beautiful river which flows down further and mixes with the Kushi river. At Manihara stands the steam engine, ready to carry the passengers who disembark from the steamboat from Sahebgunj.

Rajmahal: Rajmahal is situated along the bank of River Ganga. It is actually a piece of land lying along Rotsgarh mountain, which is a part of the Vindhya range. Raja Man Singh had founded this city hence it was named Rajmahal. In 1637, Subedar Suja had built Sangidalan on the bank of the Ganga and the place still exists. We were fortunate to meet the local Santhal men and women who had come to the market to sell wood. The claim is not unfounded. Even though the Santhals of Damini and Koho did not bow down before the Muslim rulers, they were finally won over by the clever manipulation of Mr Cleveland. He won their confidence by giving them a hilly tract of land to live in and then imposed a tax upon them. Cleveland was only twenty-nine years old then.

The physique of the Santhals indicate that they are born to undertake hard physical labour. You'll be disappointed if you expect an elaborate answer for your questions. Whatever you ask they will retort with a big 'yes'. It is as if they are always in a hurry to escape at the earliest. Hence, a yes is their only way of responding. The chief of their community is known as Majhi. He has never been known to have misused his power. According to the British imperialists, it is the torture inflicted by the Bengalis upon them that drove the Santhals to revolt. But according to the forest dwellers, had the British rulers enquired about their sufferings, this state would not have occurred. Some of the Santhals have now been converted either to Hinduism or Christianity. These conversions have taught them the art of cheating.

The Mountain is their chief god. And he is known as Merongburu. Maybe he is actually our Hindu god Lord Shiva, who knows. Like the Bengali Charak festival (held in mid spring) they too celebrate their Pota. Unfortunately, they have now forgotten the use of bows and arrows. According to a journalist, during their Badna festival, they feed on pies, meat and wine. And as a part of the celebration, they sing and dance and indulge in free mixing. Has using expletives during the Hindustani Holi festival originated from this custom?

Santhals call themselves Har, and Har women are extremely fond of music and dance. Jamhir is a dance form very similar to the dance sequence of Ras Lila. Drums and flutes are played and the women in Dravidian hairstyles find a male partner to dance with in circles.

The headman of the village is not entitled to sell any land. Their pertinent question is if we have to sell the land then why name the place Santhal Pargana?

Interestingly, many Sanskrit words have been incorporated in the Santhali language. Likewise, many Santhali words have infiltrated into Prakrit. These forms of infiltration however are not strange at all because they do not change the structure of the languages. Verb and few other grammatical elements comprise a language. And only when these structures are changed or modified does a new language emerge. Normally the case endings in any language remain untouched. Later when required they are modified. But they never lose their individual identity in the language, just as we have seen in Bengali.

There stood many cow-carts at Rajmahal to carry passengers to Malda, Dinajpur etc. The forest of Gaur is not far from here. While stepping out of Rajmahal and entering the mountainous terrain, one is in the heart of Bengal. The language and customs change drastically to pure Bengali. Thatched huts became visible. A group of women had travelled from Teen Pahar to take a holy dip in the Ganga. Their ways and attires reminded us of the Santhals. They wore lac bangles on one hand while on the other they had brass bangles. On the bank of the river, we found a colony of several small villages with Hindustani population of different castes.

The soil of the bank here is not hard. In fact, hard soil is completely absent in this region. The same soft land is to be found in the territories of Bengal as well. On the bank we found ladies standing with pitchers resting on their hips. Their way of wearing saris showed they were Bengali.

We reached the village of Farakka and instead of going on the main river, sailed down its tributary, Bhagirathi. On the banks we heard people talking in both Hindi and Bengali. The Hindi-speaking people residing here have a typical tone and accent while talking in Bengali. But when we had to address a person at Dhuliyan, we were of two minds—should we talk to him in Bengali or in Hindi, we kept wondering.

A person of the Gunri community was seen sailing a boat home after attending an invitation. Interestingly, the males wear Bengali attire while the females prefer wearing Hindustani style attires. All the land that we saw on our way was full of people carrying pitchers of water. Most of them were women. The ornaments they wore differentiated them as Muslim and Hindu women. Muslim women wore bangles and ornaments on their ankles, while Hindu women wore elaborate ornaments on their limbs and nose pins. They still continue with the art of washing their hair with mud. Someone must have worshipped Goddess Durga in the village, whose straw remains was seen resting on the bank. Any person who crosses this part of the country during Durga Puja will have the fortune of seeing the celebrations in the village.

The confluence of Chapghati has dried up, so we had to come to the confluence of Farakka and reach Jangipur. Across Jangipur is Tulsibihar. Here they have a toll house for boats. In order to maintain the cleanliness of the Bhagirathi, there are government appointed tax collectors, who are perpetually vigilant. Where the water has dried up, they have set up bamboo plantations so as to divert the water flow. The language people use at Chapghati is peculiar. Here people utter palatal sounds and hence, even the known words sound different. This has led to the growth of a new language.

Murshidabad: The other name of Azimgunj is Sahar. This place is full of merchants dealing in Balucharis (a type of silk sari). The place appeared to be full of affluent people. Except the luxurious residence of the nawab there is really nothing important to see in Murshidabad. Crossing the royal palace of Maharani Swarnamoyee[45] we reached Khagra, in Berhampore. It is clearly an old and sufficiently affluent place still standing strong on the bank of River Ganga. Our eyes grew tired, yet there was still so much to see and enjoy. The Shiva temple had an Arabian architecture, but the trident at its peak bespeaks of its Hindu identity. Women here wear various types of bangles made of conch shell, silver and wooden and golden neck wears.

In order to view the battleground of Plassey, we had to leave our boat. Human habitations have come up there, yet we felt it our sacred duty to visit the place and shed a few drops of tears. After a search we were able to trace the victory stand made of stone. On it was written:

> 'Plassey
> Erected by the
> Bengal Government
> 1883'

Standing under an ancient mango tree I had to read out a canto from the poetic work *Battle of Plassey*. Before we could control

---

45. Swarnamoyee was born in a poor family and was extremely beautiful. She married Maharaja Krishna Nath Nandy of the Cossimbazar royal family and took over the reigns (1844 to 1897) after her husband died at an early age. She is remembered for her several significant charitable works.

our emotions, it was time to return. On reaching Katoa we saw the Ajay river. Then when we reached Metiri we found people dressed in the style that is followed in the Burdwan region.

Nawadip: The water of river Padma here has got mixed up with the waters of the Bhagirathi. The British call the Ganga as Hooghly here. On the bank stood a few people with tufts of long hair. They were offering food and water to their dead ancestors. A few were completing their evening prayers. Students belonging to Kanauj, Mithila, Telangana and Bengal were delaying their ablutions because of their late classes in the Sanskrit village schools. Their lessons would resume soon, in the afternoon. We might debate about procrastination, as the people here clearly manifested a leisurely pace in their lifestyles.

I was curious to know the exact buoy where Nimai (Sri Chaitanya) used to steal prasad offered to the gods. Old king Lakshman Sen used to live here when he desired to spend his final days near the Ganga. In 1203, Bakhtiyar Khilji, instead of attacking the capital, had come to Nawadip. But he did not seem to be much impressed since there were no soldiers to oppose him.

Here standing on the bank of the river I could see bel leaves and flower garlands strewn far and wide. At Kalna we were happy to view Lalaji's temple established by the Raja of Burdwan. The wooden image of Lord Jagannath was offered pulses. The walls made of bricks were artistically designed. On reaching Sukh Sagar we heard people speaking a language with which we were familiar. But the language across the place was different. Colloquial language is different from the language that is used in writing and written language was originally introduced in Birbhum and Burdwan. All folk arts like kirtan, jatra and narrating mythological stories were their properties initially. The first Bengali newspaper was brought out at Srirampur and the books that were later published in Calcutta used the language which this newspaper used in print. Now that is officially the language that has come into use.

The language people use in Birbhum has typical words and phrases which we do not use colloquially but we use them in our writings. For example, language found on the eastern bank of Ganga is somewhat like this: Hari's to be called. Language found in the western bank of Ganga is: Hari has to be called.

We reached Tribeni and after assessing the ebb and flow of the river decided to commence our journey. On our way we visited Hanshewari temple and approached the Hooghly bridge. Our guide informed us that Calcutta was almost 32 miles from there. Since my servant had not seen Calcutta before, he presumed Hooghly to be Calcutta. This was because the affluence of Calcutta had indeed spilled over to Hooghly.

Calcutta

(The Great Exhibition)

Mid-November (or December) 1883: Today we went to see the inauguration of the grand international exhibition. Invited by the British empresses' Indian representative Lord Ripon, the third son of the empress, the Duke of Kent inaugurated the grand exhibition. The interesting lecture of Lord Ripon was followed by a glimpse of the Governor General's durbar (courtroom). And that was really the icing on the cake.

My three simple reasons for visiting the exhibition every day for three months at a stretch were—to acquire knowledge, for entertainment, and to breathe in fresh air. But to be frank, other than enjoying beautiful sights, how much knowledge I managed to acquire is a debatable issue. Fact is, without proper initiation it is impossible to acquire knowledge in any subject. Same is the case with education. But because we Bengalis lack the required commercial mindset, our visit to the exhibition remains confined to entertainment only. For instance, in the last exhibition I had seen British men and women working hard to acquire the weaving skill of our local master weavers. This time they will possibly learn the art of making brass vessels, thereby depriving the local artisans of their works. Yet, handmade objects can never compete with machine-made ones. And because we are far behind in technical skills, there is really no chance for us to benefit by this exhibition. Other than getting assistance for few almost extinct folk works of artistry, we will not gain much.

The British immigrants of Australia, who have organized this exhibition, will undoubtedly be benefitted by it. Government has already formed an alliance with Australia for commercial transactions. The exhibition displays both living and non-living items. On the opening day of the exhibition, I was not able to view and remember all the items that were on display. Hence, every day I would search for new items with the following mindset—okay, today let me see what more the exhibition can offer.

On reaching the stall set up by the state of Punjab, I felt transported to the land of five rivers. Everywhere there were Punjabi items. There were even Punjabi men displaying their wares and talking to us in chaste Punjabi. And what was more interesting was the odour of the stall—the beautiful fragrance of deodar trees that permeate the entire state of Punjab prevailed here! I had the same experience when I visited the other stalls too—Bombay, Madras, Rajputana[46], North-western region, Assam and Cochin. It was as if they had lifted a part of their state and brought it here. Actually, if someone visits these stalls and looks at them carefully, he need not visit the states separately. They have everything that is there in the (different) states, either in the form of pictures or models of wood or stones. Right from birds, animals, houses and the dresses people wear, all are exhibited here. Those who have not seen the Taj Mahal of Agra, the Gurdwara of Amritsar,

46. Old form of Rajasthan

the Qutub Minar of Delhi, the temples of Vrindavan, or even viewed Varanasi from this side of river Ganga can view it all here, in this exhibition. From the perspective of showcasing art and artistry, the exhibition has been a roaring success.

The varieties of ethnic objects that are being displayed here are as follows–papier-mache works and Damascus shawls of Kashmir, Benarasi saris, zari embroideries from Ahmadabad, sandalwood items from Mysore, arms from Rajputana, the carpet King Man Singh had procured from Kabul, frilled dresses from Jaipur, artistic objects from Agra, the fine ivory works of Tanjore and Murshidabad, the works of transparent stone from Gwalior and Khamb, chandeliers of Ashlars, musical instruments of Hamilton, the ivory mat from Tripura, mats from Tanjore, the diamond crown of the King of Cooch Behar, the golden throne and diamond headgear of the King of Burdwan, the diamond writing materials and stars of Empress Eugene, the pearls of Badri Das, the statues of the queens of both Delhi and Lahore and pictures of overcast cloudy sky, snow-covered scenic beauties, etc. Likewise, varied factory manufactured items of Europe for houses, weapon stores, etc. are displayed in a separate place. There was also Mr Woodruff making glass threads. At another place steel was being converted into soft cotton-like substance. The granules of both steel cotton and glass thread appeared soft to me. A house was being cooled by a water cooler too.

Banga

(Bengali Vaishyas)

In between Bengal, Bihar and Orissa lies a small place called Chotanagpur. The place is still inhabited by people belonging to the most ancient tribes. Since the place has Bengali, Bihari,

Oriya and Santhali population, ethnologists take great interest in it. The British scholar Dalton has based his ethnic study on this place and written his book.

Language changes but not people's attires, whether they be Aryans or non-Aryans. It takes time to change people's habits. The attires of people living in Bankura or even Calcutta are same but not the language. Formal language has almost died off here. While writing we prefer using the colloquial language and not the bookish formal language. But in Bankura some of the words indicate they have still retained a few formal words in their vocabulary. So, attires do not indicate the regions people live in, but their language does act as pointers to their place of inhabitation. However, the demarcation between Aryan and non-Aryan is not possible through language. It's only their culture and habits that indicate their origin.

After the development of the railways, commuting for people has become quite easy. They can travel back and forth and hence never have to leave their homes permanently. Consequently, losing one's identity by renouncing one's root—a Bengali turning into a Hindustani or a Hindustani turning Bengali, is no longer possible. Some might feel that a Bengali has always been a Bengali likewise a Hindustani always a Hindustani. But reality was very different. Earlier, whoever shifted base, lost his or her roots and identity and assumed the culture of his or her place of residence. Now with the improvement of communication, chances of losing one's identity is really remote. Now people go and settle at some other place for earning their livelihoods, but when it comes to marriage and bringing up their families they go back to their communities. Previously however, this was not possible. Once they shifted base, it was not possible for them to return, so they had to settle there permanently and make an unknown land their home. Now, when you have an opportunity to find someone of your caste to cook your food why will you opt for someone who does not belong to your caste.

Nine Hindu communities comprising of spice dealer,

garland maker, weaver, milkman, barber, grower of betel leaves, blacksmith, potter, and the confectioner is known collectively as the Navashak. Here they are called Navasena. In our region, people belonging to Navashak share only their smoking pipes with one another. Here however, they share their rice and food as well. Even though they call each other kinsmen, but when it comes to marriage, they do not permit anyone outside their own specified caste.

Both natural beauty and society change markedly when one shifts base from urban to rural settings. In the rural world there are mountains, green fields, little cottages, humble villagers leading a peaceful and satisfied life. In cities women belonging to rich business communities or the milk-vending classes are not allowed to take a dip in the open or in the Ganga, nor are they free to visit their neighbors openly. For both these activities they have to travel in palanquins and remain completely invisible to the external world. Here women dressed in waist-hugging clothes indicate that their family business is either selling oil or milk. This is because they have to put in hard labour and wearing tight waist clothes help them to work freely. Brahmins carrying baskets full of betel leaves from Bankura can be seen here. While kshatriyas wearing the sacred thread can be seen husking paddy. Vaishya women wearing the sacred thread were seen selling puffed rice in the market. The new class of soldiers was seen employed in carrying on trade and commerce. City dwellers should not be astounded at this drastic change of professions, because their ancestors too belonged to these kinds of mixed castes. And naturally they all bear a distinct kinship with one another. They are addressed by varied surnames.

Here potters are not allowed to offer water to people of upper castes. Potters and blacksmiths are divided into two different classes. The class of potters who allow widow remarriage are considered heretic and are known as Maghai. This clearly shows their proclivity to retain their Hindustani roots.

In Purulia there is a community that speaks a mixed language of Hindi and Bengali. They follow a custom of widow remarriage. Though this is not publicly acknowledged by them. When someone tries to point it out, they backtrack saying 'It has happened to someone. We do not deal with such deviants.' Yet, during the Vedic age, widow remarriage was very much prevalent. And this is clear from the mantras which are recited during funeral rites: 'These women without suffering the pangs of widowhood have managed to get a compassionate husband. Let them enter their new lives with proper prosperity. Let these women not shed tears of sorrow and getting married to a good husband enter their new abode. O woman you who is lying beside your dead husband get up. Go to the community and marry someone who is ready to marry you.'

The illiterate Vaishyas call themselves Visi or Vis. People of Bengal who are not willing to acknowledge castes other than brahmins and sudras, I appeal to them to look at this class. I have learnt from a reliable source that in Pabna district Sanhkya banik[47] of Chatmohor and Kansha banik of Dainhata take the sacred thread (meant mainly for the brahmins). At Ranichak the Tambuli banik have the thread ceremony. But they are undoubtedly Vaishya by caste.

In reality brahmin, kshatriya, Vaishya and sudra are castes which assume different connotations in different regions. Now the rigidity of this division should be questioned. No wonder novelists who talk about caste divisions talk about the need to abolish these divisions and creating a new caste.

The Puranas narrate that it was from Lord Brahma that this four-tiered caste system originated. Hence, to consider the sudras as mere bifurcation of one family and not something derogatory is rational. Brahmin, kshatriya, vaishya and sudra should be considered to be different parts of the same body. But it is also normal for people to want to find out the original

47. They are Vaishyas basically.

source of this division. And because the origin is not known, people tend to take the help of imagination.

In some cases when the number of men and women are really small in number, inter-caste marriages occur out of desperate need. But when this need disappears, the new mixed caste that arises out of inter-caste marriage survives as a distinct class. This is how in Bengal different sub-sections have come up with time—different forms of brahmins like Kulin, Bangshoj, kshatriya etc. But these sub-sections should not be treated even among the brahmins as lesser mortals. However, at present the man to woman ratio is almost same hence inter-caste marriage is strictly prohibited.

In the ancient world, a man's caste was determined by his profession and accordingly came the caste divisions brahmin, kshatriya vaishya sudra. In case of a change of profession, their castes too would change. (substantiated by *Vayu Purana* and *Hari Vansha*)

With the increase in population and the advancment of civilization, cultural changes took place. Consequently, various professions came into existence, leading to the widening of the caste structure. New names for castes based on new professions started developing. Interestingly, till date a boy belonging to a brahmin family is considered to be a sudra till he has the sacred thread ceremony. Likewise, a woman till she is married to a brahmin remains a sudra.

A person belonging to a different family may enter the caste if he/she follows the same religion. The Shak race of northern Himalayas had ruled over different parts of our country. Initially they were not assigned any specific caste because they did not follow our religion. Later, after they adopted Buddhism, they were redeemed and were accepted as kshatriyas (the ruling class). According to Western historians, Parihar, Pramar, Chalukya and Chauhan Rajputs actually originated from the Shak race. The Buddhist ruler of Kashmir, Kanishka, was a Shak, and he formulated an almanac which was named after him, called the Shakabda. This almanac is still followed both in China and Japan.

In India, before the arrival of the Muslim invaders or just during that time, brahmins and Rajputs invaded Nepal, and started converting the Mugs, Gurungs and Newars into Hindus. The Mugs who adopted the brahmanical rulings of Hinduism were absorbed into the kshatriya caste and could take the sacred thread. They were conferred the title of the Sun dynasty. And from them the Thapas, Gharti and Rana clans emerged. These new kshatriyas were known as Khas. Children born of brahmin father and Mug mother had the right to assume the sacred thread and were part of the new kshatriya caste. This constant caste and religious flux led to the modification of the existing language and the mixture of Tibetan and Indian languages led to the formation of the Khasku sub-language. The Gurungs were not allowed to take the sacred thread and socially they belonged to a caste below the kshatriyas but above the Vaishyas. The diasporic Gurungs however, till date, remain committed to Buddhism and have resisted conversion. But their interaction with Khas has in many ways changed their beliefs to a large extent. The British Gurkha regiment comprising of Gurungs has many members living at close quarters with the Hindus. With time and intimacy, they have adopted the Hindu ways especially regarding their toilet habits.

The Newar clan is divided into sixty-nine sub sections. Out of these, sixteen are Buddhists, thirty-eight follow a middle path while the rest fifteen are Shaivites. The followers of the middle path comprise of both brahmins and shramans and they employ priests for domestic worships. Newars have a script of their own. They have their literature too. Their art and literature strongly reflect a Chinese influence. Chinese scripts do not have alphabets. It is primarily a language to express feelings or emotions. A reader attributes different meanings to the same expression according to his or her habits. Chinese language has more than two thousand expressions.

Nepal is a Hindu kingdom since the king is a Hindu. If Hindu religion prevails, both the Gurungs and the Newars will undoubtedly remain within the Hindu fold. Defeating the Newars, a Gurkha king has established his sovereignty in Nepal. The Jetro clan did not permit them to enter the army. Newars therefore have to remain satisfied with trade and commerce. In the given context, society will not be able elevate them to the status of a kshatriya. They will have to remain vaishyas.

The Vaishnava Bengalis of both Manipur and Tripura are basically kshatriyas. Their physique indicates their mongoloid origin. In 13th century AD, the Assamese Mugs of Kamrup set up their kingdom and became worshippers of the mother goddess or Shakti. But after the Muslim invasion, the Mug priests fled from Chittagong and gradually entered the Hindu folds. They celebrate Durga Puja by sacrificing animals. In places, as per their previous association, they even sacrifice hens and cockerels. At present, instructed by the ancient priests many of them have become Buddhists. And significantly, two members of the same family follow two different religions as their names indicate—Kali Charan (Hindu) and Barkat Ali (Muslim).

The Tibetans have learnt both Buddhism and Tantra from Nepal. Hence, at present in Bhutan we find images of goddesses along with the traditional gods. In Darjeeling (the most important place for Tantra) we came across a rudraksha-wearing long, unkempt-haired and bearded Bhutia.

Despite being converted into Hindus, the Bhutias will never give up their habits of eating pork and chicken (two meats that are a strict no no for Hindus). But the Hindu rule of not eating animal flesh and not even touching them, is not universal. It varies with time and place. The monks do not consider any food to be untouchable.

Initially men thought all human knowledge was acquired naturally, but now people have realized that most of our knowledge has been acquired from our ancestors. Knowledge, when coupled with rules and ethics, is also applied in practical life. When this happens a distinctive class of knowledge develops, known as religion. But knowledge is progressive, and it keeps changing with time and situation. Likewise, religion too keeps changing. Language cannot be created, and similarly religion, too, cannot be created. Hence, both language and religion are considered to be eternal. But both language and religion can be developed by man. Whatever is new—language or religion—should have an origin. Progress is a continuous process and is inevitable.

At times circumstances force us to take the assistance of another language, but it is impossible to renounce one's mother tongue completely. During the Roman rule, Latin as a language had gained tremendous importance in Europe. Likewise, when French rule prevailed, French language became the second-most important language in Europe. At present it is vying with English for eminence. In India, during the Muslim rule, Persian became an important language, and similarly at present English has become an extremely important second language in our country. But during the Hindu rule Sanskrit did not gain an eminent place as a language.

Just as it is impossible to renounce one's mother tongue, similarly it is absolutely impossible to give up one's religion. Religion, language, kingdom, race or even trade and commerce are destroyed with time if there is no motivating force or life force behind it. Just as a constant supply of wood is necessary to keep the fire burning, similarly, to improve the above-mentioned issues, people will have to work hard constantly and improve their status. Whether the life force of a religion or a race is diminishing can be accurately measured by comparing them with their previous status. To develop Hindu religion, it is mandatory to remove its narrowness and make it open and liberal. Divisiveness in the name of castes is the hallmark of Hinduism. But to help the nation progress, this divisiveness should be done away with and a liberal outlook has to be developed. Unity in diversity in terms of race and caste should be widely practiced. Equal access to national wealth and national rights should be provided to all.

There are three types of Hindus depending on their physical features, their language, and their economic status. For instance, Kashmiris have Caucasian antecedents, Nepalis have Mongoloid origin while the Dravidians are from Coler race. In general Indians are a mix of Caucasian and Coler. If the complexion of a person is indicative of his origin, then there are many brahmins who are both fair and dark, clearly pointing to such mixing. According to a few rigid authors the concept of two races comes from the context of Aryans versus the non-Aryans. History clearly shows the occurrence of cross breeding.

Second comes the question of language. Aryan language comprises of Bengali, Turani, Tailangi. Sematic Aryan is the language of Urdu-speaking Hindustani. Hindi is a sematic coinage. Third comes profession or occupation. Professions are of two types—ancient and modern. Ancient professions depended on the castes of the people—brahmin kshatriya vaishya sudra. The modern professions are of the florists and the weavers. And because we remain committed to our traditional classifications, we brand the modern professions as the professions for the sudras.

Other than India, in many other countries too, this practice of segregating people based on their caste still prevails. In Europe, even though this concept of untouchability does not exist, there is a rigid distinction between the aristocrats and common men. They neither communicate socially nor allow marriages to take place. But even a common man can become great. In that case he is automatically elevated to a higher social order. This approach indicates the flexibility of their society. At present in Bengal some people are trying hard to uplift their social status. But without self-respect no one can really become great. Among the Satsudra the kayesthas are trying to rise up to become kshatriyas, while the middle order sudras like gold merchants are trying to become vaishyas. And finally, the chandals are trying to become sudra. These efforts collectively keep the society alive and moving.

Individual effort is needed to uplift a person's social status. No collective effort of any specific caste can ensure the betterment at the individual level. One can ensure the rights, but not the progress of society as a whole. Those who are trying their best to uplift their social status will have to change their daily habits drastically along with a change of their surnames. For instance, let the kayesthas be addressed as Burma Mitra instead of Das (servant) Mitra. Similarly let ladies instead of calling themselves Dasi, call each other Devi.

In Bengal the Satsudras lead such a pure and pious life that compared to their counterparts in other states they have already attained the status of vaishyas. The Satsudras of Bengal learn the scriptures and enlighten themselves so as to renounce their stigmatized caste of Sudra. Let them renounce their demeaning surnames, indicating their inferior professions and adopt surnames suited for the vaishyas.

Men of all the castes can elevate themselves by studying the scriptures. If many receive education, learn Sanskrit along with the scriptures, and manifest their adeptness they will surely find a way to uplift their social status. For instance, King Rajballabh was born of a vaidya and redeemed his caste. Likewise, any great man can redeem his caste by personal achievements. Vaidyas were allowed to take the sacred thread, a distinction earned by King Rajballabh.

We are gradually losing our traditional respect for the caste system after coming into contact both with the Muslims and the Christians. Personal achievement is now being acknowledged instead of one's caste. If a large section of people of one particular caste is enlightened and wins the respect of people universally, the entire caste then wins universal respect. But mere mimicking any caste to uplift oneself socially is simply not wise. Since most of our country men are illiterates, they prefer to revere the caste system as a mark of superiority. And taking advantage of this narrow outlook many well-educated men give undue importance to the practice of caste distinction.

The Aryans started coming to Bengal in the 5th century BC. They came, and like everywhere else, started dividing the existing society in a new manner, based on the caste system. As a result of this there sprang up two distinct castes—the Satsudra and the Navanash. Consequently, the learnings of Tantra became widespread. And it was due to this popularity, scholars feel, that Tantra originated from Bengal. The fact remains that many texts on Tantra were composed in Bengal. However, the origin of these texts was as old as the Vedas.

In all likelihood the Aryans brought with them the practice of worshipping gods like Indra and Varun. And when they settled down in the land of five rivers, they were introduced to the non-Aryan practice of worshipping the phallus of god, i.e., the Shiva lingam. This was originally the traditional practice of the Dravidians. With the co-mingling of the Aryan and non-Aryan culture, maybe society started following both Vedic and non-Vedic practices of worship, i.e., worshipping the Vedic god Rudra and the non-Vedic Shiva lingam.

When Alexander the Great came to India in 300 BC, he came across this practice of worshipping the Shiva lingam. Now from Kashmir to Kanyakumari, this form of Tantric worship of Lord Shiva has become extremely popular. In the text *Malatimadhav* that was composed in 7th century AD, we find a reference to a Tantric worshipper, Aghorghantik. In 6th century AD, Tantra infiltrated Buddhism and made its way to Tibet. But by 10th century AD, the Tibetans started rejecting Tantra. However, for the Vedic practitioners of India, Buddhism coupled with Tantra became a religion of dissipation.

Buddhism that became popular in Nepal, Tibet and China was known as Mahayana. But the Buddhism that spread to Ceylon, Cambodia, and Japan spread the message of non-existence of soul and God. In Buddhist theology this form came to be known as Hinayana. Likewise, the practitioners of erotic Tantric rites called themselves Vir (hero) and the southern practitioners of Buddhism were termed as animals. But the practitioners of the first form of erotic worship could not retain the purity of their religious practices hence, after a time this class of Buddhists started preaching to the Bengali society the values of self-control.

In the Vedic age, ordinary Aryans were known as Vish or vaishyas. But with foreign invasions the same population was branded as sudras. Some scholars however think that the term sudra connotes dark Dravidian. But they are not the only sudras. Sudras are of various types. Unlike the Vedic age now there is no difference of language or castes and complexion. Now the difference depends upon social status, affluence, and heredity. The physical appearance of the sudras in Bengal is closer to the Aryans, rather than to the Dravidians. But because they are debarred from mastering the Vedas, they are unable to belong to the proper caste structure. Tantra, however, acknowledges them. Tantra has assigned brahmin and sudras the same God, the same mantra and the same Guru. Sudras are even allowed to practice the Gayatri of the Tantra though not the Savitri of the Vedas. Consequently, the sudras started following the rules and customs laid out for the brahmins. But significantly, the sudras of northern India and the sudras of eastern India do enjoy the same caste status. Their customs and regulations vary considerably. Sudras of eastern India do not consider themselves debarred from pursuing the Vedas. Quoting the tenth sloka of the *Brihatkarma Purana* they claim their rights to learn the Vedas. Tantrics however, pay more importance to Agam, Nigam and Jamal over the Vedas.

Buddhism, which had influenced one-third of the world's population actually originated from eastern India. And that it had spread vastly here is now an established fact. The destroyed Buddhist structures still bear the names of many merchants. The leading business community, the Jains, have started following the ancient Puranic customs closely. But the Buddhist merchants of Bengal have gradually lost their religious traits. Consequently, they were not allowed to re-enter their previous Hindu caste structure.

In Anandabhatta's *Ballal Charita* there is a mention of the caste system followed during the rule of Ballal Sen. It says that other than barber and kayestha, all the other castes are nothing but offshoots of the vaishya category. Milkman, gardener, tambuli, kanshari, weaver, shell carvers, potters, karmakar, teli, gandhabanik and vaidya are basically vaishyas as per their acquired skills. Common people too acknowledge their skills and admit their excellence. The community of milkmen claim that according to *Brahmavaivarta Purana*, the father of Lord Krishna was a milkman, hence a vaishya. So, by deduction they all are vaishyas. The weavers claim that according to sage Manu, weaving is a profession of the vaishyas, hence they too are vaishyas. Gandhabaniks claim that the name of their caste category has the tagline merchant (banik) hence, they too are vaishyas. But this argument does not hold good for all. As mentioned earlier, the caste categorization of the ancient times has not been destroyed completely. Despite various changes the basic caste structure is still extant in society. Whoever desires to belong to a certain caste category will not be easily accepted till his customs and behaviour pattern conforms to that specific class. Even his profession is considered in this matter. Hindu society pays great importance to a person's profession and accordingly his status in society varies.

Kamrup

Life without curiosity is meaningless. Curiosity helps a person to make life meaningful. When someone is fed up with life, he could undertake a journey round the world, just to satisfy his curiosity.

British ethnographers[48] have said that the people of Bengal are of Mongoloid and Dravidian origins. According to them the people of Assam belong to the Mongoloid faction. Comilla is situated right in between Bengal and Assam, hence is termed as the entry point of both these regions. Present-day Bengali language bears marked resemblance to the language of eastern Mymensingh. But the language of western Mymensingh is different from the eastern part. Sylhet has a different language. The mountain range of Kamrup divides Mymensingh into two parts. One range which is near Goalpara is habited by the Garo tribe. The appearance of the Garo and Tipra people tell us that originally they did not belong to the Aryan race. 'Tripura' is actually the Sanskrit version of Tipra.

On reaching Tripura we found men and women carrying fodder on their backs to the market fair. The women wore one kind of fabric to cover their bosoms, and another kind around their waist. They adorned their ears with flowers. A few men had tufts of hair at the back of their heads. The crown prince of Tipra dynasty, Nawadip Chandra, was seen wearing European headgear and driving a car.

Fine architectural aspects, as reflected in their Shiva temples, give us a hint of the Tipra people's skill. Their homes are surrounded by betel-nut trees. Adjacent to these stands an engraved boundary wall, which bears testimony to their lineage. We saw the royal library, the court and a large market and then returned home to sleep on a bunk. Due to excessive humidity the bedroom is often constructed upon a bunk. Tipras call their houses chung. They employ tribal Assamese for jhum cultivation in their agricultural fields. The eatery which we visited give us an inkling of their class distinction. The people who were raised from the category of Jugi to become brahmins

48. A) Ethnographic appendices and B) *The Tribes and Castes of Bengal*—edited by H.H. Risley C) *A History of Assam* by E.A. Gait, D) *Upto the Clouds (Darjeeling)* etc.

were called Nath brahmins while the others were called the superior brahmins.

For bearing loads they use a wooden plank which is wide at one end and narrow at the other. They use these planks to sell agricultural products. I asked a person about his race. He said that he was a namasudra, i.e., a class lower than the sudras. A brahmin was mimicking the pronunciation of Calcutta people. I found two Assamese ladies trying to hide their faces with an umbrella. The sight aroused my curiosity, and I went forward to find out the cause. But the more I advanced the more they tried to hide their faces.

We started our journey from Comilla and in the morning opened our eyes to view Badarpur, a place near Sylhet. We had reached a valley. Surrounded by deep green foliage on all sides, there was a river with blue, transparent water flowing down the rocky terrain, creating a superbly picturesque sight. There were a few Manipuri men and a woman with her child mounting a carriage. They had long signs drawn across their foreheads down to the nose, indicating their belief in Vaishnavism. One among them appeared to me to be a Gurkha.

Gradually we entered Nagaland, crossing endless dark tunnels. Our steam engine rushed forward cutting across rocky terrains (the rocks looked like slates), tea plantations and gorges. The hill we viewed was covered with various plantations like bamboo, banana, cane, and varied creepers. Here and there were scattered green foliage-covered cottages of the Naga amidst agricultural fields on the slopes of the mountains. The Nepalese were selling curd to the passengers of our train. Labourers who had previously come to construct roads, have now turned into thriving businessmen here. We spent the night at a place called Lamding, and in the morning, after sunrise, proceeded towards the plains bordered with mountains. The crimson sun started playing hide and seek with us. Sometimes it was visible while at other times it hid itself behind the mountain ranges.

*

Bhairav Devi island in the middle of the Brahmaputra, Kamakshya

For long I had been waiting for a bridge to get us to Assam. Right now, I am in Guwahati, on the bank of river Brahmaputra. There is a steamboat on the white waters of the river. Afar stands the mountain range, merging with the horizon. First to Khanjagiri then via Vota to the Himalayas, that was to be our route for the next phase of travel. The temple of Bhairav Shivananda at Kamkshya stands on the submerged water body. The place is full of European-style houses. Panbazar is where the Bengalis work. We had to go to Ujanbazar to find the local people of Assam. Panbazar did not satisfy me actually.

On the other side of the river, north of Guwahati, we found a few shops. A milkman's hairstyle and language, which was distinctly Oriya surprised me immensely. A little distance from there we found shops which were selling items we could cook, and fish. The lady selling fish had a large face with no vermilion mark in her hair parting. She was wearing big red-coloured earrings and no bangles on her arms. She drew my attention at once for the mekhala she was wearing. The cottages here were all surrounded by greenery and the terraces even though not as beautiful as those found in Faridpur, were sufficiently beautiful and eye catching. From one of the cottages peered a lady who was covered from her breast to knee by a knotted cloth. Her long hair was like the girls from Kerala and the moment she saw us looking at her, she simply disappeared.

We reached the house where bhajans were being sung. The owner was asleep, and his wife woke him up the moment we reached. They had a Bengali almanac. Assamese script is similar to the Bengali script and even the colloquial language is quite similar. The story of Lord Krishna forms a part of their ancient literature. Their renowned saint, Madhav Dev, who was a non-dualist, was almost contemporary to Sri Chaitanya. His followers are known as Mahapurushia. Since bhajans are not sung except at some specified times, we had to satisfy ourselves with loitering about the place and taking in whatever we found around. In the evening devotees arrived to sing bhajans for the entire neighborhood. The owner served me betel leaf and betel nut and asked me to dress them appropriately. It is not the custom to serve the guests with dressed betel leaves. Here they do not use the brown- coloured stuff for dressing the betel leaf.

In ancient times, the Assamese needed money only to pay the royal tax. And for that they had to sell their paddy. The fish in the pond, producing salt, grinding mustard from one's own field for producing edible oil, molasses, pulses, and weaving helped people to thrive on their own. They had their cowsheds too for steady supply of milk. For fire, they had a supply of husks which they would ignite for illuminating the house. Interestingly, they still haven't learnt the art of warming milk for consumption. Here Bengali cloth and Bengali salt is very popular. Since Bengali traders supply them all the foreign goods, they call them Bengali goods and not foreign goods. The Marwaris are now gradually replacing the Bengalis.

Since we were unable to visit Hayagriva, we could not see the witches who were once driven off from Kamakshya. The Mohinis of this place did not appear more adept than the Devadasis of Puri or prostitutes of Calcutta. In the afternoon we went for a horse ride on the banks of the Brahmaputra. When we reached there, we found ourselves surrounded by a group of opium-addicted priests. There we sat, to listen to their chanting of the *Ramayana*, composed by Krittibash (renowned Bengali rendition of the original Sanskrit *Ramayana*). But their pronunciation was so different that we could not recognize the language as our mother tongue Bengali. For instance, instead of 'chandra' (moon in Bengali) they pronounced it as 'shandra'. Likewise, 'sarba' (all in Bengali) as 'harba' and 'chida' (flattened rice in Bengali) as 'hira'. Ch is h for them.

Even though the ladies were religiously attending this *Ramayana* session, they were talking among themselves in Assamese. To us, the language sounded more like Oriya. Since both Orissa and Assam are border states of Bengal, this affinity is quite understandable. Other than language, the other similarity that struck us was their hairstyle. For an outsider these similarities might appear quite mysterious. Interestingly, there are quite a few ancient poems composed in the remote parts of East Bengal where we come across several words in Oriya. Yet, generalization should not be stretched too far. Actually, the influence of Bengali has been far-reaching. It has kept modifying itself and assuming different forms. For us it is just a change of form, but to others it is the chief language. In fact, we were struck by the similarities we found in regions ranging from south west to north east.

Unlike the people of lower Assam, the people of upper Assam do not speak Assamese. Their language is called Dhekeri and this language is closer to Bengali. They refer to their Guru as Gonsai. He is the head administrator of the village. He selects his representative, who works for him in absentia. The number of representatives in a village is directly proportional to the number of his disciples. They have to work in unison to pass a judgement. Previously, one could approach the Guru for redressal in case of misconduct of his representatives. But now they must approach the British court. They are, however, entitled to decide cases relating to land and other issues. In case of physical torture, a fine of rupees one or two is imposed.

I was introduced to a Hazarika and his wife who is known as Hazarikani. His ancestors received land directly from the king of Assam. This royal gift exempted them from paying any tax for the land. In return he was to provide the king with thousand labourers who would work for him without pay. This ensured him a regular grant, and also the title Hazarika. It is still not easy to find labour in Assam. Previously, only a person in dire need would accept slavery. If a person owed rupees fifty to anyone of higher social status, in lieu he became his servant. After the arrival of the British, this practice ended. But because there is no steady occupation, many people prefer tilling land. However, there is also a scarcity of agricultural labourers. The daily wage of a labourer is six anna, and no one accepts any less than that. And even when they work, they refuse to undertake excess labour.

There is an interesting story about this. Once a person at Dangoria had employed a person to take out thread from flax. In the evening when the labourer asked for payment, the owner said that 'I don't have money, I will pay tomorrow.' Next day he told the labourer, 'You sell the thread and collect your payment.' The fellow replied, 'The thread will fetch only three annas.' The owner replied, 'You are to be paid six annas, but the work you have done is only half of what you claim. In that case I am not ready to pay you.' From the next day the labourer started working thrice the amount. The story teaches a good lesson to a materialist.

Assamese are not adept in making varied dishes like the Bengalis. Gourd and green being very tasty are used extensively. The greens bear an Assamese name and appeared quite foreign to me. The most popular festival that is observed here is during the vernal equinox. During spring another festival takes place for a few days and is celebrated by all. During this festival people wear new clothes. In order to gift new clothes to all the family members, housewives start weaving them long before the festival. Except the Bengali servant, all native people receive new clothes. They are also given a few days' leave, which they spend in playing games of dice, singing and other such entertaining activities. They also visit the families of their kinsmen. Bachelors play drums, sing and dance. And when no older people are around, they also sing obscene songs. The lower caste women are also well versed in playing drums and dancing. No ritual worship takes place during this festival.

Pragjyotishpur was the capital of Bhagdutt. It was his father Narakasur who set up the Kamakshya temple during the Puranic times. The temple is still there, a testament to times gone by. On the bank of the Brahmaputra there is the temple of Sukleshwar. Underneath the temple a stone figure was found, which supposedly belonged to the age of Lord Buddha.

Early in the morning we travelled about a mile in a horse carriage to visit the Bhuvaneswari temple. All the while we could see the beautiful Himalayan range. After a time when we reached a spring, we had to alight from the carriage. Before going up to the temple we saw the remnants of a large entrance. At places there were steps. But the entire pathway was steep with smooth places here and there. So, we walked up slowly and carefully. It was easier while alighting. The place was full of trees, especially champak trees. The entire area buzzed with the sound of varied insects. The profuse amount of champak flowers filled the air with a heavenly fragrance. At the second entrance sat an ash-covered ascetic wearing a garland of rudraksha. Looking at his face, I felt that for the sake of worshipping the goddess, he could go to any extreme—either sacrifice himself or, if necessary, any other human being. After viewing the temple of Goddess Chhinnamasta, the lake of fortune, and an alley of mountain cottages, we reached the small house of the priest.

After bathing in Kampith and then having our breakfast, we went to visit Goddess Kamakshya. We just had to promise a bath at the lake before entering the temple. People are fond of visiting temples because temples indicate the faith of a race and their behaviour pattern. Right in the middle of the temple we saw an image of Goddess Durga and proceeded towards the flower-clad sanctum sanctorum, dimly lit by lamps. We sat by a small puddle and dipped our hands into it, to feel the touch of the sacred mountain spring. At night yajna is held at the mandap which was constructed by Gourinath, the king of Assam. Animals like sheep, buffalo, duck etc., are sacrificed. Sacrifice of pigs has been prohibited now.

Three hundred years ago the king of Cooch Behar, the brothers Mallyadhwaj and Sukladhwaj, had constructed a temple to Parvati, the daughter of Himalaya. Mithilesh had tried to destroy it. But King Nripendra Narayan had not permitted him to do so. Viswa Singha had constructed the temple at the top of the mountains, and a low-caste musician was appointed as its priest. It is said that when the goddess danced, the priest used to play his drum. And because he permitted others to see this divine sight, the goddess beheaded him with just her hand. That head, now turned into a stone, is still preserved within the temple premises. Since then, the kings of Cooch Behar have been prohibited from seeing the goddess.

The moment I came out of the temple, I saw the temple girls and paid them about one-fourth of a rupee. Later I heard that the priest had taken it from them as his due. Like the Trambakeshwar temple which stands at the origin point of River Godavari, here also, a pilgrim is served his meal at the residence of the priest. After leaving Calcutta this was the first time I relished the food that was served. The three sisters of the priest were exceedingly sweet natured and the very incarnate of simplicity. Here I found the betel creepers embracing tall trees and growing merrily. On rare occasions elephants from the bank of the Brahmaputra come and destroy the garden. However it was impossible for me to trace the sweet water source below, where tigers come to quench their thirst, and get a glimpse of the Bhuvaneswari temple which stood above it.

The devotional song or kirtan that are sung here is very similar to those of Bengal. The lead singer sings a few lines first, and then the rest repeat them after him. The song the ladies were singing in front of Goddess Durga had a strange story to tell. Lord Shiva had fallen down unconscious due to excessive consumption of alcohol. I have never heard of such theme in a devotional song. This is typical of Tantric practice. The Assamese brahmins, who worship Shakti the Divine Mother, have to adopt the Tantric mode of worship. The other brahmins, not belonging to their clan, are not respected by them. They do not touch the feet of the brahmins as a form of salutation. They do not accept either water or rice from them. This might be due to either Vaishnava influence, or a general hostility towards the Shaivites.

When a Tantric practitioner after completing his novitiate becomes a Koula, he enjoys the freedom of acting out his role as he wishes. The people who assume the ochre robe are divided into many different categories in Tantra. Other than Saraswathi and Ashram all the other ascetics of the Dasanami group practice Tantra. In India the Gonsai of the Sringeri Math do not practice Tantra. In this group, people of all castes can become a Paramahansa. However, except a brahmin one cannot become a Dandi. But at Panchakroshi in Varanasi, even the cobblers in desperate need to beg, carry with them the usual accessories of a monk, like a water pot used by ascetics, and a stick.

Tantra is a modified Vedic practice which has evolved naturally. Vedic gods have assumed symbolic forms with human characteristics and this has enabled human beings to worship them with what they consider to be sacred and auspicious, like flowers, frankincense, ignited lamps and also food offerings. The yajna fires set up during the Vedic age have now been recreated too. Likewise, different slokas and mantra were composed for chanting while performing the yajna. And instead of Soma rasa, alcohol started being used. In the Vedic age, however, wine used to be used directly. In order to satiate the urge of human thirst various mudras were modulated. They formed a major part of the yajna ritual. Similarly, animal sacrifice instead of hunting an animal became an easier solution. And in some places where animals were not easily available, fish were used for conducting the ritual. From the Vedic age till the age of the *Mahabharata*, the fidelity in marital relationship was not a strong issue. So, following these loose ends, the threads of Tantric practice do not give much importance to the sacredness of the husband-wife relationship.

In order to gather full knowledge about a place that one visits, it is necessary to travel by foot. We started an uncomfortable journey on a double-horsed carriage towards Til mountain from Guwahati. The journey became steeper as we proceeded. The path however was not curved. The natural beauty was not visible at all as we found emaciated Garo men and women suffering from Kala azar working hard to reconstruct the roads. Late in the afternoon when we reached the capital Shillong, we found it to be a beautiful place surrounded by mountains and green foliage on all sides. Despite being summer, Shillong was cool. Shimla is full of cedar trees while Shillong is full of pine trees. The city is situated 4000 feet above the sea level, amidst the mountainous terrain of Jayanti hills. Most of the local population belong to the Khas community, who have quite interesting ways of living.

Satyasrava had once remarked that 'Assam is nature's most cherished land'.

India is bounded by seas to the east and south-west. In the north the Himalayas protect the country. The invaders therefore could approach the land only through the mountainous terrains of our north-west and north-eastern boundaries. Aryans, Greeks, Huns, Pathans, and the Mughals entered the country from the western side. The Mongols entered the land from the east via Kamrup and the western part of China. They came and mixed with the local Dravidians and consequently lost their Mongoloid traits. Their physique changed, their language changed and even their religion changed. They became Assamese and Bengali, Hindus and Muslims. But a few of them who still retained a large portion of their Mongoloid traits are now known as the Khas tribe, and they reside in the Jayanti region. They still converse in their original tongue which is nowhere similar to the local language, and their religion too is the ancient religion of their ancestors. There are a few tribes even in Kamrup who have remained unmixed Mongoloid, and their faces indicate their antecedents.

There is no tradition in our country to record our national history. But here in Assam I found the Assamese have a wonderful written history of their own, right from 13th century AD. The Muslims however were unable to fly their half-moon engraved flag here in Assam. Bengal being a plain land and

Pragjyotishpur, a mountainous terrain, they termed the entire region as Assom (uneven). Hence the name Assam. This was a presumption of the past. Now however, this theory does not hold good. Clearly the name Assam has evolved from the local word Ahom.

The betel-leaf chewing, artistically attired, beautiful Khas girls carry heavy loads on their backs. They have beautiful faces and cover themselves with two pieces of long cloths, one to cover their upper part of the body, while the other starts from their waist and reaches down to their ankles. They use another piece of cloth to cover their heads. The males wear dhoti and a coat and also a creased cloth as their turban. Men who have names like Ravana Roy or Buddhadev Babu, use Roman scripts to write their names in Khasi language. Unfortunately, before they could establish their racial identity, they lost their freedom. The Christian missionaries, instead of helping them to establish their racial identity, preached universal love. Late Assistant Commissioner Jivan Roy, being a Khasi himself, had tried hard to prevent the conversion of the Khasis either to Hindu or Christian religion. Spirits and demons are the gods of the Khasis. The Khasi leaders however try to prevent the common people from adopting the religion of the learned people.

Without faith neither material nor spiritual goals can be reached. And this holds good both for the literate and illiterate tribals. The difference between an educated and an uneducated person is this—an uneducated person readily believes in things but an educated person thoroughly searches for the source of a thing and then decides for himself what he should believe and what he should not believe. That his belief may be wrong he will not accept. In other words, in both cases faith is fundamental. Just as a weak person bows down before a powerful person, or a fool before a scholar, similarly man too bows down before overpowering nature. And it is this submission which makes the common man worship nature as gods and goddesses.

There is difference of opinion regarding the existence of

this universe as well. A class of people does not believe in the existence of God, while another set of people believe that everything in the universe belongs to God. The non-believers can be said to be believers of Maya philosophy, while the believers can be termed as materialistic. Both however, are believers of Advaita (monotheism) philosophy. The non-believers say that both the internal and external worlds are same, just a collection of few things and a temporary experience. The universe has no existence of its own. The believers say that both the material world and the inner world are inseparable, and one accentuates the other like fire assumes motion and generates heat. The human mind, when set in motion, experiences joy and sorrow. To them even the atom has an existence of its own. But both believer and non-believer give due importance to consciousness. It is only their perception that is either correct or wrong. The sky whether it has an existence or not exists everywhere. A person by concentration and meditation can send thought waves to other minds and understand the thought process of all, thereby impressing them and subjugating them. But it needs a lot of spiritual practice to attain this state. Since ether exists everywhere it is possible to produce waves in it and collect information from miles away and also extend one's thought process. This is very much possible. It is a hidden process and the one who has mastered this technique is bound to win everyone's respect.

It is but natural that a strong person will win the respect of a weaker person. A disciple unquestioningly believes in his Guru because he has faith in him and depends upon him. Faith and dependence come naturally to man. Shankaracharya did not believe in the existence of the universe, yet believed in gods and goddesses. Buddha, even though scientific in approach, believed in the karmic cycle. And none of them felt their beliefs to be inconsistent. One who does not have knowledge beyond his capacity believes only what he knows. So, Brahman can be both with and without attributes. It is really not required to talk much about God. The fundamental concept of religion is to seek individual wellness and then the wellness of the world. And it is because of this we have to protect our own identity. Without it, both nationalism and national interest cannot be sustained.

Fruits and vegetables are available twice a week in the market fair. Compared to Srihatta, all types of oranges that are available here are less sweet. I was tempted to taste a few known and unknown fruits. Mango and mustard pickle were piled up in a place but I dared not buy them. Agricultural products sold by Khasi women, dresses of both Bengali and Marwari men, betel leaves, were all available, but they formed a small amount. A little down the slope various types of meat were displayed for sale along with firewood, frankincense, and building materials.

Since it was difficult to shop in open spaces, the king was constructing a larger enclosed market. Large, white-coloured pillars were constructed to beautify the place. The high pillars helped people to locate the marketplace from afar. Mr Fuller had come to inaugurate the market and in all likelihood the gods in heaven, displeased with the occurrence, sent down a heavy downpour of rain. A Roman-scripted Khasi invitation, written on a red cloth in white alphabets, was stuck at the entrance. That too was getting drenched. Under the covered enclosure, unable to do anything, the entire Gurkha regiment was waiting patiently and enduring the torrential rain. The Khasi administrators of the Til Mountain were sitting on one side. They were dressed in silk garments, and were wearing swords and golden necklaces, which hung up to their waists like sacred threads. Bedecked in large-sized diamond-studded golden necklaces, which were visible from afar, they kept on munching betel leaves. In the afternoon, images of gods and goddesses were brought and placed on a horse-driven chariot. The benevolent British superior addressed the gathering and read out a congratulatory letter. The letter was placed in a silver receptor to which the gentleman pointed out and asked why was it brought from Kolkata instead of it being a local product.

Clearly, the Khasi king was not much in tune with his subjects. They did not have to pay any tax and the entire region was divided into twenty-five smaller regions. In the Panchadash region, even though the king is selected from the royal family, it is the subjects who have the final say in choosing the king. Here a caretaker is employed. Sardar rules five states while the Lingto rules four states and they all are elected. At present the British government has to endorse the elected representative. The British government receives half the share of items like minerals of the regions, elephants, and the revenues from the forest products through the representatives. Consequently, they readily endorse the elected candidates. The subjects themselves decide legal matters. But in case of serious crimes like murder etc., they rely on the British government's rulings. The lime that is found in abundance at Srihatta is produced by the Khasis of the region.

Like the ladies of Kashmir, Shimla, Darjeeling and Shillong, the women here cover their heads with a piece of cloth. The practice possibly is foreign in origin. But that region is beyond my travel itinerary. The breast covers Manipuri, Tipra, Nepali and Assamese girls use bear marked resemblance and that too has foreign origin. The Mug girls of Arakan use similar covers. The scarves the Assamese use are slightly different in style from the one used by the ladies of Arakan. But there is quite a lot of similarity between the people of Kerala in the southern part of India and the eastern Indian people of Kamrup. There is a Mongoloid touch in both cases.

*

I have visited many hill stations. Of these Darjeeling is unparalleled. You are not disturbed by any kind of domestic activities there. It is an ideal place to soothe one's agitated nerves. Constant visual treat of the majestic Kanchenjunga and the interplay of the clouds cannot be found elsewhere. It is as if a cluster of cotton-like clouds keep moving constantly across the clear sky. A pungent odour permeates the place, and I was amused to find this combination in such a beautiful natural setting.

While travelling across Shimla we were troubled by recurrent sandy storms. Only once in a fortnight we were soothed with a rainfall. Here, of course, the natural sights are different. The inhabitants of Darjeeling and Shillong are non-Aryans. But in Shimla that is not the case. There we had the fortune to meet an ancient Aryan farmer. A fair-complexioned luggage carrier being questioned had replied that he was a brahmin. And because his elder brother does not have to live outside their ancestral home, he uses the sacred thread. But he does not use the sacred thread because he cannot observe the rigid rules accompanying the sacred thread. We met a kshatriya stone cutter and came to know a lot about them. Due to dire economic condition, only the eldest son of the family gets married, and the younger ones thrive on them. If every one of them had different wives, the family size would increase and there would be scarcity of food, which they cultivate on their ancestral lands. At times a man is allowed to have three wives as well. There is no restriction regarding acceptance of food from a different caste. At the Shipar fair a beautiful fair-complexioned lady reminded me of the Kashmiri pandit people. Though she belonged to the family of a farmer, but her actions appeared ethereal. The Muslims, however, have not been able to penetrate these hilly terrains. The behaviour pattern of these people is very different from either the foreigners or the orthodox Hindus. Inside the mountain terrains there are several small kingdoms, and the progress of these states is entirely dependent on the rulers. This has been the practice since ancient times.

The mountains of Uttarakhand are not very far from Shimla. Even the neighbouring region of Kedar is within Uttarakhand.

Kanchenjunga peak, Himalayas

The people of these regions are renowned for their honesty and truthfulness. Because of the remoteness of the region, I decided not to proceed further the moment we reached Hardwar. While sitting on the wide space near Brahmkund in the evening, the melodiously flowing Bhagirathi transports one to a different world. 'When I turned my eyes towards Chandi Mountain right across, I felt 'o art thou new, forever new, whenever I look at you'. The water was ice cold. In Garhwal region, small human habitations are found scattered here and there. Just as the material world lies dormant in the hearts of the ascetics and only emerges when the mental turmoil settles down, likewise, human habitations are seen at times hidden within the mountainous terrains. Ascetics from different Maths or organizations have constructed their hermitages in Hardwar. Isn't that a manifestation of their materialistic outlook? True they have withdrawn from the material rat race and stopped themselves from propagating the human race, much to our benefit. But just to earn handful of meal they remain forever busy, forgetting their spiritual practices. However, I found the hermitage hospital of Vivekananda and Dayananda's Gurukul bit different.

The Garhwalis were found carrying water to the plains in containers covered with Himalayan birch leaves. They resembled the Nepalis. They supply holy water to different pilgrimages for six months and then return home. The amount they earn in these six months is spent in agriculture and looking after their families. Blankets are worn during the chilly winter. The village women approach the passengers going to Badri shram and ask for small aids like thread and needle to fulfill their needs.

Similarity played an interesting role, right from Shillong and Darjeeling till the Shivalik range. In my mental world I had travelled from the land of non-Aryans to the land of the Aryans. Now again I have returned to the world of the non-Aryans. History always preserves the glorious past but sometimes this proves to be destructive. Sri Ananda Ram Gonsai is an Ahom and he expressed deep regret at the fact that they have lost their power now and brahmins have become scarce for carrying out priestly duties. He wants to return to the old-world order, since it is becoming increasingly difficult for men like him to lead such an ignominious life. He insisted that I return to Kolkata and request the protectors of Hindu religion to find a way out. Without a historical record such a distortion of view would not have occurred. He would have lived happily being absorbed in the existing Aryan and non-Aryan system followed now.

From the point of material composition, there is no difference between lifeless and a living object. That even an apparently lifeless object too can respond has recently been proved, thereby dismissing the age-old misconception. Hence, social science and geology are intrinsically linked. The state of land, weather, and natural setting act on the physical existence of human beings.

The land of Bengal is soft but the land in the western part of India is not like that. Hence, the Hindustanis living here are stronger than the Bengalis. The Assamese people living on a fertile land like Bengal have turned soft and cowardly. But their ancestors who lived in arid lands were valorous and had repeatedly deflected the attack upon the Hindus by the Muslim invaders. Just as Jaichand had sought the assistance of Sahabuddin to crush Prithviraj, the people of Gujarat had taken the help of the Marathas, similarly the king of Assam had begged the British to retrieve his throne and thereby destroyed the pride of his kingdom and also his race.

It is not possible to thrive for long on borrowed powers. If you don't work, you become incapacitated. But you need a cause to drive you to work hard. Lazy people misuse their own capacities as human beings and are finally destroyed.

The king of Assam had become incapacitated and hence had turned into a tyrant. Moamaria was a Vaishnava sect, who were forcibly converted into Sakta, by sacrificing animals and anointing their forehead with the blood of the sacrificed animal.

Revolting against these ghastly practices the subjects turned against the state. To that was added the general outlaws.

Many courageous Buddhist soldiers of the Shan tribe had arrived at Kamrup from upper Brahma[49] and as per their greater capacity to rule had established their supremacy. But later they were weakened morally and lost their ability to rule. Why they are called Ahom I really can't say. Their history is known as Burunchi and was written in the Shan language. The ancient priests were Buddhists. The priest whom I was acquainted with looked like the inhabitant of Brahma. But his daughter Kshiroda had a Bengali look. In the middle ages, the Assamese kings had Hindu names with Shan attached to them. For example, Suhitpaksha or Gourinath Singh. Sudinfa or Chandrakanta Singh etc. The Ahom kingdom survived for 600 years. Barua, Gonsai, Gohai, Phukan etc., were titles conferred by the Ahom king.

I could not visit Shiv Sagar and had to remain satisfied seeing these royal activities. But I saw the Kamrup Math, established by the uncle of Chandrakanta from Varanasi. He had spent 60,000 rupees to construct this Math. The king could not perform any stately duties without consulting the Gonsai. Barua were social and military protectors, under the surveillance of the Gonsai. This prevented the king from turning into a dictator. The king could dole out punishments. These consisted of tearing off ear lobes or cutting off the nose. With time and changed scenario we now consider the punishment pronounced by the British rulers as light in nature. But the British make no distinction of caste or race when passing a judgement for the wrongdoer. This is because they believe in equality.

At present, the Ahom king whom British imperialists helped to win, has his inheritor on the throne. But unfortunately, he has recently lost his kingship. And his direct lineage having refused a paltry allowance of 50 rupees, has left the state. He is

49. Bengali old name of Burma (Myanmar)

in Shillong now, earning his living as an ordinary employee at rupees 150 only. It is essential to strike a balance between one's living and one's principles.

There is a striking similarity between Ahom's rural gods and Bengal's rural gods. At Goalpara, Bisahari or Manasa[50] (goddess of snake) and Hubachani or Subachani[51] (goddess of sweet speech) are worshipped. Snakes are worshipped throughout India. But the worship of the manasa plant, other than Bengal, is found only among the Garo. This clearly indicates a link between the two races. During Paus Sankranti they have Bihu festival in Kamrup and prepare sweet pies similar to the ones prepared in Bengal on the same occasion. Hindustanis do not prepare sweet pies. Maybe we have learnt the art from the Ahom or else they have learnt it from us.

The Koch community forms the largest part of the entire population of Assam. Their approximate number is 2,21,000. In Yogini Tantra they are called mlechas[52]. Inheritors of Koch are related to the king of Beltala in Bengal. The Koch dynasty ruled Kamrup for 200 years. They however had to battle against the Ahom. Kachari, Lalung, Mikir and other races have to follow Koch ways before becoming Hindu. In North Bengal they have lost their old social status and are now looked down upon. They are called Rajbanshi there. The community however has lost its original language and now the language they use is somewhat like the language of the Garo. Previously a Koch could marry a Mech, but after they adopted Hindu religion this practice stopped. These changes cannot be prevented.

Nobody cares to preserve the ancestral history if it is not a glorious one. In 1790, King Krishna Chandra of Kamrup had tried to establish himself as kshatriya and claimed that Bhima (of the *Mahabharata*) was the originator of their tribe.

---

50. Bengal version

51. Bengal version

52. Foreigner and not of the same religion.

In Naogaon region, at present known as Dimapur, there still stands the capital Hidimbapur. But this royal tribe is among the oldest inhabitants of Assam. They are also known as Bodo. Narakasur probably belonged to this tribe. They ruled over Assam for 300 years. This royal tribe had terrible enmity with the contemporary Ahom kings.

If we had gone via Srihatta, we would have been able to view the copper idol of Goddess Jayanateswari Kalika. This temple is one of the famous fifty-one peeths[53] of Sati like Kamakshya.

From the perspective of language and physical appearance, the Khasi and the Jayanti tribes are almost identical. The Khasis live on the upper terrains of the mountains, while the Jayanti tribes reside in the plains. Like the Khasis, their villages too are ruled by representatives. Probably they have not renounced their original religion. Right from Parvat Roy to Rajendra Singha, that is for a period of 335 years, (1500-1835) Assam was ruled by them.

Someone had once stated, 'I prefer describing the tribes instead of the place I visit.' Likewise, at present my travelogue too is turning into a tribal history. Anyway, ethnicity cannot be established only by physical appearance, anthropological proofs are also required. So, before proceeding to give a short account of these tribes, some background information is necessary.

As mentioned in the *Kalika Purana*, at present no human being is sacrificed for worshipping the goddess Jayanteswari. But during the rule of Jayanti Raj, human sacrifice was inevitable to celebrate any occasion, whether be it the birthday of the prince, or any kind of achievement. People used to volunteer to sacrifice themselves to fulfill the demands of the ceremony. And

53. According to the Puranic myths, when Lord Shiva carried the body of his wife Sati and went round the universe in rage, Lord Vishnu sent his chakra and cut her body parts into many bits. The body parts fell into different part of our country and each one became a sacred place for worshipping the Divine mother. They are called the peeths.

nobody ever stopped such people from such terrible acts. If by chance the person decided to flee before the sacrifice, the king would get hold of another person from anywhere and sacrifice him. During the British rule, such an incident took place and immediately afterwards the place was annexed to the British empire.

The British rulers, however, did not accept the barbaric logic behind human sacrifice. Consequently, people of Kamrup felt reassured under the new ruler. People rarely admit their own faults. If a sovereign commits a mistake, he is never ready to rectify it. This leads to tremendous dissatisfaction among the subjects. Forcibly performing human sacrifice is a heinous crime and the king was a part of this terrible practice. So, his destruction was inevitable. Naturally a foreign ruler with logical outlook was more than welcome.

Various kinds of divisiveness have persisted in our country. The anarchy of the kings, their misuse of power, corruption and love for material enjoyment coupled with political peace had turned them into a bunch of useless, lazy monarchs. This finally led to us losing our independence. At present we are ruled by a group of foreigners. Their interest is very different from the local rulers. Their rule too cannot be called perfect. Yet, we have benefitted by the British rule, just as they have benefitted by ruling our country. It is by assisting each other that we are progressing. Britain is a nation of the vaishyas. So, their tendency to acquire material wealth is understandable. Even our native kings were vaishyas by nature and not kshatriyas, hence their greed for wealth. While talking about the British rule, we often talk about their positive sides for about a page and their negative aspects for four hundred pages, by way of showing our patriotism. This approach is misleading. From the point of material achievement, our country is undoubtedly progressing. And when we are unable to achieve a target within a fixed time, we are worried. This is the right approach, or else we will lose our national zeal to develop our country. Expressing gratitude is the sign of a proper human being. Hence, we should respect the British rulers. National or foreign, representative rule is necessary for the benefit of the subjects. And India, with her cultural divisiveness, can never develop without the assistance of the British rulers. The new political theory states that the subjects of a nation are her real rulers. But in a country like India, without a strong ruler, it is not possible to control the multiplicity of ethnic identity, leave aside her development. The rulers have now turned into imperialists, trying to crush the subjects. So, our present aim is to become self-reliant.

If we compare old Assam with present Assam, we observe notable changes in all spheres. The civilization of this region is developing at a fast pace. By assisting each other, the tribes too are being enriched. The presence of British merchant rulers in Kamrup is just an ideal example of it.

The people who would willingly submit themselves for human sacrifice were allowed varied privileges by the state. Because the materialistic rulers of this state considered lechery as their legal right, practices like human sacrifice etc., thrived gloriously. Even the Tantric pundits were not above these kinds of perversities. The pundits, by way of imaging the natural procreation of human beings, conceptualized the female sex organ as the active element and the male organ as the inactive element. The sculpted figure of unification of these two organs was then portrayed as an exemplification of monotheism to the civilized world[54].

It is impossible for us to disbelieve our own existence. But those of us who are not well-versed in either philosophy or theology are often convinced by the learned philosophers and religious preachers to believe otherwise. And when their arguments fail to convince, people take measures to mend them carefully through logical deductions. Saktas[55] and Vaishnavas,

---

54. Here he is clearly talking about the Shiva Lingam that is worshipped by the Hindus.

55. Worshipper of God as the Primordial power

whose philosophy at times bespeak of animality, take immense care to subvert the issues and confer divinity upon them. And for that they take the help of Sankhya philosophy. Philosophy of existence is pretty complicated.

Often it is difficult to understand one's own ideologies. And to interpret the ideology of a population is tougher. It is equally impossible to clarify one's thought through other's thoughts. The information that is at present stored in the brains of children within the age group of three to fifteen years, is the result of acquired experience of thousand years by human beings. We easily imbibe them within a short span of time because of the advantage of inheritance. All acquired knowledge, thus, cumulatively forms our basic knowledge. For a child who knows about his past life, the memory stays on with him up to five or six years. At precisely what age the perception of smell strikes the human brain is yet to be ascertained. Perception of music is the acquired knowledge of 5000 years after persistent effort and practice. And a youth becomes adept in it within a span of a few years, just by inheriting the information of his ancestors. Knowledge of ethics is the result of 10,000 years' constant cultivation and practice. And we at present master it at the tender age of fifteen, as a matter of inheritance. Hence, to consider oneself as the sole proprietor of all knowledge, is grossly incorrect.

The concept of faithfulness or fidelity of women is rather lax at Kamrup, due to Tantric influence. Right from the ancient times, many untoward practices are allowed to thrive here because of it. Except the Bengalis, all other non-brahmin Indians approve of widow remarriage. And in Assam legal marriage is rare, hence, marital ties can easily be snapped. In 'agchalua' marriage, for instance, the guests are entertained with betel leaves and betel nuts, but for conducting the marriage ceremony, approval of the guardians is not essential. In another kind of marriage only the approval of the bride and bridegroom is needed. The groom gifts clothes and ornaments to the bride and fixes up the match. The bride's guardian welcomes the villagers with flattened rice and molasses. Goldsmith, potter, barber, blacksmith, actor etc., follow the latter form of marriage. They are generally addressed as chotokalita. In the ancient texts this kind of marriage is known as Gandharva marriage.

Brahmins, kayasthas, astrologers and borokalita conduct yajna while formalizing the marriage. This form is supposed to strengthen the marital bonds. At present even the chotokalitas acknowledge this form of marriage as superior. But both brahmins and kayasthas are foreigners here and hence are exempted from these social rulings. Kayasthas are allowed to marry borokolita grooms or brides. This is possibly because of the dwindling number of kayasthas.

Taking into account the royal marriages of both Tripura and Cooch Behar, the British government had tried their best to stamp them as illegal and thereby choose heirs according to their convenience.

Accompanied by the beating of drums and other musical instruments, the brahmin groom travels in a palanquin to marry. The women of the groom's family accompany him singing songs of blessings. The groom's invitees at times travel on the back of elephants. Marriages take place only during the day. The groom wears a golden-coloured dhoti and a scarf along with a lot of ornaments. He uses a turban for the occasion. Brahmins, in order to retain the sanctity of their caste, do not consume rice served by anyone other than their own kinsmen. Hence, they often partake of food comprising of moist flattened rice, plantain, and yogurt.

One day, while loitering in the village of the Khasis, I came across a Bengali gentleman from Sylhet. He had married a Khasi woman following the Brahmo rules of marriage. His son was dressed in Khasi outfits. Even though he had changed his religion to Christianity, he had retained his previous surname, Sharma. Added to it since he was now a Christian, he seemed to be quite happy and contented. On another day, having climbed to the top of a range to reach a Bengali village, I met a priest who was preaching sermons to an empty hall of a church. No one was around to attend his service. In the same region I met a large crowd, precariously balancing themselves upon a bridge, in order to attend a Hindu service.

The mountainous terrains of Shillong are not as steep as either Shimla or Darjeeling. Loitering aimlessly along the red petal-strewn path, I went straight ahead into the dense forest. There I came across a huge palatial European house. I was happy to have found the royal palace. When one walks in confidently, no one dares to stop you. And that is exactly what happened to me. Ignoring the Gurkha guard I walked straight towards the lake. The poor fellow, proudly displaying his gun, could do nothing to stop me. Mr Cotton[56] had converted the place into a wonderful garden. This is possibly the best sight in the whole region. The beautiful bridge proved too tempting. The sight of gushing water kept beckoning me. I was happy to tread on the nearby alleys as well. Everything seemed so beautiful. From above I viewed the lush green deserted pathway and was stupefied. Then after exploring a few more paths, I returned home.

Since I was suffering from severe cold, I decided to leave the place. I recollected the beautiful mountainous sights while sailing from Goalpara on a steamboat. While returning, I got down at Jagannathgunj and walked into a dining hall in the midst of a paddy field. It was then I realized that I was suffering from malaria. Then from Narayangunj I travelled to Gawaland. The memory of that voyage is blank. I knew Assam was not a healthy place and this long stay there proved it to me.

56. Possibly Henry Cotton, Chief Commissioner of Assam

North

The Himalayas

Our journey commenced from Rawalpindi when we took the Butemal-Karachi train. Within three hours we reached the Himalayas. From there we took a carriage which drove us up the mountain slopes. Viewing unfamiliar trees and shrubs on two sides of the road, we kept going on the serpentine route. At night, the driver, on the pretext of going off duty, dropped us off at an unknown and uninhabited place, without caring for the arrival of his substitute. To make matters worse, it started pouring with rain. The cold coupled with rain nearly froze us. Desolate place, heavy rains, extreme cold and darkness—undoubtedly it was a unique experience.

We had heard about the rich mountains, but next morning when light broke in, we viewed a rather gloomy and sleepy land. The sun hadn't risen, and the desolate mountainous paths were all wet. The doors of all the British bungalows were tightly shut though postboxes were installed at frequent intervals. It clearly indicated that the place was once inhabited. The carriage dropped us at a place where we could not see a soul. After frantic search when we managed to reach a person or two, they seemed extremely reluctant to talk to us. One said, 'keep climbing' while the other replied 'go to the market and find out'. Where do we go by climbing upwards, we didn't know, so we walked straight into a nearby office. There we asked a gentleman, 'Does anyone know a Bengali working here?' The gentleman whom we had approached provided us an escort who would take us to our promised host. So, after getting thoroughly drenched once again, we walked up the broad and straight path. The wayside shops were all shut. Finally, we reached the house of Sri Surendra Deb Majumdar.

After an adequate meal we went to a nearby rooftop to get a view of the mountains. Since the sky had cleared by then, we beheld a beautiful sight. We viewed several paths dotted with houses on both sides. Running straight down the mountain slopes they all seemed to head for a deep crevice. And from each crevice new mountain ranges kept emerging. The ranges, covered with shredded cotton-like materials, shone brilliantly under the sunrays. To me they seemed like clouds dropped from the sky, but later I was informed that they were not clouds. They were the far-off snow-clad ranges. My visit to the mountains was indeed fulfilling. I was reminded of Mussoorie where there is hardly any plain land. No two houses can be built side by side. Consequently, separate paths were created to reach each house.

Next, we travelled to Kashmir from Murree, on horseback. The path had high mountain cliffs on one side and deep crevices on the other. But tall trees on the cliff side provided shade to us. The view was somberly beautiful, and the scenario brought to my mind a picture of the ancient sages who spent their lives in the Himalayas practicing austerities. Since I intended to see the mountains, I had decided to visit Masuyavat, but then opted for Kashmir because it would serve that dual purposes of seeing the mountains and also the heaven on earth about which people talk so much; hence, this journey to Kashmir.

Previously I had thought mountains were tall stony structures but now I realized it was nothing of that sort. It was a continuous large and tall stone cluster, with intermittent gaps in between. The taller cliffs were all snowcapped. Even though most of the snow at the lower altitudes had melted, snow was still strewn around here and there. By and by we reached the rest house and after having our meals, in the evening we sat on the wooden seats of the balcony to view the mountains. It was sheer bliss to observe the view all around us.

We decided to avoid further horse riding, and walked some way to view a garden. It was set in a valley named Karnar which was exquisitely beautiful. Since we had to travel from one range to another, it was necessary for us to come down to a valley and then again climb up a steep range. On our way we reached the shore of River Jhelum and viewed the waters flowing down a steep cliff with a deafening noise. We stood mesmerized for quite some time. We also found another saffron-coloured river penetrating its way down the mountain slopes and finally submerging itself into the Jhelum. A bridge was constructed upon their confluence. The sight was magnificent.

The distance from Masidi to Kohala was about 30 miles and involved steep descent. And the distance from Rawalpindi to Masidi is about 60 miles involving steep climbing. Consequently, we had to keep going upwards to finally reach our rest house, or as the natives call it, padao. Sri Sashi Bhusan Dutta, whom I had met in Puri, was also a classmate of Shib Babu. He joined us here to accompany us to Kashmir. Instead of the beautiful rest house we shifted to a nearby free guest house meant for pilgrims. Since the guest house is run by a Sikh, every morning one wakes up to the chants from the Guru Granth Sahib. The owner, a senior Sikh, looks after the guests with great care. He provides pilgrims with room and with utensils to cook their own food. Night lamps are lit throughout the night at the expense of the guest house. Since the room we were in was extremely small, we had to share it with gents and ladies who came from Punjab. The door of the room couldn't be shut so we stayed up the entire night chatting among ourselves. However, I enjoyed the stay thoroughly.

Kohala is a part of Hajara region and there is a bridge there. On the left side of the bridge is the kingdom of Kashmir. Because of bad weather and imminent rain, we decided at first not to travel that day but, when has weather been a deterrent for a traveller? So, soon crossing the Jhelum, we left the land ruled by the British imperialists behind and reached a Hindu kingdom[57].

Out of the several routes to Kashmir, the route via the valley of the Jhelum river is the most convenient. The reason for it is simple—rivers cannot climb up. Hence, if one keeps travelling along the shores of a river to reach a destination, his journey will be less hazardous. The route from Kohala to Kashmir is just that. In fact, the roads are so smooth and broad that vehicles can move about very conveniently. We kept walking on that road soaking in rain that was making the road muddy. There were potholes and trenches in several places. At places large boulders had fallen and were blocking the road. The blocks of the mountainous stones that were lined up all the way looked menacingly at us and we felt it safer to walk fast, away from them. As we viewed the falling stones from afar, we grew mortally afraid. How could the poor goats carrying our luggage escape these boulders, we kept wondering. A momentary slip of feet would take us down the abyss and land us into the fast-flowing Jhelum. After walking for some time in this state of mind, we found a horse stable. On enquiry, we came to know that since there was no bridge ahead, a blockade stood before us. Finally, out of desperation, we decided to take a circuitous route to reach the top. Since the man-made road had failed us, we thought it wise to opt for an alternative natural route. My state, however, was pathetic, since both my hands were engaged—one carrying an umbrella to prevent the onslaught of rain, and the other hand tightly grasping the metal rope on the side of the narrow slippery pathway. Danger lay at every step that we took.

After some time, much to our relief, we reached a plain land. We kept on walking that unending road, striking with our sticks the stones and pebbles that came our way. At home we hardly use our warm garments, but here, though it was summer, we were clad in several layers of warm garments and yet we

---

57. Kashmir as we know was ruled by a Hindu King for a long time.

could not generate the required heat. We kept on exhaling fumes (water vapour) from our nostrils and our limbs were gradually going numb. Our guide controlling the goats couldn't tell us the exact distance to our rest house, since he had never come this far. His normal route for plying was from Maseri to Patan. So, we thought it wise to ask the passersby we met about the exact location of our guest house. Even they couldn't help us since no one knew its exact location. In the meanwhile, we found a new road which was both slimy and dangerously slippery. It was really very difficult to go any further. Suddenly, our eyes fell upon the guest house standing right in front of us. Oh, what a relief!

Since we were completely exhausted and knew if we sat down, it would not be possible to get up and move forward, we had not stopped anywhere on our journey up to this point. Consequently, when we reached the guest house, journeying almost 24 miles, we were half dead due to exhaustion. And in the guest house when they served us only salt and puree for dinner, we were only too glad to eat that up ravenously. Next day we cooked rice and lentils for lunch. And because none amongst us favoured chicken, we thrived on vegetarian dishes only.

Transport appeared to be a major problem now, due to the heavy rains. So we kept toying with the idea of cancelling our trip to Kashmir. But before finally calling it off, we espied a few local ladies trudging along in this bad weather. The sight recharged us and we grew brave. The caretaker of the guest house informed us that we had to walk another 24 miles along the newfound road, only to reach the ancient but easily accessible road. This road would finally take us to Kashmir. Gradually as the rain subsided, the prospect of undertaking a new journey grew brighter. And because all of us were extremely tired, we decided to opt for litters for the rest of our journey. Litters were available where local people lived, we were told. So, we again went up another cliff and reached the nearest village.

The village headman[58] was not at home so we decided to wait at his place till he returned. We had with us an introductory letter from the king of Kashmir, and when an employee of the village headman saw it, he reverentially touched it to his forehead. A contractor came and informed us about a British citizen from Ahmedabad who was also on his way to Kashmir like us. He had plenty of luggage with him and needed several luggage carriers to carry them. In the meanwhile, the village headman returned and greeted me ceremoniously with a loud 'Ram Ram'. We observed a frenzied movement in the village and on enquiry were told that they were all busy searching for suitable luggage-carriers who would be able to carry the luggage of the visiting British Sahib to Kashmir. Even though the British Sahib was yet to reach the village, his luggage had arrived in advance, hence the frenzy. The village headman was therefore summoned to make the required arrangements. When he returned home, he called one of his assistants and wrote on a piece of paper the number of people who would accompany us and the number of people who would accompany the British citizen. After sending off his assistant, the headman turned to me and politely offered his personal palanquin for my journey. He promised to fetch two litters for us from the nearby Alaway market. However, because of the Vaishakhi Fair we could not begin our journey that day. Finally, two dilapidated litters arrived. Clearly, they had to be mended before commencing the journey. The assistant to the headman got the litter bearers to meet us and after we met, the responsibility of the employees of Tehshildar Dayaram too ended. They insisted that we give them in writing that we had received everything and that done, they simply disappeared.

A litter looks somewhat like an improvised palanquin but is different in terms of its wooden handlebars. They emerge from below the seats instead of above. So, the passenger practically

58. Known as teheshildar

rides on the shoulders of the bearers. Interestingly, the two bars are tied to one another by a thick rope so that at times a single bearer can carry it all by himself. This is done keeping in mind the narrow mountainous roads where it is impossible for two people to walk parallelly. Hence, this system has been improvised by the local litter bearers. Both Shibu Chandra Babu and I mounted the two litters and journeyed forward. The natural view of the place was exquisite even though the trees were bare. There were mostly tamarisk trees all along with a few cedars standing tall and obstructing the passersby. The lower part of the ranges comprised of oaks and pine trees.

The woodcutters of the region use a novel method to obtain wood from these trees. They ignite the lower part of a tree and when it collapses and falls into the river, they see to it that the woods are carried to their specified destinations. We espied a few scattered houses on our way and wondered how people managed to reach there. And when they have to convey anything to their neighbors, they generally yell out their message, because to reach a neighbouring house one has to traverse a long winding path. Most of the inhabitants were either farmers or cattle owners. Even though there were a few Sikhs and men from different communities among them, professionally they all were same—farmers or cattle breeders. They were all mostly Muslims. Since I am not at all conversant either in Punjabi or Kashmiri, I neither could understand a single word of the local people nor trace the growing change in their languages from Punjabi to Kashmiri. To worsen matters, our carriers were our teachers in this regard!

Kashmir

One cannot be an artist without a poetic flair. But here in Kashmir even if you are devoid of artistic sensitivity, you will find abundant material to draw beautiful imageries. One doesn't have to reorganize and beautify Nature here, since it is already overflowing with scenic beauties. In fact, there isn't much scope to eulogize about the beauty of Kashmir because one remains spellbound just viewing the place silently.

We began our journey from Uri and had the fortune to behold the magnificent natural beauty scattered on all sides. Clusters of short-statured plants and trees dotted our entire route. And the more we advanced towards Kashmir, Nature grew more beautiful. In comparison to the somber beauty of the Himalayas, here Nature appeared to be in her prime, giving rise to an aura of positivity and joyousness. Gradually, we came across plants bearing multihued flowers. Normally the trees shed leaves in winter, and with the coming of spring, they are filled with buds. As leaves start sprouting, most of the flowers fall off. A few flowers that remain behind give birth to fruits. The order is interesting—first bloom the flowers then sprout the leaves. The trees lining both sides of the roads were filled with fruits and flowers from top to bottom. It looked as if someone was displaying wreaths of white flowers everywhere. I saw two leafless apple trees and felt my journey to Kashmir was complete even without seeing anything more. I also plucked a few leaves which smelt heavenly.

Baramulla: After climbing the Baramulla range, we viewed the entire valley of Kashmir. River Jhelum looked like a mirror spread out across the plains. We could see its long route. The tall sapodilla trees stood in straight lines like a troupe of soldiers lining the road on both sides. There stood a bridge across the river. But the place seemed asleep. It looked new. In order to avoid the onslaught of snow, the roofs of the houses were sloped. After reaching the riverbank we saw a few Kashmiris. A woman was rowing our boat. The steering, however, was in the hand of her male counterpart. The boat stopped at a place called Sopore for us to spend the night. In the morning, we started once again. This time, keeping Ular lake on the left, we rowed down the canal and reached Shadipur, only to meet the Jhelum once again. There is an accompanying river, the Sindhu, here. And at the confluence there is a submerged mountain. On it stands a white-coloured chinar tree and at its foot is a Shiva lingam. Suddenly we encountered a storm, and our boat was almost on the point of being capsized. So, we spent the night at a safe place and in the morning started our journey towards Srinagar.

Srinagar: We reached Srinagar. Since it was difficult to row the boat against the tide, we travelled down a canal. Srinagar, however, did not appear outstanding to us. In fact, the wooden houses appeared extremely repulsive. Here and there were washermen washing their clothes and spreading them out. We had probably arrived at the ugliest part of Srinagar. Dressed in Kashmiri clothes and forehead anointed with saffron, we found a few lady priests. They looked beautiful. We reached the house of Sri Nilambar Mukopadhyay, a minister of the king of Kashmir. Sri Sashibhusan Srimani, a doctor of the royal hospital of Kashmir, welcomed us and took us to our residence. We rented a house situated upon the bridge Amira Kadal. A cook, four boatmen and a boat called shikara was fixed for us.

Here it is very impolite to leave one's head uncovered. So, on the request of Dr Sashi Babu, we started using caps. We had to order pajamas and coats to cover ourselves adequately. Mr Makhanlal Chattopadhyay came to meet us. Then we all went out for a boat ride upon Dal Lake. Having read a book named *Kashmir Kusum*, I had visualized Kashmir to be a land where flower beds would be strewn any and everywhere. But on reaching Kashmir, that illusion was shattered. The book has unnecessarily magnified the beauty of Kashmir. On enquiry, I came to know that there is a place called Gulmarg where after a few months that kind of flowery sights can be seen. On reaching Sashi Babu's residence, we were treated with lamb meat.

We visited two beautiful gardens called Shekhbagh and Khazirbagh. Friday being a rest day for the Muslims, they organize flower fairs in the gardens. At Shekhbagh I came across a bottlebrush tree covered entirely with white flowers and practically no leaves. My eyes which so long were thirsting for such a sight were finally quenched and so I asked our servant to spread the mat for me to sit under the tree. Another servant advised me to sit at a distance from the tree to view its beauty completely. But I preferred to sit under a flowering tree first and enjoy the beauty of these flowers of spring. After a time however, as per the advice of the second servant I sat at a distance to view the beauty of the garden. That was the last day of the flower fair held in the garden.

From there we went to Nishat Bagh. A great festivity was on at Dal Lake. So, we took the road below a bridge. The road itself was a sight to behold, with tall straight trees lining both sides. We embarked on a boat which swiftly bypassed all the larger luxury boats and kept moving forward. As people from these boats glanced at us, we heard sounds of loud music and dancing emanating from them. The occupants were served innumerable cups of tea in these fast-moving boats. We also caught sight of a few boats where smiling young and beautiful ladies were strolling on the open deck. They kept looking at us, and we at them. It was really an enjoyable trip. Even though I was melancholic at first, but gradually my spirits soared. Life after all is made up of sorrows and happiness.

Finally, we reached Nishat Bagh where the sight of varied types of flowers further enlivened my spirit. The first phase of Nishat Bagh was brightened with violet flowers which bloomed in nearly all the branches of the trees. It was a magnificent sight. We couldn't resist sitting there for quite some time. Then we saw the yellow roses. The sight of yellow roses seemed to glorify the entire Kashmir valley.

In order to make our stay comfortable, Sri Nilambar Mukopadhyay had sent a letter to the governor of Kashmir. It was therefore necessary for us to make a courtesy call to the governor. Dewan Badrinath is employed as the justice to the court of King Ranjit Singh, the nephew of King Dinanath. The governor greeted us politely and then bade us farewell. But soon afterwards, Dewan Saheb sent us a few chairs for our use. Deputy Governor Pandit Ramju expressed his desire to meet us. I was really pleased to meet him. Pandit Saheb is very fond of Bengalis. He gave me a book, *Happy Valley*, to read. We discussed many things. It is customary for the Kashmiris to offer tea to guests. So, I had to accept tea at his house. The most revered and senior-most scholar of the place is Pandit Dayaram. I went to his house and managed to get the *Neel Purana*. Our acquaintance grew to friendship and his son Devram visited us every day. I came to know a lot of things about Kashmir from him. *Neel Purana* is nothing but a collection of stories about Kashmir. I had carried *Rajtarangini* with me from home. Sitting in Kashmir and reading about Kashmir tickled my sense of humour.

Our house was located at a beautiful spot. It almost grew out of the Jhelum. My room was at the bottom of the bridge. On both sides of the bridge, there were markets. The bridge had upon it the central road of the place leading to the palace and the main offices. Expectedly, the entire place buzzed with activities throughout the day. Near the house, our boat was anchored, guarded by four boatsmen. It awaited my orders. Lakshman Pandit was a great cook. After our dinner, he served us sedatives in the form of local tales. There were tales about the local customs, beliefs et al.

Nine Bengali gentlemen were invited for a meal one day. Sri Nilambar Mukopadhyay sent us a lot of food for our consumption. Since Sri Nilmabar was a perfect Bengali gentleman and much respected here, we being his associates, basked in reflected glory. Unfortunately, a few Bengali gentlemen had once come here some time ago and had behaved shamefully, thus tarnishing the image of Bengal.

Dal Lake was the place where we used to sail. Shalimar Bagh, Naseem Bagh, Hazrat Bal after a time grew monotonous. Then we went to see Chashma Shahi and a vineyard near it one day with Makhanlal Babu. The water that sprung up from there was our source of drinking water. The office of Makhanlal Babu, which was the royal distillery, was very near to our house. That side of the city which was enriched by the flowing Jhelum river became a hot spot for sightseeing for us. Then we decided to visit Amira Kadal and Safa Kadal next.

We rowed down the Sindhu river to reach the fair being held at Kheer Bhavani. Our house was in a lotus garden. We anchored our boat at a place where there were many beautiful ladies, their smiles as brilliant as blooming lotus flowers. We alighted from the boat to view the temple of Kheer Bhavani. There is no idol there except a cavity full of water connected to a nearby spring. It is said that at times the water in the cavity changes its colour. However, the priests do not allow visitors to touch the water possibly because they are afraid that their myths and resulting spells about Kheer Bhavani would be busted. We returned to Kheer Bhavani the same night and found the place illumined with white light. The entire place teemed with beautiful ladies, clad in white clothes, offering their prayers to the cavity. The whole ambience was both beautiful and somber. I visited the place next afternoon when it was relatively empty. As I was looking deeply into the cavity a gentleman walked up to me and said, 'Do you see the umbrella shielding the empty golden seat inside the cavity? There is a serpent upon it.' Once again, I looked hard and yes, I did find a serpent, not a real one but made of silver. Slowly the crowd kept swelling and there was a lot of jostling going on; and I without realizing the cause of this sudden surge decided to escape from the place. Later on, I came to know that a gossip of the goddess appearing in the form of a serpent had given rise to this maddening rush. The priests, sensing trouble, had at one point of time removed the controversial golden seat and stopped the inflow of people. On reaching our boat, I heard that a few pilgrims had seen the serpent wriggling as well.

Our next destination was Manas Bal, which is smaller in size than Dal Lake. The colour of the water here is yellow and is crystal clear. We found fish swimming in the water, just below ten or fifteen arms length. The deeper water was of a darker shade of yellow. We had our bath on the shore of Lake Manas and then went back to the boat for lunch. Lunch at the heart of the lake was a different experience altogether—looking at the beauty of the lake and simultaneously taking a bite. The more we saw, the more it pleased our senses. We washed our hands and mouth in the clear water of the lake. It was so refreshing and purifying.

Then we went on to climb the chinar cliff. The trees provided us such soothing shadows that we were refreshed in no time. From the cliff we could clearly view Manas Lake. Chinar trees are magnificent to look at. The leaves are broad and white in colour, while the trunks are large, tall, and sturdy. It is said that they were brought here from Persia. It looked like five or six chinar trees were covering the entire land. A small river meandered amidst the shadows of the trees.

Our boat carried us towards Ular, which to the Kashmiris is as large as a sea. It's about 6 miles wide and 4 miles long. We reached an island, a place not visited by human beings. There is a dilapidated house and forest here. I entered a broken-down Hindu temple. Instantly I was aware of the smell of tiger and rushed out. Our boatman, hearing the news, prayed to God and said 'tauba tauba'. It was impossible, he insisted. Removing the creepers, I made my way and reached an ancient mosque. Shib Babu, as a token of remembrance, engraved his name there. We had our bath and finished our breakfast with the wild fruits we

Manas Bal, Kashmir

managed to collect. On the other shore of Ular lay a road to Tibet.

Next day we reached Ancharas, which is nothing but a water body comprising of clumps of reeds. There was adequate water in it for our boat to sail through. The entire stretch was filled with floating lotus leaves. We could well imagine the beauty of the place when lotuses were in full bloom. The boatmen pluck the stems of the plants and make garlands to wear. We saw two ladies singlehandedly steering their boats at lightning speed. Their boats were full of reeds. And when our boatmen tried to tease them, they hurled expletives in return and steered away. These water bodies confirmed Mr Vignette's statement about Kashmir[59]. Even Kalhan's *Rajatrangini* appeared to be quite authentic here.

Previously, there was a large pond here known as Satisar. And it is said Sage Kashyap created the land that we now see here. We kept sailing across streams and canals and finally reached Dal Lake. But when we reached, we found its opening shut. The reason, we were told, was the increase in water level of River Jhelum. The excess water of the river could flow down to Dal Lake and inundate the entire valley. So, to prevent a possible catastrophe this method of shutting the entry point of Dal Lake was devised. If the water flows in reverse direction, there is a safety valve here which automatically shuts off.

Bijbehara: The fair of Mir Baba Haider Saheb is famous among the Muslims. The fair starts from the grave of Mir Baba and then shifts to Islamabad and finally ends at Achabal. I was keen to see the fair. Viewing a fair even for an hour is more informative than staying at a place for more than a year. That was the reason why we sped towards it. Sri Souresh Dev Roy of Naldanga and his assistant accompanied us on another boat. We took two hours to reach an ancient affluent city that

59. Unfortunately, the statement is not there in the text for us to re-confirm.

is said King Abhimanyu once, out of rage, burnt down. There is a small temple there. According to British archeologists, the structure of the temple resembles the Egyptian pyramids. Next day, we went to see the Bijbehara fair. Essential rural items were being sold there. The fun in the rustic atmosphere appealed to us. The grave where the mortal remains of Mir Baba rest was crowded with people who were shedding tears. I stood there for a long time. An aged person was saying something about the ancient sage and looking at me, he blessed me and wished me well. Wherever we went people looked at us, and realizing we were outsiders visiting their place, conveyed their good wishes.

Next day we went to Avantipur. Previously this was the capital of Kashmir. King Avanti Verma had set up this place. Later, King Pravar Sen had established Srinagar. Avantipur is full of dilapidated stone houses and temples. The stones that were initially malleable, had now turned into hard rocks.

Anantnag: River Jhelum flows at tremendous speed here. But it is narrow and shallow too as it is near the origin of the river. We left the Jhelum now and rowed down a canal to reach the garden of Wazir Pannu. Then we went to view Anantnag. There was a pond amidst a garden. The water was clear and full of fish. We threw a piece of bread into the water and watched the hilarious activities of the fish. Then we took a circular route and climbed up. There was a smaller pond there and its water was flowing to another nearby pond, and from there the water was gushing down at a great speed to a stream near the main road. We climbed up a small cliff in search of the origin of the water source but could not find it. Then to console ourselves we argued that maybe it was coming down from the third storied pond where stood a house. Maybe there was a spring there.

At night, while sailing on the boat, we sang our national song full-throated and the entire forest was filled with the cacophony. Then we landed at a green, covered place full of moonlight for our dinner.

In the morning we started our journey towards Martand. At the tableland of a mountain range stands the Kuru Pandu temple and we went to view it. It is considered to be the largest archeological ruin in Kashmir. Clearly it was a huge temple of the yesteryears, with a large courtyard surrounded by numerous rooms and cottages. But now people hardly visit the place. Had the place been infested with wild animals they would find an ideal shelter here among the ruins.

All the ancient temples that are here were constructed during dynasties of both Dharmashok and Avanti Varma, within 250 BC to 875 AD. A temple situated at Mattan had an idol of the Sun god. We sat there for quite some time and refreshed ourselves observing the beautiful architecture and then left for Bhayan, which was another pilgrim spot[60]. We found a cavity there, from which emerged a stream of purified water that flew down the shaded pathway. The landscape was a visual treat and we sat there for a long time. Our guest house was right at the top of the cavity. When we reached it and looked below, we found numerous fish swimming in the clear water. The water was so clear that we could see the ground below. There are no sights worth seeing within the cities of Kashmir. All the beautiful sights are to be found in the outskirts. *Kashmir Kusum* tells us that Kashmir is worth visiting even if one has to spend one's life's savings for the trip. But on reaching here I realized they are nothing but exaggerated claims.

From there we moved on to view the Achhayal spring. The garden from where the spring emerges is three-storied. We went up to the third layer to view the origin of the spring. It was a fantastic sight—it was as if the very heart of the earth was torn open to permit the water to gush out and flow down the foothills. It seemed as if a river had formed down below. There was a second smaller outflow of water adjacent to the

60. Clearly it was a pilgrimage at that time. But now this place has either been renamed or is not as important as it was then.

main spring and when both these outflows merged at a point on the second layer, a colossal water body was formed. On the second layer there were numerous smaller springs too, which after merging with these two big springs collectively flew down to the main road to appear like a river.

Emperor Shah Jahan had seen the spring and had constructed this three-tiered garden. The garden was constructed in layers, first layer right at the bottom, and then followed the second layer or tier and finally the third one. However, with the spring flowing down, and vegetations sprouting along with it, the layers have now increased in number to three, four and five. Similar, many-tiered gardens comprising of Shalimar trees can be found in Lahore. The garden indeed was a visual treat for us. Small light sources were placed in between the springs making the entire place look like paradise. Clearly Shah Jahan had built this luxury garden for his personal enjoyment.

The view to Verinag was extraordinary. We had to journey down the valley of the Jhelum. The mountain range here is relatively lower in height and the vegetation less dense compared to the higher terrains. Numerous rose plants dot the entire region. Interestingly, these rose plants are without thorns and are covered with large-sized rose wreaths. Small, fast-flowing shallow rivulets run throughout the region. And because our litter kept climbing, to avoid the discomfort of the journey, I reversed my seat and turned backwards. The carriers had a tough time ascending the slopes. After a time, we reached Verinag which is about 480 miles from Rawalpindi. That is the distance we had travelled till date in the Himalayas. The gorge of Verinag which we were about to visit is octagonal in shape and the water is blue, like the sea. I have seen a sea but never have I come across any water body whose water resembles the water of a sea. The water, though crystal clear, assumes the blue hue because of the depth of the gorge. Interestingly, the water emerging from the gorge is fast flowing and flows rapidly down the rose garden to reach the foothills and form a river. This gorge is actually the origin of the River Jhelum. But according to the people of Kashmir, Behast, or Paradise, is the origin of the Jhelum.

We went to view the gorge after our meal and found several springs flowing from different directions. The distance separating each spring however was very small, perhaps that of a finger; hence, perhaps the name of the river was Jhelum. Verinag was a favourite place for both Nur Jahan and Jahangir. There were sweet-smelling rose plants all over the garden illuminating the entire ambience. One plant bore at least thirty roses. In order to produce rose water, the king had constructed a room where all the roses would be gathered. We entered the room and spent some time there. We even slept on a flower bed there.

The day was cloudy and soon it started drizzling. The cold was really enjoyable. Any number of woollen garments could not reduce the chill we were experiencing. I am used to bathing every day. But after coming here, to this land of perennial cold, I was forced to skip my bath one day. Even on our way from Mussoorie to Srinagar, I was not inclined to bathe either. I didn't even open my stockings. That wearing socks could be so comforting was beyond my imagination!

We started our return journey from Banhal. The carriers carrying us said the pain of carrying you all will never be repaid. We will not be paid adequately. The money that you will give us will be instantly grabbed by the munshi, and in return he will give us just a day's rice. I reached Islamabad by boat and summoned the munshi. I refused to pay him the dues I owed to our carriers. Finally, I threatened to send him to the District Magistrate sahib. Then the munshi said, 'In that case it will be the Saheb who will take the money, the carriers will not get anything.' Having no other alternative before me, I started bargaining. Half the money I paid to the munshi the other half to the carriers.

On the Maripat route where the British travel, this

malpractice does not exist. The carriers are paid the full amount. It is indeed a terrible practice. The person who is toiling is cheated of his dues. The Britishers assure that their carriers are not cheated in this manner. So, the deduction was clear—the subjects who live in that part of Kashmir which is outside the jurisdiction of the king and is ruled by the British, are relatively better off only because the Britishers keep an eye over the misdoings of others.

The boat started sailing and we had our meals. In the evening we anchored near a village. I got down for a stroll. Here horses are bred and reared for commercial purposes. There were many horses roaming about freely and they appeared healthy and pretty expensive. A caretaker tried to take them back to their respective stables but two of the horses refused to comply. They kept running here and there.

We sailed the entire night and in the morning, reached Pampur where we found several large fields of saffron. Time was not ripe for kesar yet. At places poor people had consumed the roots of the saffron in order to avoid starvation. In our country saffron is produced only in Kashmir. We dug out the root of the plant and found it resembles an onion.

Two of my wishes remained unfulfilled. We couldn't visit Gulmarg, since it was not time for the flowers to bloom. Had we waited for some more time we could have seen the flowers blooming all over the place. The second was not being able to taste Kashmiri mewa. Mewa too had not ripened yet. Since both mulberry and strawberry had already ripened, we were happy consuming those. Green groundnut and khobani were made into curries. Many ascetics had gathered to visit Amarnath. The route to Amarnath is very dangerous and no litter was ready to take us there. So, our desire to visit Amarnath, too, remained unfulfilled.

The central road of Srinagar is very wide, and the river is lined with houses and quays on both sides. The local ladies are extremely beautiful and very efficient in household works. A lady vendor selling vegetables, while rowing her boat, narrated various stories to us in a language we failed to understand. There was the wood seller rowing his boat while a Muslim bridegroom was making his way to a hammam (Turkish bath). Likewise, a Hindu bridegroom was walking with an umbrella covering his head, and a loud sound of conch shells accompanied him. A minister was rowing his way back home.

We came across the Hamdan mosque and entered it. The place was filled with beautiful carvings of verses from the Holy Quran. We also saw Varsha, the scared grave of the Jain saint Uluddin. He was a Muslim king who initiated the architectural developments of Kashmir. And it was under his specific instruction that a part of *Rajatarangini* was composed in Sanskrit. We climbed the Shankaracharya hill, which is a part of the Tibetan range. Despite being dog tired after mounting about a thousand steps, we were enthralled by the spectacular natural beauty. The distant villages appeared to be floating in the water of Dal Lake.

Kashmir originally was a Hindu kingdom which the Muslims had conquered. But after five hundred years of Muslim rule, King Ranjit Singh had won it back through a bloody battle. But the Hindu temples that were converted to Muslim mosques (obviously during the Muslim dynasty) could not be reconverted. There is however an interesting variation which we observed and noted—Buddhist prayer halls, possibly created by a Hindu king two thousand years ago, had been converted to Hindu prayer halls (with Hindu idols and images). The Muslims came and plucked off the Shiva lingams and constructed mosques there. King Ranjit Singh reintroduced the Shiva lingam in Kashmir. The place can therefore be marked as a pilgrimage for freedom fighters. At the top of the cliff there is a Shiva temple, and a few houses. The houses unfortunately are all dilapidated and not worth inhabiting. There was a waterfall previously which has dried up now.

Next, we visited Raghunathpur Panchakki. The small water

source of Sindhu was diverted into a canal and was employed in turning a wheel at a great speed. That wheel acted as a husker, husking the paddy to bring out the rice.

The cotton industry of Babu Nilambar was now facing severe crisis. The entire storehouse of his silk was almost empty. Since we had no time to visit Gulmarg, we visited the garden of the British gentleman Mr Arman and viewed the flowers that bloom at Gulmarg. One day we visited the place where shawls were being woven. The king had abolished the tax upon these woven shawls. The reason for the Kashmiri city's disfigurement is this: we in the other parts of the country procure essential goods from different countries, but this place being extremely inaccessible cannot avail that sort of assistance. Here people have to live contented with things that are available within a span of a few miles, within the valley. For people who live here, Punjab represents entire India. A person who has visited Verinag has actually visited a distant land to them.

It was Manu, a sage of the ancient world who had first introduced the caste system based on man's profession. But here in Kashmir the Aryan dwellers of the prehistoric times did not follow this caste distinction; hence, Kashmiris are not affected by the segregations rampantly practiced elsewhere in the country. Other than brahmins there exists only another caste called the Buhas. The dress code of the Buha girls indicates that they are basically tribal in origin. However, regarding the complexion of the Kashmiri Pandits one can compare them only with the texture of a rose. Looking at their complexions even the British imperialists surmised that they actually had originated from the Jewish communities. Even the ancient triangular arches found in several buildings of Kashmir are quite similar to the ones found in the temples of Jerusalem. A Hungarian scholar who specialized in ethnology had once visited Kashmir and declared that he had never come across such an ancient unmixed race in his life. Kashmiri Muslims are, however, not as good looking as the Kashmiri Pandits. But the converted Muslims, who initially were Hindus, are still as handsome as the Pandits.

The approximate population of Kashmir is four lakhs. And out of every ten Kashmiri one is a Hindu. The native dress of Kashmir, for both male and female is the angrakhha[61], while the males use a headgear or turban in addition to it. Both males and females of the Buha community wear red-coloured caps while the Kashmiri Pandits wear white-coloured headgears. Only married women wear earrings to differentiate themselves from either spinsters or widows. The Pandits use slippers made from a type of grass and wear silver bangles on one hand. If they wear bangles on both hands the bangles differ in design.

Academic learning is not very popular among the Kashmiris. Their native language is colloquial Kasur which has no script. Both Hindus and Muslims pursue learning in Persian. But there are no formal schools here. The Pandits are not at all conversant in Sanskrit. The Shastri community of Kashmir are professional astrologers employed in preparing astrological charts, which is their ancestral profession. Persian is their state language since Persia has always inspired the Kashmiris. The shawls made in Kashmir also have a Persian origin. Everything, right from paper mache, enameling of ornaments, tea containers, or pots and the musical instrument called rabab, bear marked signs of Persian influence.

The staple food for both Hindus and Muslims of Kashmir is rice and lamb meat. Our cook had prepared a Kashmiri dish for us one day. It was a mixture of lamb meat, lotus stem, sugar, leafy vegetable, and mushrooms. They consume a type of chapati called bakharkhani and biscuits with tea. Two types of tea are available in the shops of Kashmir—green tea and Surati tea. Surati tea is somewhat like the one consumed by the British. Both these types are supplied from Lafda and the Punjab. The preparation varies between Mughal tea and Surati tea. Mughal tea is prepared in the following manner: five bowls of water is added to one ounce of tea leaves and boiled for half an hour.

61. A cloth to cover the upper part of the body.

The mixture is allowed to cool for some time. Then water is added to it along with sugar and spices and again boiled for half an hour. It's only after the second half an hour of boiling of the mixture that milk is added, to prepare the red-coloured Mughal tea. Surati tea, on the other hand, is a combination of tea leaves, soda, sugar, butter and salt. The process is more or less similar, boiling in two phases—first with soda and tea leaves for half an hour, then adding the rest of the ingredients and re-boiling for another half hour. Tea is also imported from Lhasa and China.

Selling of meat during Ekadasi[62] is strictly prohibited by the king. The Muslims in Kashmir are not allowed to eat beef, since cow slaughter is considered to be equivalent to homicide. The punishment meted out for cow slaughter is same as murder. Previously, Muslim servants were allowed to supply water to the Pandits, but after the ascendancy of the Hindu king, this practice has been strictly discontinued. The brahmins, while eating, place their plates and utensils on a linen cloth and then enjoy a community meal. Other than Bengal, no other state is particular about food leftovers.

Kashmiri music is not at all pleasant to hear. One day when we decided to opt out of a musical session, the local people warned us that it was an unpardonable offence and that we would be branded as uncivil and be reported to the royal court. Most of the musical sessions are held at Dal Lake.

We sailed in a canoe to our next destination, which was Dal Lake. The canoe danced its way towards the great lake. We reached Dal and found a musical soiree had just begun. A lady dancer dressed in Afghani attire was accompanied by an adolescent female performer. Her accompanying musicians both sang and played musical instruments. Previously the Muslim emperors of Delhi used to detest music, but once a

62. The eleventh day of the lunar fortnight; fast is observed by the Hindus of this day.

clever musician not only entered the emperor's court but also mesmerized him with his rendition. Since then, they became sponsors of Indian music. The reason for such illogical hatred was due to a stricture in Islam where music is strictly prohibited. And possibly because of its prolonged Muslim dynasty, Kashmir still does not permit musical programmes to be held in the heart of the city.

The land revenue is paid by the citizens in the following manner: half in silver coins and the other half in rice. The king runs a flourishing business in rice and half of the salary of his employees comprises of rice. The farmers here are known as zamindars. Even though they own the lands, their economic condition appeared pathetic. Kashmiris, even though physically strong, have repeatedly lost their independence since times immemorial. Even their king is a Punjabi and not a Kashmiri. Most of his officials are either Punjabis or Kashmiri Hindus. There is hardly an impoverished Hindu here in Kashmir.

Punjab

Lahore: Here we stayed at Shah Almi Darwaza. Previously, the city of Lahore was surrounded by deep trenches. But the British, after filling these trenches, converted them into parks and gardens. That has beautified the city. Whichever side of the city you look at, a beautiful garden greets you. The sewerage system of the city lies embedded in them. And scattered among them are several bathhouses for women. Since women here wear ghagra (type of long skirts) they have to completely disrobe themselves for a bath, hence bathhouses are essential. Same system prevails in Kashmir, as seen in Srinagar.

Earlier I was of the opinion that most of the residents of Punjab are Sikhs, but after coming here, I realized that Sikhs here are in minority—probably only farmers and soldiers, known as

Jats, are Sikhs. Once while researching on Gurumukhi scripts, I had failed to trace any reader of the language. And according to my study the language did not have the following two vowels á and ó. But I had found them in printed books. The alphabets generally used are as follows—ū, á, é, s, ȟ, ɋ, kh, ɓ, gh, én, ch, chh, j, jh etc. similar to Bengali script.

Most of the Hindus here are kshatriyas by caste. And kshatriya women are very beautiful. The women among the people who have migrated and settled here permanently, either from Calcutta or Banaras, wear saris. To me they look better than the local ladies wearing ghagra.

All buildings, including shops and institutions, have signboards in front of them displaying either their wares or professions—there are signboards for doctors, lawyers and even a dancer. The signboards are all written in Roman script. Even residential buildings have signboards in front of them. For instance, the signboard in front of a dancer's house specifies the following information: 'People interested to see dance recitals can come here; chance meeting of acquaintances is remote.'

We went to see the tomb of King Ranjit Singh and found the entire interior part of the ceiling covered with intricately decorated mirrored glasses. Elsewhere, too, we found similar architectural use of decorative mirrors. The three-storied Shalimar Garden is situated here. It is said to have been set up by Emperor Shah Jahan. The thousand-headed musical fountains caught our fancy and we sat before it for quite some time.

One morning we saw a procession walking down the street. It consisted of a group of men, a band comprising both English and Indian musicians, and two dancers singing and dancing alternately. The occasion was the Chuda ceremony of a boy.

Here brahmins multitask. They cook, clean utensils, and if necessary, also polish shoes. The popular Bengali adage—from stitching shoes to reading the *Chandi*[63], seems to hold good

---

63. A sacred text of the Hindus, praising the prowess of goddess Chandi or Durga

for these brahmins. However, for the resident Bengalis this practice seems highly advantageous, because once you employ a brahmin cook, you don't have to employ a separate servant in the house to perform the other tasks.

Three castes predominate here: brahmin, kshatriya and Jat. There are no kayasthya or vaidya[64] here. And in likelihood because they consider men from either Calcutta or Banaras to be brahmins, they readily accept to work for them.

Amritsar: Darbar Sahib is the most important building of Amritsar. It stands right in the middle of a large man-made pool. Guru Ramdas had dug this pool and Guru Govind had enriched it. As the story goes, when the Muslims invaded the place, they defiled it by shedding the blood of slaughtered cows in several places. Guru Govind, to avenge this wrong, had smeared the blood of Muslims upon those very sites. Guru Tegh Bahadur, father of Guru Govind Singh, was killed by the emperor of Delhi. Consequently, the otherwise pious and peace-loving Guru Govind and his disciples learnt the art of revolt. Had that not happened, the Sikhs would not have been so adept at warfare. Till date all Sikhs are ever ready to undertake war. It is mandatory for them to carry a knife and wear a steel bangle.

The story goes, when Guru Tegh Bahadur was taken to be killed, the emperor asked him, 'Do you desire anything?'

'Get me a paper and a pen with an inkpot,' he had said. He wrote down something upon the paper and tied it round his neck. Instantly his head was cut off. When the paper was opened, they found the following words written on it: 'I have given up my head but not my religion.' The Sikhs had lost their freedom for a very short spell of time, but their valour is still visible everywhere. The Christian missionaries always criticize other religions. Once, when a missionary was criticizing Sikh religion, a person came from behind and struck his head with

64. These other two castes are found among the Bengalese mainly

a log and killed him instantly. When the judge asked him why he had hit the man, the Sikh replied, 'Our religion tells us that if a person defames our religion, hit him seven times with a log. But this fellow died at the first stroke.' Both the valour and the honesty of Sikhs are commendable.

The king of Delhi was terrified of Sikhs. Punjab was invincible as long as Punjab Kesari Ranjit Singh was alive. But after his death, English soldiers had to be summoned to subdue the domestic disturbances. The British soldiers indeed proved to be superior. It is said that even Ranjit Singh used to lose his night's sleep on receiving summons from British rulers. Yet, the British rulers had enough proof of the valour of the Sikhs.

During the battle of Chillianwala, the Sikhs were in possession of the British flag, yet finally they couldn't win because they didn't have a valorous captain. And as history records, Jaichand, in order to subjugate Prithviraj, invited Shahabuddin. This smoothened the entry of the Muslims to India. While Lal Singh Khalsa, in order to defeat his army, took the help of the British and assisted them to rule the country. Seven years after the demise of Ranjit Singh, the princely states lost their freedom due to internal conflicts with their ministers.

As mentioned above, Darbar Sahib sits in the middle of a pool of water. It is connected to the land by a marble bridge. Interestingly, the architectural design of the gurdwara is not that of a temple, rather it resembles the courtroom of an emperor. It's built entirely of marble. It is an intricately designed large auditorium with four doors. The walls of the auditorium are decorated with fine golden-coloured designs. The top, or mast of the gurdwara, is made of pure gold. A large volume of *Guru Granth Sahib* placed on a wooden platform is seen inside the room. An aged and somber-looking priest, sporting long beard and bushy moustache, dressed in immaculate white and with a white headgear on, is to be seen seated in front of the *Guru Granth Sahib*. A group of singers and instrumentalists playing different musical instruments are found singing mellifluously a

Gurdwara Darbar Sahib (The Golden Temple), Amritsar

dhrupad (Indian classical music). Both the melody of the song and its rendition mesmerized us. At the far end of the bridge is another palatial structure—the Akalmunga, with a large, intricately designed marbled courtyard. There are several singers sitting inside it and singing mellifluous bhajans. We were told that every day, in the wee hours, before sunrise, priests carry the *Granth Sahib* on their heads from Akalmunga to the main hall or Darbar of the gurdwara. A troupe of musicians, playing various instruments accompanies them on their journey. It's only after reaching the central hall that the morning worship is concluded.

After sunrise a long list of names of the sponsors are announced. Following it the priest reads out only a few lines from the *Guru Granth Sahib* and then covers it up once again. After that, the same text is read out for quite some time in many of the other temples like Gurubagh and Baba Atal that encircle the pool. Even women are permitted to read from the said text.

In the afternoon, we found a person reading out from the *Bhagvat* and explaining it to a group of people. At another place there was a person narrating the life of Guru Nanak. The entire ambience of the place was spiritually surcharged since there was a constant discussion and reading out from different scriptures. Music and singing were also being performed uninterruptedly. It is undoubtedly a wonderful pilgrim spot. There is a constant flow of devout followers of different age groups. It is mandatory to remove ones shoes before entering the gurdwara, and this has been clearly stated outside the premise. Other than that, there are signboards which say that you have to broaden your vision to accept all religious beliefs. Guru Nanak did not believe in idol worship, yet, in the gurdwara the sacred text is worshipped like an idol.

Unlike Lahore, Amritsar is not dirty. Enclosed by a boundary wall, the city shows clear signs of affluence. The Muslim ladies of Punjab wear a typical type of pajama, known suthyan. It is wide enough at the top but extremely narrow at the bottom making it very difficult to wear. Hindu ladies wear ghagra or long skirts, but the little girls are permitted to wear pajamas. For whatever reasons, both little boys and girls wear earrings made of shells. The ladies plait their hair into innumerable strands and adorn them all over their heads. Here Hindu women are allowed to use slippers[65]. Very few ladies have a dark complexion. The Jats are, however, not so fair. Probably the fair ones belong to the Sikh community. They are actually the Punjabi agriculturists. Most of the kings and princes of Punjab are Jats. The king of Kashmir is a Dogra.

Having seen only Punjabi soldiers I had formed a notion that Punjabis as a race are tall. But after reaching Punjab, I realized that my perception was totally unfounded.

Both Lahore and Amritsar are no longer ruled by Punjab, yet, in both the places there are many Sardars. This is possibly due to their tendency to cling on to their past glory. Consequently, when in public, they behave as their ancestors did. For instance, when they have to attend any social function, they never move alone, instead are accompanied by a large entourage of ten or fifteen horsemen. The number indicates their capacity of having similar battalions of soldiers. Ten horsemen stand for ten thousand soldiers and fifteen horsemen stand for fifteen thousand soldiers. Possibly during the reign of Ranjit Singh all these Sardars used to work as captains of his soldiers. The word Singh means lion. And all Singhs were possibly as valorous as lions.

In Bengal, an adulterous wife is not accepted by the family, but here people are generous enough to accept a wife who has committed adultery. No wonder the residents of Punjab are full of praise for Bengali women for their loyalty towards their husbands.

Rice, chapati, and meat are sold in the market for the consumption of the Sikhs. One day, I tasted a dish which

---

65. This is an interesting observation in relation to the practice of Bengal where women were prohibited to wear any form of slippers.

later I was told was a Muslim dish. Tinda is their favorite vegetable here. Just as in Varanasi, where wood apple is found in plenty, likewise here adoo is found in abundance. Adoo tastes somewhat like a peach. No white puris can be found here, only dalpuris.

We went to Durgani, to see a temple. Nearby there's a crematorium, which is separated by a boundary wall. There were ladies striking their breasts and wailing aloud, near a burning pyre.

The structure of Punjabi houses was something new to us. Most of them have an enclosed balcony and a fireplace. The toilets are all situated on their terrace, and as a result, the scavengers have to cross their interior rooms while carrying out the night soils. Nobody seems concerned about this unhygienic practice.

One day we went to see Govind Garh, a fortress built by Ranjit Singh. But now every bit of land is owned by the British Queen.

The easiest way of learning a foreign language is by reading its translation of the Bible, because Bible has been translated in all languages of the world. There is a Punjabi Bible as well. Unfortunately, we found no translated version of Guru Nanak's *Japji* here in Punjab.

When we had first entered Punjab via Ghaziabad, we were struck by the unique qualities of the place. Their dress, their language, their food habits, and their social customs were very different from people of other provinces. But by the time we reached Ludhiana, everyone around was a Punjabi, and we could only hear the Punjabi language around us. It felt like we had reached a new country altogether.

Rishikesh

Almost fourteen miles north of Hardwar, on the bank of River Ganga, stands the city of Rishikesh. Situated at the foothills of the Himalayas, it is considered to be the sacred land of Lord Shiva. I have never seen such a beautiful place in entire India. Most of the pilgrims' spots of our country don't seem sacred at all. Everywhere it is densely populated. Whereas, once you enter a hermitage in Rishikesh, you feel the presence of true ascetics. The place is dotted with small grass huts with little verandahs that add to its sanctity. An ascetic, having collected a wood apple, was preparing a drink of this sacred fruit. When I glanced inside his little hut, I found only a woven mat as a bed, a book, and a water pitcher. Most of the huts standing side by side are furnished in this spartan fashion. I wandered around from one path to another. The entire village seemed to be immersed in deep meditation. There was no sign of opulence and I noticed an abundance of eatables. This village is ideal for meditation. There is nothing that one would like to buy from here. And no unwanted people are found loitering around. Sightseeing is a passé in Rishikesh. Silence is being interpreted in so many ways. Any visitor will realize it. A person sitting inside the hermitage hardly cares to even glance at any passerby. When being greeted, he hardly responds. Once in a while, a person may be addressed and conversed with. An ascetic clearly indicated that it was best for him to remain quiet.

In the afternoon they go out to the nearby locality to beg for food which sustains them only for the day. The community kitchen provides simple rice, chapati and pulses. The person distributing the food appears so gratified at having served the meal. A person offering drinking water humbly requests a person, 'Do gratify me by accepting the drink.' There is a proverb which says that once a god had come here and sent his assistant to collect drinking water for him. When the person failed to return after a long time, he personally went out in search of him. After a time, he found his assistant deep in meditation. When he asked his assistant the reason for it, the poor fellow replied, the sacredness of the place had forced him to meditate. In reality, Rishikesh is a place of renunciation. And renunciation is in the air. I will discuss it at length at first.

Divine medicine: Human psychology is guided by both desire and the renunciation of desire. Renunciation is the pathway to liberation, say the sages. Yoga is the chief method to achieve it. Deep concentration can ensure spiritual (occult) powers and most people are eager to achieve this power and not liberation. Many methods of yoga are employed to achieve it. Out of them, the most important one is the yoga which helps to soothe the nerves. It is not easy to practice perfectly all the activities that are mentioned in the *Ashtanga Yoga* of Patanjali. Breath control and exercise is really difficult. Likewise, it is also difficult to do true meditation.

When one is in a state of ecstasy, one realizes one's true self or identity.

1) Mind is then in the normal state. When one withdraws his mind from the material world, the mind remains unchanged without any external disturbances. A person who is desireless can easily attain a state of ecstasy.

2) By renunciation, one can remain detached to all material objects and thereby attain a state of liberation. A permanent state of ecstasy is actually called the state of liberation. And because one has to withdraw one's mind from the material world, the method can be called a state of void.

In order to attain that state of ecstasy, one has to practice renunciation.

Our spiritual journey begins with non-attachment. And non-attachment is actually the pathway to attain ecstasy. One has to arise from a state of honesty, dishonesty and become materially totally non-attached. This leads one to rise above all sensual pleasures. Only then can one realize his true self.

3) One has to constantly strive to arouse the conscience which will lead to the destruction of all darker sides of life.

4) Desire is the cause of all that is ignoble in us. That will automatically be destroyed.

5) This is the end result of renunciation. Only then can man be truly liberated. The noble qualities then assist one to attain the state of self-realization.

6) When man can fix his mind towards his actual identity then comes liberation. Renunciation and non-attachment are directly related to one another. When all sense perceptions withdraw themselves from the material world and fixes itself towards self-realization, the state he attains is withdrawal.

7) Even an atheist can pursue this kind of spiritual practice. Hence, Patanjali has not emphasized the concept of God in his yoga-sutra. Both believers of non-dualistic and dualistic philosophy have the right to pursue this form of yogic practice. There is nothing called soul or spirit in Patanjali.

Occult powers may appear as an impossibility and hence can be discarded as improbable. But at present there have been cases where thought reading has been explained through vibrating waves sent in the ether. According to scientific explanations, when a thought arises in someone's mind, the atoms travel through the ether and produce vibrations in someone else's mind. And because ether is permeating everywhere, whether in living or non-living objects, it acts through the vibrating atoms travelling in it in the form of waves. However, the act of entering into someone else's body by travelling through the air may be a symbolic representation and need not be believed. It's one's experience that decides what to believe and what not to believe. Just because one impossible happening has proved to be correct, it need not be taken as the parameter to believe everything that seemingly appears improbable. Just because someone has thought about someone who is living afar, need not necessarily mean that his thoughts will be sent through the ether and that person will physically appear before him.

Since both animate and inanimate things are inseparable, people tend to hypothesize that all is the work of the ether without going into any kind of logical analysis. This isn't right. To believe something that is terribly absurd or improbable tends to thwart human rationality and logic. If a petty thing proves to be wrong, that may act as a beneficial impact.

Brahma Sutra has provided ten types of interpretations for ten different types of people. Each one has expressed his own theories with proper explanations. And we tend to accept those explanations which suit our temperament. The way these sutras were composed in the philosophical age changed during the age of the Puranas when philosophers tended to synchronize everything. One school of philosophy not only refers to another school of philosophical thoughts but also subsumes within itself everything that does not tally with its line of argument. Consequently, everything that is there in one school of philosophical thought is not always completely logical or rational. But when a person meditates and tries to shift his mind from one thought to another, finally making efforts to make it absolutely free of thought, then occult powers come into the way and prevent the occurrence of ecstasy. Occult power comes naturally to some and either through medicine or constant practice to others. To be in a state of inert ecstasy is, according to some, an inferior state of spiritual attainment. The heart stops beating and even though the man appears dead to the world, his body does not decay. He can stay in that state for a long time. A man becomes inert like this if bitten by a snake, but the function of the body does not stop, hence, excreta is found in his clothes. But Patanjali has described a state of conscious ecstasy. In yoga, if a person does not use all the body parts, then he cannot be completely liberated—this hypothesis is not true. Every yogi is seen to meditate upon one particular body part. This is very much possible. But one must have a fixed target.

A yogi need not perform any ritual. But he has to fulfill

his karma, which will help him to control his sensuousness. A person who has really mastered the art of self-control will never utter a lie. He will be self-satisfied. Hence, purity will be his natural attribute. Desire and desirelessness can be adopted according to the varying orientations of human minds. Both these approaches will make man a complete human being.

While meditating, sit in a comfortable posture and try to vacate your mind of all material thoughts. Stop looking, hearing, or responding to all other senses. Thoughts will come floating in the mind, likewise, one cannot stop listening or seeing. But use your conscience to stop them from entering your consciousness. Your eyes may see, but your brain will not perceive it, your ears may hear, but your mind will refuse to listen, and thoughts will come but you will not ponder upon them. State of ecstasy cannot harm you, but it is difficult to achieve it right at the beginning. Thoughts will crop up in your mind which proves that it is active. Gradually this tendency will cease. Consequently, you will reach a state when you will be detached from everything. In this condition, one thing that cheers up the mind is the feeling of universal love, e.g., feeling happy at the happiness of all living beings on earth.

Patanjali has said these very things only in different terms. Empathy for others, sorrow, joy, honesty actually refer to the following concepts—friendship, kindness, happiness. If a person can master these feelings, he will be happy. Added to it, if you can free your mind from thoughts, that will bring happiness. If you can rise above joy and sorrow, your mind becomes calm, and you enjoy a state of bliss. The other name of this state of mind is renunciation. Since ascetics practice the art of renunciation in search of perpetual happiness, they have 'ananda' (happiness) attached to their names. Merely by renouncing the material world one cannot become a true ascetic. One has to be desireless to become a true ascetic. But staying within the boundaries of the material world it is not easy to become desireless. Particularly when one begins his spiritual journey. But one who can internally conquer the material cravings of the world will never deviate from the spiritual path.

In order to sit for a comfortable position while meditating, one has to pay attention to one's physical condition. For instance, the place where you want to set up as the altar for prayer, has to be paid attention to. Hence, withdrawing into the forest is the best possible alternative. Fact remains, even if you withdraw yourself to the forest and still not completely free from material longings, the problem will persist.

Discussion: As mentioned above, your eyes will see but not perceive, your ears will hear but you will not listen, your mind will work yet you will not think—these are the things one has to try to follow. In other words, you will not pay attention to anything. You have to be detached. Physical needs like hunger, thirst, feeling cold, feeling hot, bitter taste, sweet taste are the things that will be there. You have to attend to them. Same will be applied to other feelings. Whatever your assignments are in this world, they have to be done. But the moment they are complete, you have to be dispassionate towards them. Rajas or tamas feelings should not move you to any action. You have to be sattvic. You have to be dispassionate towards all your actions and treat them as a part of your duty. This will not affect your actions. And if you can work with this kind of mindset, you will be self-satisfied. Then sacrificing yourself even for the cause of others will not matter.

Before ascertaining your duties, try to work towards the general good of all. But even in that case you have be very careful. Whatever you do to survive is not considered to be an action. You have to learn to ignore both favoured and repulsive feelings. You have to learn how to remain dispassionate. But without tremendous detachment, all these above attitudes are not achievable. A person who is self-contented is an extremely reliable person. Come what may will be his attitude, and he will be able to depend upon the Almighty. Self-contented means self-reliant too, or in other words, dependent on Almighty only and no one else. In *Shrimad Bhagwat Gita* this is how Sri Krishna describes the reliance on God or Brahman. Bhakti is the manifestation of this reliance. Reliance and detachment are inseparable. And to become reliant on God one has to meditate deeply. Only the method of meditation differs from person to person according to his or her capacity. The main sermon as preached in *Gita* is dispassionate action. There is also the preaching about detachment elsewhere but whether one has to do his work or karma even after being detached has not been specified in the book clearly.

A person who is truly self-contented, dispassionate, detached, and is completely dependent on God, is really a person without any desire. He does not need any other religion. He can never commit any sin. Hence, if a person has completely surrendered himself to God, he need not perform any ritual worship, and even if he renounces his own religion, he will not be erroneous. And as Sri Krishna says, even if he commits a sin unknowingly, he will not be punished. So, he need not repent for it.

Moksha, according to Patanjali, is a state when one can transcend the state of good and evil and be a realized soul. *Bhagwat Gita* terms this state as desirelessness. In the world of desire, this state of desirelessness works as the stepping stone. Hence, the *Gita* can be called the interpretation of Yoga Shastra and Patanjali's philosophy. A truly detached person will also be a self-realized person and will be able to proceed forward in the spiritual world. His senses will not trouble him anymore. This is how he will be totally detached and experience divine ecstasy.

Difference of opinion: The Buddhist sramanas have their own method of controlling the desires arising in the human minds. And that is their method of yoga. The following is the method they adopt:

1. True vision
2. True vow
3. True words
4. True actions
5. True execution
6. True work or exercise
7. True memory
8. True divine ecstasy

This ultimately leads to one achieving a supramental state. A sramana is undoubtedly a self-realized soul, and has attained a supramental state, which has brought him eternal peace and happiness. The Buddhist monks are divided into two categories—Granthadhur and Vidarshanadhur. Granthadhur achieve samadhi or divine ecstasy only for a short period. Vidarshanadhur stay in seclusion, earn their food through begging, and scantily dressed, they keep on meditating. The number of Vidarshanadhur is rather few. Their prime aspiration is to fully practice the eight parameters of the Ashtanga Yoga. For them there is hardly any division between meditation and samadhi. They do not worship any idol but have forty places of action to worship. Whichever place of action draws a sramana for meditation is his ideal place. He has to work contrary to the action specified. For instance, a person who is choleric has to cultivate friendly attitude, or a person given to sexual dissipation will have to think about the transiency of the body, etc. If a person is able to overcome these weaknesses, then he does not require contrary thoughts to ponder upon. The person then reaches a supramental state. Buddhist samadhi is the final stage of person's spiritual life, and like Patanjali, is a state of inertness.

If a person is able to reach the state of desirelessness, the only thing that is left is his consciousness. And that consciousness is the person's true state. The person is then above joy and sorrow.

Refutation: Patanjali's philosophy can be established through Shankar's theory. There is nothing in this world other than knowledge. The world and worldly feelings are all chimerical and elusive. Vedanta's main philosophy is a derivative of Buddhist theory of temporariness. Different feelings are the results of different actions. It keeps changing with changing circumstances. Hence, there is no reason to surmise that other than one's own feelings or knowledge, the world has no other conscious existence. Consequently, no material joy or sorrow exist in reality. Once this false knowledge is removed, detachment automatically occurs and man is liberated. Then both truth and untruth appear identical. Man's desire will completely vanish. But from the point of material progress or development, this kind of knowledge is totally unfavourable. However, at times man experiences such a state in life when he has no other option but to withdraw his desires in order to attain peace. That is good for him. Knowledge, bhakti and karma or action have their own special features, and they are applicable to a particular set of people with typical orientation or mindset. But demolishing of desire should come naturally, it cannot be imposed forcibly. If imposed forcibly, the impact does not last long. This is indeed true; but one must forcibly try to withdraw one's mind from desire through regular practice. From practice this withdrawal comes naturally.

Just as the state of samadhi is not permanent, likewise detachment or withdrawal from desires cannot be a permanent state of human mind. But the effort must be on to lengthen the duration till it becomes the permanent state of mind. An ascetic may gradually lose his intensity of dispassion, but that doesn't mean he has lost his spiritual urge. There is always a chance of reviving it. Maybe during samadhi, or divine ecstasy, a mind may be disturbed. This is quite likely. Practice can reduce this disturbance.

Pranayama helps one to develop the stability of mind. But Patanjali never insisted that without pranayama, samadhi or divine ecstasy cannot be achieved. There are various methods that have been mentioned. A person who has adequate self-control can control his nerves as well. Pranayama is one of the methods mentioned in Ashtanga Yoga. But mental stability can be achieved by withdrawing one's mind (from the material world) as well. That in fact is safer. In Buddhist yoga, ashtanga is bit different. It does not mention pranayama.

A yogi need not practice good or holy deeds. Why? This is because if you really attain a complete state of dispassion, you transcend the state of good and evil. Whatever he has to perform, he must perform with utmost dispassion that will not harm his spiritual growth. You need to practice good deeds so that they become your natural inclination. But for a totally liberated person that is not desirable. During spiritual practice one must practice love, friendship and help others to purify their mind.

Bhakti and dispassion depend on the mental orientation of human beings. If a person is totally dependent on another person, he automatically develops a kind of humility which turns into bhakti. But when a person is drawn towards a like-minded person, this humility or bhakti doesn't come easily to him. But bhakti and humility bring about mental peace. Irreverence for material things can also bring about bhakti for the spiritual life and thereby lead to dispassion. But to a person who has totally surrendered himself to the Almighty, such things become immaterial.

Local: Many people have asked me 'since you have travelled a lot, where did you find a spiritually enlightened ascetic'? At Drona Ashram, I met a novitiate monk named Satyavan. He had travelled for eighteen years around Uttarakhand, on the banks of River Narmada, and to the Girnar hills. He had studied every place in detail. Yet, he never met a person who could satisfy him. He was in search of a Guru who would help him to realize God. So, his Guru had to be an enlightened soul with a lot of occult power. But there are many ascetics who do not consider it necessary to cultivate these occult powers. I prefer asking such people to practice magic in the theaters rather than pursuing a spiritual life. Yogacharya Shyama Charan Lahiri had once rebuked me saying, 'Yoga should be practiced for realizing God, not for manifesting occult powers.'[66]

In old Varanasi at Rishipattan hermitage, I had the opportunity to discuss Buddhist yoga with Sri Sumangal. He advised me to go to Rishikesh for attaining samadhi. Here I found a monk who came here from Uttarkashi. Having stayed there for thirteen years, he had come to Rishikesh.

In order to learn true renunciation, one must become a monk or sannyasin. If a person undertakes spiritual practices to acquire occult power, then he will sink deeper and deeper into the world of desire and lose all mental peace. No wonder, Sage Manu has advised Vanaprastha for man after completing his family life. Vanaprastha will teach him the art of self-control. A person who finds no peace in his conjugal life will not wait to withdraw himself from the material world. He will enroll himself into the group of either Dasanami or Nanak Sahi or even Ramanandi etc. and become a monk.

I was wondering why I did not meet a true ascetic till date in the ashrams and the hermitages. But suddenly one day on reaching Mounakari I found several of them permanently residing on the way to Badri ashram. A few had the Narayan idol with them and had settled there. I instantly realized why they had chosen the specific spot. Here they would meet the pilgrims on their way to Badri and manage some copper coins from them for worshipping their Narayan idols. Otherwise, why would they decorate their gods with ornaments and allure passersby to contribute something. Then why pretend this life of seclusion? Clearly material desire had overridden their spiritual feelings.

---

66. Yogacharya Lahiri was the Guru of Shri Yukteswarji who in turn was the Guru of Yogananda, the saint who wrote *Autobiography of a Yogi*.

Except the Dak bungalow, there is no other place in Rishikesh where you can stay, paying a rent. There is, however, an excellent dharmshala, Sindhu-Punjab, where one can occupy a room, even for a fortnight without requesting anybody. The people managing the ashram take good care of the guests by supplying lights, drinking water, bed, servant and even a doctor when required. When you feel hot, the bank of the Ganga is close by. The tranquility of the place is not disrupted even though there are a few shops around. For four months this place becomes extremely unhealthy, and people shift their base elsewhere. Hence, there is no chance of the place changing into overpopulated cities like Hardwar or Kankhal. Even the forests will not be converted into human habitations. To a spiritual aspirant who desires to practice dispassion and attain spiritual salvation, Rishikesh will provide the ideal backdrop.

North-Western Regions

Delhi: Since we had no acquaintances living here, we had to put up at Kalibari[67]. In order to help the visiting Bengalis find a proper accommodation, the local Bengali community had at one point of time collected funds from people and constructed a guest house adjacent to a Kali temple here in Delhi. Any Bengali can find an accommodation here. The first Kalibari was set up at Danapur, near Bengal. But at present, numerous Kalibaris have come up in different parts of the country, extending even up to Peshawar. Being assisted by Sri Shiv Chandra Basu, a Deputy Commissioner of Delhi, we however managed to hire a house at Dharampur.

To me the language of Delhi sounded really sweet. I have never heard such beautiful Hindi anywhere else. I had heard

67. The oldest and perhaps a typical Bengali guest house—where rooms are obtained at a very nominal rate.

Hindi sweetly spoken by the kshatriya women of Calcutta. But after reaching Delhi, I realized that this is the actual birthplace of that sweet language I had previously heard. I prefer calling it Urdu instead of Hindi.

Delhi is an affluent city. At present, Delhi has been constructed and reconstructed over six times. Emperor Shah Jahan was the founder of present Delhi. The entire city has been strongly fortified like a fortress. Cannons have been fitted at places. There is a fort on the bank of the river Yamuna, constructed by Shah Jahan. We acquired a permit and entered the fort. The central courtroom[68] of the Mughal emperors has not been destroyed by the British. It still stands intact within a palatial building. It is exquisitely decorated with delicate gold floral designs and is known as Diwan-e-khas. It is from here that the Muslim emperors ruled India. And it was here the fate of our country used to be written and re-written. But now the place is utterly devoid of any sound other than the sound of the merrily flowing Yamuna.

Tranquil[69]
Down the ages your water has viewed so many sights and happenings,
The foams of your water have created and destroyed so many things.
Your tinkling sound is narrating so many tales, both heard and unheard,
I am reminded of them and they touch my heart.
But now you have been completely silenced o river Yamuna,
Your pure water now keeps flowing down uninterruptedly.

Both Moti Masjid made of marble and the Turkish bath (hammam) are beautiful structures of Delhi. The Diwan-e-aam

68. Takh e tauz

69. The name of the poet had not been mentioned, it will not be wrong to presume that the author himself had written these lines.

Diwan-e-khas at the Lal Qila, Delhi

has now been converted into a pub for the British soldiers, yet the podium for the emperor's throne still stands intact. On another day we went to Old Delhi to view the relics of the past. But to our dismay, the more we advanced, we caught site of more ruins. Finally, after crossing the Jantar Mantar (Mann Temple) we came across King Ashoka's pillar and the highest minaret of the world—Qutub Minar.

Qutub Minar looks quite new as it has been renovated on a regular basis. It is made up of layers of intricately carved stones. Stanzas from the Quran have also been carved upon them. Mounting the broad stairs of the minaret, we reached the top and viewed miles of arid land where lay heaps of scattered bricks and stones and a few dilapidated houses. Far away, we saw the large marble tomb of Emperor Humayun. On the other side of it, we espied the white structures of Tughlaqabad. Ancient Delhi lies embedded in the fields of Tughlaqabad.

Even though Prithviraj Chauhan's red house has been utterly destroyed, the idol of Goddess Kali whom he worshipped is still intact. Then we saw the temple of Goddess Yogamaya and journeyed towards Boot Khana which is actually the remnant of a Hindu temple. The Muslims have named it Boot Khana, which means a place where idol is worshipped. There is a metal pillar inside the place, which people say was constructed by King Dhav in 319 BC.

Prithviraj (Chauhan) had started building Qutub Minar but was not able to complete it. Finally, it was Qutbuddin who completed it. For me the most attractive sight of Delhi is the Qutub Minar. All around the place stand finely carved marble graves of many Muslim aristocrats. All these carvings are unparalleled. It reminded me of the lost heritage of Delhi.

One day we visited the Purana Quila situated at Indraprastha. According to Mr Cunningham,[70] there is not a single stone

70. Sir Alexander Cunningham was a British army officer and archaeologist who excavated many sites in India, including Sarnath and Sanchi, and served as the first Director of the Indian Archaeological Survey.

which bears signs of King Yudhishthira's[71] rule here. So instead of finding the relics of the *Mahabharata*, we had to remain satisfied seeing a mosque. Interestingly, this place stands as a living relic of the wonderful co-existence of both Hindu and Muslim cultures in the ancient past. Traces of the destroyed Muslim dynasty reminded me of the destroyed Hindu empires.

> When will India finally tide over the immense sea of sorrow?
> Immersed in the glacier of depression, will she finally drown forever?
> Enslaved in one's own land will she surrender all her rights?
> Dispersing all her wealth will she accept the shackles imposed?
> The cities are illuminated by lights of others,
> But you remain in a state of perpetual darkness[72].

Chandni Chowk of Delhi is sufficiently wide and extremely beautiful. Rows of trees both in the middle and at the side of the roads make it really attractive. The roads too are quite wide. It was truly meant for the entourage of the emperor to move about freely. There is park called Malika Bagh very near, containing a beautiful picture gallery. Here we saw the replica of a small peacock, as a reminder to the emperor's Peacock Throne. Then we went on to see the Sepoy Memorial, Jumma Masjid, and a few other memorials. Architectural relics coupled with meeting numerous men and women, overhearing their conversations, and observing their customs satisfied us sufficiently. A flower fair is held here and the enthusiasm of the local men and women for organizing the fair is really remarkable. The entire ambience of Delhi left a lasting impression in our minds as we moved on to our next destination.

---

71. Indraprastha was the supposed capital of the Pandavas, after they returned from exile.

72. The poet's name has not been mentioned hence presumably it was written by the author himself.

Mathura—Vrindavan—Giri Govardhan: It wasn't difficult for us to find a place to put up here and it was all due to Sri Shital Chandra Mukhopadhyay's care and co-operation. So, we were finally able to tread upon the holy land of Vraja Bhoomi.

Even though Mathura from this end of the river Yamuna appears like a small hamlet of Varanasi, in reality it is sufficiently beautiful. All the roads of Mathura are paved with stones. Mathura's architecture too is unique; beautiful floral designs are engraved on stones. A British gentleman, Mr Growse, has set up a museum to preserve these beautiful architectural relics. It's really a wonderful initiative. The room dedicated to the memory of Govardhan Chetri is worth seeing. A small booklet written by Mr Grouse helped us see the museum thoroughly.[73]

The Seths of Mathura are exceedingly rich. There was one Gujarati Seth, Gokuldas Parikh, who was the treasurer of the state of Gwalior (Scindia). Since he had no issue and did not share a rapport with his siblings, he left all his inheritance to his Jain employee Maniram. Gokuldas himself being a Vaishnava, did not hesitate to bestow all his wealth to a person of a different religion, instead of his own siblings. Clearly, to him the ties of blood relation did not really matter.

At present, it is the successors of Maniram who are the famous Seths of Mathura. According to hearsay, it was these Seths who built the Rangaji temple of Vrindavan at the cost of Rs 43 lakh. Now they have renounced Jainism and have become Vaishnavas. But they have constructed Jain temples as well. Swami Rangaji, who was a Dravidian, was their original Guru. The temple, therefore, has Dravidian touches, including in the idol that is worshipped. The idol, in fact, has clear signs of Tamil style. I have never seen such a huge temple of the followers of the Ramanuja sect.

---

73. Sir Frederic Salmon Growse was a British civil servant, Hindi scholar, archaeologist and Collector, active between 1860-1890. He founded the Government Museum at Mathura in 1874 and a notable work by him is a translation of the *Ramayana* of Tulsidas.

Hari Temple at Kusum Sarovar, Girigovardhan, Vrindavan

The red marble temple of Shah Kundan is like an exquisite picture. The architect of this temple had come all the way from Lucknow. The story about the opulence of these Seths is as follows: There was a minister at the emperor's court of Delhi. He fell in love with a daughter of one of the merchants of this family. At one point of time, when the minister came to power, the merchant insisted that the minister should now make him rich. Accordingly, the minister sold a throne made by the Seth to the emperor, at hundred time's higher rate. Valued at several thousand rupees, the minister quoted several lakhs. So that's how the merchant became rich. The mansion of Ramlal Badridass in Kolkata is owned by this family.

The other important site of Vrindavan is the ancient temple of Govindaji. According to the British archeologists, the temple was constructed by Man Singh, in European architectural style. Hats off to Mr Growse, because it was for his persistent effort the British government finally took over the temple, for both renovation and preservation, as a part of Hindu heritage. However, unlike the other temples, one cannot visit it other than at specific times. The rule reminded me of a royal court, where a king does not entertain men at any odd hours of the day. And like the king, the deity too accepts only money as offering and not trivial gifts like flowers.

Bihariji, the presiding deity, like any affluent person, wakes up at ten o'clock in the morning and then spends time in brushing his teeth. 'God did not create man, rather it is man who has created God'—the temple reminded me of this adage. Before coming to Vrindavan, I had imagined it to be an idyllic pastoral world full of trees and beautiful flowers. But having come here, I realized I was totally wrong. It is congested with buildings and the novelty of visiting an unknown place fizzled away soon. Even the local language, Vraja, did not sound pleasing to my ears. The people of Vrindavan ape the Marwaris, consequently both their customs and etiquette are not pleasing at all.

According to Vaishnava philosophy, love is the prime element of religion. Hence, both Sri Krishna and Sri Radha are worshipped together in the temples, despite their socially illicit relationship. The concept of adultery hardly has a place in Vaishnava philosophy. This moral laxity is visible even in the Bengali community living in Vrindavan. A Shaivite conceptualizes himself as Lord Shiva and meditates accordingly. But when people conceptualize themselves as Lord Krishna, this moral laxity is bound to creep in.

The Bengali Guru, who had inherited the Goswami title from here, after scrupulously following the ideals of his teacher, treated his disciples as his personal property—their money, body, and everything else. Therefore, enjoying the company of his lady disciple was not considered an aberration. Both in north-western India and Bombay, this practice is extremely popular among the Gujarati merchants and kshatriyas, most of whom are Vaishnavas.

Gokul is situated on the other side of Mathura. During Jhulan festival a few maharajas appeared sufficiently lecherous in their behaviour. At present, some Vaishnavas consider it appropriate to assume the garb of a female, presuming their presiding deity Lord Krishna to be the only man in the universe. Late Keshab Chandra Sen of the New Brahmo Samaj, during a weekly mass, had dressed a few of his men in the guise of females to indicate an inter-religious fusion. Since Brahmo religion does not believe in idol worship, he perhaps meant to show his followers that man ought to be as subservient to God as a woman is to her husband[74]. Yet, it's an undeniable fact, that Vaishnava religion did assist Bengal by practically obliterating the tantric Shaktas[75].

---

74. Clearly he was quite opposed to Keshab Chandra Sen who tried to ratify the intrinsic fallacies of old Brahmo religion.

75. Those who worshipped God as a woman—the primordial manifestation of power

Agra: Taj Mahal intoxicated us. Only a fortunate one is able to see this relic. The entire structure is made of white marble, and intricately decorated with colourful floral drawings and studded with precious and semi-precious stones. For instance, a flower is carved out on the wall and decorated with green emerald to magnify its beauty. It is impossible to communicate verbally the beauty of Taj Mahal. One has to see it to realize it. And anyone who sees it will be gratified for life. Due to scarcity of time, we couldn't visit either Fatehpur or Sikandra.

Kanpur: For long I had heard that Kanpur is commercially the most successful city of India. So today when we reached Kanpur at about 8 a.m., we headed straight towards Collectorganj. The people of Kanpur are early risers, hence, when we reached Collectorganj, we found the market was already almost empty. The market is nothing but a large, square-shaped patio with small, room-like structures on all the four sides. When we reached, most of the small dealers had already left. Only the wholesale dealers were sitting inside these so-called rooms. Customers can buy things only through the mediation of these wholesale dealers. All marketable commodities are put in bullock carts and placed right in the middle of the patio. There were men on the roadsides sitting on gunny bags selling their wares. Before coming here, I had heard that at least 8000 kilograms[76] of ghee are transacted in this market every day. But today we found only two or three persons selling hardly 5 to 10 kilograms of ghee each. Likewise, there were other men too, along the roadside, sitting on gunny bag mats and selling turmeric, salt etc.

After lunch we went to view the Sepoy Mutiny Memorial. An Indian has to procure permission from a magistrate to enter the place and since we had got them beforehand, we were able to enter. At first, we went to see the well, a beautiful piece of

76. Clearly this system wasn't in existence then, he has given an estimate of 200 mounds of ghee and 5/10 seers of ghee.

Intricate carvings on the Taj Mahal, Agra

architecture, decorated with engraved grape leaves. Upon a grave stands the stone figure of the Lady of Peace (Virgin Mary perhaps). Looking at her, you feel really sad. The British accuse Nana Saheb of being responsible for the great massacre, but in reality, it was his followers who were the actual culprits.

Our next place of visit was Chora Ghat, where a British fleet was set ablaze.

Prayag[77]: The name has been derived from the confluence of the two major rivers of our country—Ganga and Yamuna. We sailed up to the confluence point and were thrilled to note the distinctly different colours of the water. The red marble stone fortress built by Akbar Shah is the second-most important place in Prayag. We saw another interesting thing there—a white-leafed banyan tree planted inside a dungeon. The leaves of the tree have turned white instead of yellow. The fortress is a beautiful specimen of Arabic architecture.

Lucknow: In Lucknow we had the fortune to put up at the royal bhatiyarin inn of Balarampur. The word 'bhatiyarin', we were informed, meant 'hostess'. And this was the last phase of our present journey. Prior to it we had the experience of putting up at varied and weird places like grocery shop, Bengali hotel, house owners' rooms, railway inn, friend's father-in-law's house, old people's home, completely unknown person's house with only a letter of introduction, British Dak bungalow, pilgrim inn run by benevolent Sikhs, rented house, boat, Kalibari, and finally this royal hostess's inn.

The dilapidated British Residency at Kesar Bagh still bears the bullet marks which Indians had fired at the British. We visited the Imambara, Chowk, museum and also the Chattar Manzil. The walls of Lucknow are beautifully decorated with floral designs. The city of Lucknow may not be really beautiful,

77. The name of the meeting point of three rivers, Ganga, Yamuna and Saraswathi

but the citizens here love to lead a life of ease and luxury. There are vendors selling sweetmeats that are generally consumed by all and sundry, but if you are in search of a particular delicacy, your hunt may be rather long and time consuming. Foods that are generally considered to be a rare delicacy elsewhere, is available with the wayside food sellers.

West

Rajputana

(Rajasthan)

Jaipur: We reached Jaipur in the morning and put up at the pilgrims' inn of Thakur Fateh Singh, just adjacent to the railway station. Clearly Nature here is very different from what we had previously seen and were familiar with. It is a land of sands, and distant hills. There are fortresses surrounding the foothills.

We had our bath and went to visit Govindaji's temple and the city. The entire city is surrounded by a boundary wall and as we entered the city gate, we saw a long and wide main road in front of us. All the structures, including the houses and the roads, are built of stones. The concept of brick structure seems alien here. We reached a point of the road where it got divided in four different directions—east, west, north, and south. The houses which stood on both sides of the roads were identically constructed and were made of red stones. None of them had balconies other than bay windows. The walls had decorative stone webs at the top. There were water taps all along the roadsides and there were gas lampposts. The royal palace was enormous in size. It occupied a large area of the city outskirts. To us it looked almost like a complete locality and not a single palace. In an enclosed area, there were numerous separate palatial buildings.

The Govindaji temple is inside the royal garden. It is said that the deity of the temple is actually the original deity of Govindaji from Vrindavan. It was brought here when worshippers, scared of Aurangzeb, wanted to protect it against Mughal onslaught.

The Rajpath at Jaipur

However, the temple of Vrindavan still exists and is considered to be unique by itself. The idol undoubtedly is unique too. A devotee informed me that the interesting aspect of the idol is, once you see it you develop an insatiable thirst for seeing it again and again. The priests are all from Bengal. Seeing we were new to the place, they started enquiring our whereabouts.

From there we visited a huge water reservoir full of crocodiles. Since we had got some meat for them, we hung the meat down to the water with a rope and called the crocodiles to come and feast. Suddenly, a crocodile was visible from afar swimming towards the meat, then in no time a group of crocodiles gathered round the meat and started tugging the rope. Finally, their fearsome faces were visible to all of us.

It is not possible to visit the palace premises without the permission of the British Resident, so I applied for a permit and got one. After lunch, an emissary arrived from the Residency and took us to the palace. After crossing several boundaries, we came across a number of tombs and palatial buildings. Compared to Kashmir's planetarium and Delhi's Mann Mandir, the planetarium of Jaipur is far more enriched in terms of the number of items. Added to it, it's far better maintained and looks almost new. But to us it was just a collection of instruments and nothing more.

Then we visited the technological museum and the art gallery. Interestingly, in the art gallery we came across gold coins bearing Bengali inscriptions. The rest of the day was spent under the shady trees of the garden. We left Jaipur late midnight.

Ajmer: Pushkar Lake is situated just nine miles away from here. After alighting from the train, we immediately booked a horse carriage and set forth for Pushkar. On our way, we came across two Bengali residents of Ajmer. Since it was Sunday, they too were on their way to Pushkar. Among them was one Mr Prasanna Kumar Chakraborty with whom we were to put up. The other gentleman's face appeared very familiar to me. But I couldn't place him at first. He seemed to have recognized me instantly, possibly because he had already received a letter from Shib Chandra babu. After a few exchanges I suddenly asked the gentleman, 'Aren't you Nandalal babu?' He replied, 'Yes'. It was a strange coincidence, meeting him after a gap of maybe thirteen or fourteen years. Since he had changed quite a bit, I couldn't recognize him at first.

By now we had already left the plains and were in hilly terrains, so instead of the horse carriage we had to walk our way up. I enjoyed talking to Nandalal babu, reminiscing our yesteryears, and trudging upwards. The soil texture of the hilly tracts indicated we had arrived in the land of deserts. There were no leafy trees around but only different forms of cactuses. The colour of the soil, too, looked dry and totally sunburnt.

Three sides of the Pushkar Lake are cemented and up above it stands various temples and rest houses constructed by different kings and rich merchants. The temple of Lord Brahma that exists here had been constructed by King Holkar. There is no other temple dedicated to Lord Brahma in the country.

It had already grown quite late, so we desisted from visiting the Savitri hill. The priest informed us that visiting Savitri hill is considered to be very auspicious for married Bengali women. People from other provinces don't generally visit this hill. We had to feed a few brahmins here. The priest had already procured a few soured sweetmeats and pakoras[78] for the purpose and we too had to eat them in order to satisfy our hunger.

We returned to Ajmer in the afternoon. Like Jaipur, even here the houses are all made of stones and are really very clean. The city, too, is bounded by a wall. It was almost twilight, so we spent the rest of our time at a temple premise, listening to the mellifluous bhajans and accompanying music. At night we went to see a festival called Sanjh. An interesting feature of

78. Salty fried stuff

the city is every locality has a canopy set in its middle which is illuminated with lights in the evening. And on the ground are laid multi-coloured mats. On enquiry, nobody could tell us for certain the significance of this practice. Mr Prasanna appeared to be a perfect gentleman. His family consists of his wife and several daughters. He took great care of us and we felt as if we were actually residing with our own kinsmen.

Next morning, we climbed the Taragarh fort and viewed the entire city of Ajmer. It looked as if the city, comprising of clusters of white houses, was a collection of marble structures on one side and beautiful gardens and orchards with isolated British-style bungalows on the other. Had Anasagar Lake been added to this landscape, the sight would have been simply superb! Yet, the natural beauty that we had seen in Kashmir from Takht-e-Suleman, is something beyond comparison. But as a cityscape this was exceptional, not found anywhere else.

From there we descended to view an ancient structure which could be either a Buddhist temple or a Hindu temple, Adahi din ka jhonpra. The intricate carvings on the walls were too good to describe. Some time between1211to 1236 it was converted to a mosque. At 10 a.m., we started our journey towards Abu road station and reached it at 2 a.m. The station master, being a perfect gentleman, allowed us to stay at the railway retiring room for the rest of the night.

Abuji

(Mount Abu)

Arbudachal is the highest peak of the Aravalli mountain range. It is also known as the Guru Shikhar. We got into a litter to mount the peak. The surrounding natural beauty was fair enough to draw our attention. However, there was only one tree with which we were familiar. The range is full of wild and ferocious animals. Previously, the place was inhabited by the Bhil race and it was not possible for an outsider to step into this land. But the British government has managed to quail them and their ferocity by appointing a large number of Bhil security guards. They remain ever vigilant with their bows and arrows.

Gradually, we proceeded towards Dilwara, and after viewing a few old and rather dismal looking temples, left the place. Sights of impoverished buildings all the way pained us immensely and we were left speechless. What a letdown from my imagination! Even my companion was left speechless.

On reaching our destination, we got down from the litter and entered a house, expecting to find a shelter for the night. The security guard asked us our religion. 'We are Vaishnavas,' I told him without caring to elaborate further. Poor fellow, mistaking us to be some wealthy merchants, opened the door and allowed us to walk in without further enquiry. And when we showed interest in visiting a temple, two security men escorted us and led us to a temple, which really disappointed us immensely. He opened a room which had the stone statues of the Seth and his wife who had built the temple, followed by ten stone figures of elephants in another room. Completely frustrated and thinking this to be all there was to the temple, we decided to return. Just then a man appeared with a key and opened another door. It was like opening the door of paradise. We saw a large hall completely built of white gleaming marble, shinning like wreaths of white flowers. These temples are deliberately built in this manner so as to mislead the robbers who would invariably plunder them if they knew about such treasures.

We had eleven carriers with us who also wanted to have a glimpse of the sanctum sanctorum of the temple. The watchmen, however, at first stopped them by enquiring about their castes. Had they belonged to the caste of robbers they would not have been allowed in. Fortunately, none of them belonged to that specific caste and hence, were permitted to see the marvelous

The Dilwara temple, Mt Abu

room. The place was 128 arm's length high and 72 arm's length wide. The base was about 17 arm's length high and comprised of ten small cubicles. Each cubicle had an entrance built of white marble, and inside the cubicle was a podium where stood a statue of a Tirthankar. Each of the cubicles had a separate square-shaped roof at the top. Everything was made of white marble—the walls of the rooms, the cubicles, the pillars and even the roofs. And each piece of stone had wonderful engravings upon it. The sight was so exquisite that it is just impossible to describe them all.

After crossing the hall, we found the temple right in front of us. The marble pillars of the temple, too, were wonderfully sculpted. It looked as if someone had engraved flowers and leaves upon large pieces of ivory. The most astonishing part of these engravings was that they were all done in different layers. Even the ceiling of the temple was full of finely engraved flowers and ancient Jain mythical figures. The other interesting part is, even though separated by hair's breadth distance, the figures neither overlapped nor lost their distinct identity. These engravings, I am sure, have no equal in any other parts of our country. Taj Mahal is unique for its fine multicoloured filigree works and not for its sculpture or engravings. But I insist that one who has seen the fineries of Taj Mahal must also visit this temple of Vimal Shah.

Prior to Emperor Jahangir, no other emperor or king in India had introduced such fine filigree works in stone. The British however claim that these were originally introduced by English artists, a theory I totally disagree with.[79]

The only difference that I observed was the lack of colours. None of the engravings or paintings had splashes of colors, distinguishing the flowers from the leaves, etc. Added to it the

---

79. Sri Adinath temple, also known as Vimal Vasahi temple, was built by Vimal Shah in 1031 AD. It is dedicated to Sri Adinath, the first Jain Tirthanker.

flowers they depicted were not actual flowers seen in Nature, but flowers born out of their artistic imagination. The only explanation that I have for this unique variation is that the artistic inclinations are different. To these ancient artists that which was perfect and most beautiful had to be recreated in their artistry—not the ones they saw every day. Art itself has a world of its own, which differs vastly from the real world, and this world lies in the imagination of the artist and nowhere else.

The marble of Vimal Shah temple was brought from a place called Chandravati. And according to hearsay, previously Lord Shiva and Lord Vishnu were worshipped in these two temples. But the Jains bribed the priests and managed to get hold of them. It is said had the amount of bribe that was paid in silver coins, had they been laid out here, the entire temple premise would be covered with them. In 1032 AD, a rich merchant named Vimal Shah of Patan in Gujarat had spent Rs 18 crores to build this temple. It took fourteen years to complete it. At present it is under the supervision of two panchayats, one of Sibohi and the other of Ahmedabad. The sramanas visiting the shrine offer some token donations, varying from rupees ten to thousand, to sustain the workings of the temple and the shrine.

In all, sixteen men are employed here, including the temple guards and the priests. There is no hermit living here other than a brahmin priest. In case a hermit arrives, he has to be a brahmin too. We left the temple premise to visit another temple built by two brothers, Tejpal and Vastupal. It took fifty years, i.e., from 1197 to 1247 AD to build this temple. It has several elaborate balconies, bay windows etc., very similar to the Vimal Shah temple but the intricacies and artistries of the engravings are more elaborate and also finer. Right at the entrance are statues of two ladies, said to be the wife and younger sister-in-law of the merchant. The artistry of these statues is remarkable. It is said that 1.25 lakhs of rupees were spent to construct each of these statues.

As the story goes, after the completion of the temple, the

wives of Tejpal and Vastupal had asked their husbands, 'What have you done for us?' So, to pacify the two women, these statues were built, and accordingly named after them. It is said the engravers, while carving the stones, would weigh the amount of stone dust that was collected everyday. And at par with the weight of the dust they received their daily pay in silver coins. Consequently, the engravers gave their best in carving both the statues. Undeniably, their skill and artistry were par excel.

In the evening, we went to the Vimal Shah temple to view the evening worship. We came across the yellow statue of the first Tirthankara Rishabanantha, sitting in a meditative pose. The figure was adorned with gold jewellery that glowed luminously in the brightness of the lamps that were lighted. The eyes, in particular, made of diamonds, sparkled brightly.

From there we went to Tejpal temple. Worship had just begun. There we saw the statue of the last Tirthankara, Parasnath. Bedecked in golden ornaments from head to toe, he stood watching the rituals taking place. Since I opted to take part in the ritual, I promised to donate 1.25 maunds of ghee to the temple. The priest took the lighted lamp round the temple worshipping all the deities and two of us followed him like two sramanas. That helped us to view the entire temple at one go. Interestingly, other than Vimal Shah, Tejpal and Vastupal, no other idol was made of marble.

Later, I spoke to many Jain travellers who had come there, and learnt a lot about their religious practices, before retiring for the day. The large emeralds adorning Rishabhanantha kept leaping before my eyes before I fell asleep.

Jainism is divided into two factions—the Digambara and the Svetambara. At present there aren't any practitioners of Svetambara. The Digambara faction is still thriving and is carrying on the practice of adorning their idols with different ornaments without clothing them. The philosophy behind this is—clothes are a cause of material bondage. One who continues to survive, in his birthday suit, will not be troubled by any material bondage. Just as man's mind is devoid of any bondage, likewise, his body too should not put on any external coverings to cover up his real self.

It is said that Jainism is a mix of Buddhist and Brahmanical philosophy. Madhav Acharya had laughed at Jainism and commented that they practice shaving off their head, tying up their mouth and keeping intact just a tuft of hair at the back of their head. The founder of Jainism was Mahavir. Jains do not believe in the creation of the universe but accept the existence of a supreme power. The sages, who have achieved nirvana, are called the Tirthankaras and they have renounced all detrimental human emotions like anger, hatred etc. and are accordingly worshipped in simple Sanskrit slòkas.

The merchants of Varanasi comprise of both Jains and Hindus. And at present many of the Jain merchants have adopted Hindu religion as well. I am not branding the Jains as non-Hindus, but they follow different scriptures. The Jains who worship Lord Vishnu, a Hindu god, is called a Jain converted into Hindu. In Varanasi, almost fifty per cent of the merchants whose surname is Agarwal, are Jains. When a Jain Agarwal marries a Hindu Vaishnava Agarwal, the combination that is formed is—Vaishnava husband with a Jain wife or vice versa. But none of them renounce their beliefs; rather they cook their own meals separately. In Varanasi, there is a Jain from Nain Mati, known as Buddha Mati. Religions tend to infuse in them varied cultures and practices. Both at Moradabad and Bijnor there is a group of people called Vishnoi, who practice Hindu customs but read the Islamic Quran, thereby fusing two religions.

According to some scholars, Jainism did not sprout from Buddhism. It was there since ages and was followed by many people. But if one goes through their sacred texts, one realizes that there are lot of interpolations in them which have been derived from both Buddhism and Hindu mythology. However, like Buddhism, Jainism too does not acknowledge the supremacy of the four Vedas. Consequently, they have not been included in the thousand forms of Hindu religion.

Expectedly, there are several theories countering the basic precepts of Hindu religion, since Hindu religion does not believe in a single authority's control over human fate. Added to it, Hindu religion is not the handiwork of one single teacher. Rather it is a collective effort of many people, down the ages. Hence, it has varied with time and customs of relevant ages. Many scholars and sages have included their independent opinions while giving Hindu religion its present shape. And it is also not mandatory for all Hindu societies to abide by all these diverse rulings. But the most interesting aspect of Hindu religion is its amalgamation with existing societies. A Hindu cannot dissociate religion from social strictures. So, if one doesn't abide by contemporary social rulings, he is treated as both a social and religious outcaste. But if he abides by the existing social rulings despite being irreligious, he is considered to be religious. Hindu religion tolerates an atheist but does not permit a non-practitioner of social rules to thrive within its fold. And ironically, what Hindu religion had once considered to be irrefutable, may now be treated as redundant. So, what seems unalterable now, may in near future change radically to suit the social requirements. Furthermore, since men within a society vary in nature, the rulings of Hindu religion, too, keep changing to suit everyone's palate. And because Hinduism is a collection of works by various authors of different scholastic statures, the rulings too keep varying from one text to another.

After our morning ablutions, we went to Vimal Shah temple. In order to appreciate the beauty of a place, my habit is to visit it repeatedly and stay there for quite some time. I looked at the temple and tried to imbibe its beauty. But, amidst all the beautiful objects, there were quite a few figures of the ancient world depicting their barbaric practices. For instance, in the ancient world, girls were often plundered for marriage, leading to battles. At present, the practice of beating a groom when he comes to marry is reminiscent of that ancient practice. Similar is the case with the engravings found here. There are traces to be found of the ancient uncivilized practices. Interestingly, the architects of the temple have clearly indicated that the pillars are nothing but imitations of the tree trunks originally. Just as a tree stands upon its trunk, likewise these pillars support the entire structure. Often tree trunks of unequal heights would be towed in and tied together with thick rope to provide the required support.

The Arabs set up cloth tents for their homes. This is because they are nomadic tribes unused to staying permanently at a place. Hence, now even when they construct palaces, they use tent materials rather liberally. In Bengal, too, temples of Lord Shiva look like huts made from straw and even conch shells are moulded in the form of bangles. The original structure remains intact, while it's only the ornamental part that is elaborated. So is the case with the architecture of this temple, where the pillars are in the form of tree trunks while the decorative part is both elaborate and varied.

Indian temples are of five types—Buddhist, Jain, Hindu, Dravidian and Kashmiri. But Buddhist temples structurally vary from one another in the northern part of India, southern India and Nepal. Likewise, temples of Orissa, central India, Bengal, and Varanasi are not similar structurally. Other than these there are several mixed Hindu temples in our country.

Our servant was getting tired at the guest house waiting for us, so grudgingly we decided to return. But on our way back, I kept turning back again and again to imprint in my mind all the wonderful images we had seen. It was as if someone was resisting my forward movements. Fortunately, just then the gate keeper came and shut the door of the temple. Much relieved, we reached the guest house, collected our luggage, and set out for the railway station. Since we would commence our journey that night towards Ahmedabad, we decided to bathe and eat at Abu Road railway station itself. The distance from Abuji to Abu Road is 21 miles. On reaching there we were informed there was no scheduled train for the day. The time mentioned in the travel book I was carrying was incorrect. So, we spent the afternoon enjoying the natural beauty of Rajputana. People here appear to love wearing arms and hence arms and armours have become an integral part of their dress. A camel driver driving his herd of camels too has a gun in his hand. The sight reminded me of the International Exhibition I had seen in Calcutta. The Rajputana pavilion hardly displayed anything other than arms and ammunitions. This seems to be the prevalent culture here.

Here are the names of a few of the various types of swords—lahar daria, dohari, kastidodari, dhoop, teghdalilkhani, shamsher ardam, khandalaimony, nagphana tarfana cutter. There are the bow and arrow, bhalla, nagpass, phoolhari, tabol, tamacha, gun of two types, pathardwar and topidwar and also khanjar.

Gujarat

Right from childhood I had heard about the desert of Rajputana, the mirage and also about the oasis but missed seeing them this time. I had badly wanted to see Chittor as well but, couldn't make it. So, with a heavy heart I got into a train for Gujjar (Gujarat). In due course, we reached the sandy land of Gujarat. On our way we saw endless fields of millets and little children playing in the fields. They joyously welcomed our train which was being pulled by a steam engine. The women here do not wear the heavy ghagra of Rajputana, instead they wear lighter and brighter garments. Khar Bhushan kept pointing to the red-coloured wooden boundaries at places, saying aloud to all his co-passengers, 'This village belongs to the Gaekwads and that one to the British' etc.

At the stations of Rajputana one has to buy drinking water that is classified as Hindu water, Muslim water etc. The ticket collector came to collect our tickets at Sabarmati junction, and we were informed that the next station was Ahmedabad, our destination. We travelled down the Sabarmati Bridge and reached Ahmedabad in no time. Out in the station, we came across several houseowners both male and female. We accompanied one of them and reached a guest house. Since it was getting dark, and we decided not to waste our time in the guest house. The houses are not at all beautiful to look at. We took the main road of the city and reached a place called Manik Chowk. There is a large market there, where we could not see the people—only a sea of turbans. Turbaned shopkeepers were selling different types of turbans.

After crossing several entrances, we reached a temple of Goddess Kali, known as Bhadra Kali temple. A few citizens, whom we came across, expressed their curiosity by asking our whereabouts. The opulence of the place was quite palpable. And the ancient heritage of the place also was quite impressive.

Next morning, we got a conveyance and went for sightseeing. The city was established in 1412, by Sultan Ahmed Shah. Prior to it, the city was named Ashwabal and before that it was known as Karnavata. In 1818, the city ruled, by King Rajeswar Peshawar, came under British rule. We viewed the Jain temple constructed by Hatti Bhai. On the way, we saw the house of the city mayor, Prem Bhai. Just a few months ago he married one of twin sisters and got the other one married to his son. Jumma Masjid, Rani ka Roza, Bhil queen Sipri and Shalam ka Roza, and the graveyards of the kings bear signs of beautiful architecture. Interestingly, all the Muslim rulers of Gujarat, having Hindu antecedents, did not construct anything that had the remote touche of Arabian styles.

Kankaria reservoir is a beautiful lake. Its ancient name was Hauz e Qutub. The reservoir was constructed in 1851 by Sultan Qutbuddin, the king of Gujarat. It has quays on all four sides and is about a square mile in area. It has a beautiful island in the middle named Nagina, which means the jewel of the ring finger. The island is full of trees and lovely foliage. In the middle of the island is Ghat Mandal. There is a beautiful garden path laid out to access the island. There is no connecting bridge. A few years ago, the Collector of the place had renovated the place and now it looks beautiful.

We returned to our place and were about to bathe, when a sarangi player appeared. He was about to display his skill, but because we were busy, we refused to sit through his performance. Then he showed us his credentials and we offered him some money. With that he seemed to be happy to leave us. What happened next was interesting. Informed by the said artist, another person appeared with his string instrument. This time we couldn't help him. We asked his blessings and insisted that he leave the place.

Baroda: On reaching the place in the wee hours of the morning, we took shelter in a pilgrim's inn. We heard music coming from the floor above us. And next morning, when we woke up, we found it was a temple premise. The person who had set up the temple had also constructed this inn. So, by default we had arrived in a Hindu kingdom. The city is inhabited by more than a few lakhs of people. Being the capital of the kingdom, it clearly manifested signs of opulence. After visiting Moti Bagh and Nazar Bagh, we went to see the temple of Bahucharaji. The idol of Goddess Bhavani was decorated with diamonds all over. It being the auspicious occasion of Mahashtami, the place was filled with people. A musical soirée of garba[80] was being held in the temple courtyard, and the Gaekwad himself came to offer his prayers. A lady appeared and beckoned others to join her in performing the garba. But the number being inadequate, she asked the singers to join her, saying in Gujarati, 'why feel

80. A typical musical performance of both song and dance which is very popular in Gujarat.

ashamed to dance'. The ladies finally joined the group. I could follow only one song, sung in Hindi. It had something to do with the love of Lord Krishna and Sri Radha. The lead singer, however, appeared slightly abashed in singing the song. The ladies were all exquisitely dressed. A few ladies who were attired in transparent clothing had inner wears too. They wore beautiful pearl necklaces and earrings of either diamond or other precious stones. They wore ornaments on their hands and legs too. Some of the foot ornaments had little bells attached to them.

In the evening we went to see the garba festival held on the streets of the city. They had selected a suitable spot in a locality for the programme, and girls had assembled there. They stood around a large lamp and were clapping their hands and singing. It presented an ethereal combination of beautiful dresses, brightly lit lamps, and novel music. Gradually the crowd of viewers kept swelling. Garba musically narrates the love story of Lord Krishna and Sri Radha. Consequently, only beautiful girls are selected to take part in it. Little boys and girls were sitting beside the lamps waiting to take part in the musical event as little Krishnas and Radhas. A lady was singing mellifluously, and others joined her in chorus. Even though the tune was monotonous, yet listening to her for long was not boring at all. The audience clapped along to maintain the beat and the lady acknowledged their participation by bowing down before them.

In the afternoon, a procession came out to celebrate Vijaya Dashami. Previously, both in Gujarat and Maharashtra, the kings used to celebrate the occasion through warfare. But after a time, it so happened they could not proceed with their mission any further and had to return home, only to seek a better time to attack the enemy. Now, however, there is no warfare to be undertaken, only the ritual of procession has remained. In other places the kings send either their royal umbrellas or swords to different states to mark the occasion. In our native village, on

Vijaya Dashami, people assemble in the house where Durga Puja was held, with a turmeric-covered cloth and tie a rupee in it to undertake any new venture. The priest chants a few Sanskrit mantras and the people who have assembled go round the idol several times, symbolically beginning their new journey.

Here, the King of Baroda fixes the route for the procession to follow. The procession is led by the gong men and then followed by artillery soldiers led by a British soldier. They march to the war tunes played by the musicians who follow them. A cartload of arms is a part of the procession. The bulls of this cart are decorated with jewels and other fineries. The courtiers, royal kinsmen and elephants form a part of the procession. A battalion of Kutch soldiers, dressed in their native soldierly attire, too, are included in it. They play their native war instruments like shehnai, kada and nakada. Lastly comes King Sayajirao Gaekwad, seated on a golden throne, which is mounted upon a mountain-like elephant decorated with all pomp and heraldry. The elephant walks at a leisurely pace allowing the king to greet all his subjects who are present to view the show. Just behind the king rides his ancient chief minister, Kazi Shahabuddin. Interestingly, there are no horse riders in the entire procession. The flag that is raised high bears the emblem of a sword and the limb of a horse. These two insignias stand for the uprise of Maharashtra as a kingdom.

After the procession reaches its destination, the king accepts a blood-smeared leaf and begins his return journey. Previously, Khande Rao Gaekwad used to kill a bull and smear its blood on the forehead of the royal entourage to mark the culmination of the procession. At Birul, a he goat is still sacrificed instead of a human being (supposed enemy) to mark the occasion. Expectedly, with the progress of civilization, warfare will come to an end. What an irony! When a subject kills a man, he is punished for murder, but when a king kills thousands of men in the name of war, he is never censored.

After returning to our place, we kept discussing the sight

we had viewed. I kept remembering the movements of the fast-paced horses and slow but majestic movements of the elephants. The entire congregation was saluting the victorious king as if in replication of the scenes described in the Hindu epics and puranas. It is difficult now to visualize the roaring heroes in warfare. This procession was meant to display not the actual warfare, but to display the opulence of the king. Hence, the lavish display of gold and precious stones. The royal Guru, Gukulia Gonsai, attired in lavish dress, was travelling in a horse carriage and all the royal kinsmen followed him, attired in equally lavish attires. The elephants were decorated lavishly too—an unthinkable proposition in actual warfare. I kept reminiscing all this.

The procession of Moharram followed in the evening with people lamenting, Hai Hassan, Hai Hussain. Since the king permits other religious festivals and rituals in his kingdom, an official tazia was brought out at the dead of the night and a substantial number of men had assembled to view the procession. We found three structures resembling missiles set up at the site and three fat men dressed in white were lying inertly within them. Other than these there were figures of ferocious animals like tiger, crocodile etc. displaying their catches. The accompanying songs (originating from Lucknow) were extremely melancholic in tune melting the heart of all the people who were there. Finally, when a blood-smeared horse, named Dul Dul, bearing a flag went up on top of a nearby mosque, the people attending the show started wailing loudly. The imam, who was seated inside, echoed the cries of the people and started narrating the incident that took place centuries ago. 'Just like this blood-covered horse, centuries ago another horse had returned without the rider on its back on this very day etc.' The poor horse could not stand fixed there as its body bore marks of injury all over and blood was oozing out from the injuries. Its white hide was gradually turning red with blood. The sight intensified the cries of the people. Even I could not withhold my tears at the sight. However, the Sunni Muslims, to prove their contrary belief, dressed in various styles were singing and dancing around.

In 1720, the Maharashtrian Army chief, Pilaji Rao Gaekwad had attacked Gujarat and had succeeded in collecting Chautha[81] from the rulers. Thereafter, their empire was established and had started growing. At present, the King of Baroda earns a revenue of Rs 12,500,000. The area of his kingdom is about 4399 miles and he rules over 2,000,225 subjects. The kingdom is divided into four sections, and each section, called Pranta, is looked after by a Subba. The method of ruling is commendable. The landowners of Kathiawar pay half of their land revenue to the British government and the other half to the Gaekwads. There was a time when, ordered by the king, a convict at Sathmari, was trampled upon by an elephant as punishment for his crime. There were other cruel punishments, too, like burying a person alive, throwing a person down a hill, or even nailing him to death.

At Moti Bagh, we saw a picture of Malhar Rao, openly playing the supposedly unholy festival of Holi with hundred prostitutes. He was spraying coloured waters on them in the royal courtyard. He also celebrated pigeon's marriage in all pomp and splendour. And once when a cat ate up the she-pigeon, the cat was killed gruesomely. It is said that once Malhar Rao had visited a place called Billimora, but when he heard the road was constructed by Khander Rao Gaekwad, he refused to step in. And as per royal order lands of the estates full of harvest-worthy crops were destroyed to construct a new road within a few hours. The workmen reported that Rs 25,000 was spent for the purpose.

No one believes the story of the Resident being poisoned. Jamuna Bai was imprisoned for this, and after being released from prison, she coronated the young prince who is now the

81. A kind of revenue.

ruler of the state. Sir Madhav Trambak Rao has resigned from ministership. It is said that Madhav Rao had deposited Rs 80 lakh with the British government and the King of Baroda was to receive only the interest, and not the original sum. This had displeased the king, hence Madhav Rao had to resign. The smiling face of Madhav Rao clearly indicates that he is a cunning fellow.

Queen Jamuna Bai resides in a different palace and has nothing to do with the royalty. Recently, in the absence of the queen, three people were murdered in her palace.

There is another interesting practice that is followed in the royal court—the recruitment of African performers down the generations. These people are neither soldiers nor do they do anything other than remain addicted throughout the day. But they are remarkably close to the king and hence have been nicknamed as 'children of the king'. If the king orders them to behead someone, they readily comply but when it comes to performing anything on a regular basis they refuse to comply. The present Gaekwad has assigned them a regular task which they refused to perform. The king, being extremely annoyed, stopped their salaries. Consequently, they shifted their base to Hyderabad. Unable to make a headway in Hyderabad, they returned here and have now threatened the king that they would plunder the kingdom's exchequer and collect their dues. The Gaekwad got them arrested. Three of these men used to reside at Jamuna Bai's residence and after a tough fight with the police who came to arrest them, were killed.

Sur Sagar or Nawa Lakshmi, and Bapi Tarag are a few sights worth seeing in Baroda. Jamuna Bai's hospital and school are exquisite pieces of architecture like the filigree works of Jaipur. A convoy of horsemen lead the conveyance of both the king and other royal kinsmen, and at night a group of men carrying lighted torches lead the convoy. Since the Gaekwads do not have coins worth half paisa the said amount is normally paid through physical labour. Hence, if one must account for one paisa, he must note it as five paisa. This again leads to another story. Initially, when copper coins were used for monetary transactions, then one could procure five cowries at one paisa. But now they can procure a handful of cowries with one paisa. In Gujarat, twenty-five paisa is known as paoli and a paisa is known as dheria. And a rupee is called Gaekwadi rupee. Victorian rupee is kaldar.

Surat: Our car reached Surat in the wee hours of the morning, at 2 a.m. A white-capped, elegant looking, elderly Parsi gentleman got into our car, and when we asked him whether we had reached Surat he said yes, it was Surat indeed. A few female luggage carriers took us to a house where we could put up during our stay. For the rest of the night, we spent our time combating the bedbugs, which infested the mats where we lay. As kids we had read in our geography texts about the hastamals. And now we knew that in Surat, Jains have cowsheds and other sheds to house the domestic animals. Likewise, they also have provisions to rear and care bedbugs. To help bedbugs to thrive and propagate, they pay men to sleep on beds full of bedbugs. My query was, were the mats provided to us meant to assist the bedbugs to thrive and propagate?

Next morning, when we went out to view the city, I felt rather relieved and happy. The memorial of Merwanji Horamji Fossett, clock tower, high school, hospital and adjacent to the hospital, the market, were the few places we saw before moving towards the Victoria Garden near the fort. Then we walked towards Tapi River and bypassing the English people's colony, reached the Free Thinkers Corner set up by the local Britishers. In the evening, the riverbank turns into a meeting ground for many British inhabitants. With the receding waters of River Tapi and Bombay becoming an important port, Surat has lost its ancient glory as a commercial hotspot.

In 1612, the British colonists had set up their trading center here in Surat. It was famous for building steamboats and many

Parsi workers were employed here. And even now the master builder of Bombay dockyard is a Parsi. As history records in seventh century AD, the Parsis were driven away from Persia for following their religion. After sailing through the turbulent seas, they finally managed to reach the Hindu kingdom of Surat, where they set up their colony. According to some, the original name of Surat was Saurashtra, and with usage it has been reduced to Surat. But Saurashtra is in Kathiawar region. And the name Kathiawar has been derived from its people, who belonged to Kathi race. Likewise, the name Gujarat has been derived from the inhabiting race, the Gujjars.

Surat has a population of 107,149. The city is partially surrounded by a boundary wall. In case of an immigrant, the local police super makes a thorough enquiry about his antecedents and only then permits him to reside here.

Surat is famous for sweets. Gujaratis are fond of ghee from Surat and sugar from Bengal. But at present, instead of Bengal, sugar is obtained from Mauritius. There is a popular saying in Gujarati—it is best to die in Kashi (Varanasi) and the best food is to be obtained from Surat. The most delicious sweet of Surat is ghari. It is made from condensed milk and when preparing, large quantity of ghee is poured into it. The resultant product is then cut into pieces and served. The thick coating of ghee is very much visible upon the layers of the sweets. Puris, various types of salty snacks (namkeen) and other fried stuffs are favourite Gujarati foods. Spinach and vegetables are sold only in night markets. Variety of fruits too are available in these markets. There are both tea and coffee corners. The less affluent people consume alcohol and so do the women folks. The women consume alcohol even at home.

Vallabhacharya Shrinathji's temple is an interesting place. Here men and women of the city gather every day to view the deity. There is one specific door which allows people to enter, and when the door opens for the day, there is a surge of people entering the temple. But they are allowed only a few seconds to remain inside. Hence, even if they are not able to view the deity they must exit from another specific door. If a person tends to delay the exit even for a few moments, he must bear the beatings of the watchful guard. The door is closed after a short spell of darshan. Anyone who enters the room for viewing must hail Jai, Jai. The priests then open the door for him just for a few seconds. In case the wait to view the deity is delayed for a long time, the women sit there and weave plumes for temple use. We met a few Hindi-speaking people there in the temple premise. They welcomed us with such a show of enthusiasm, that we felt as if they were our long-lost kinsmen. In this remote land, even a Bengali turns a kinsman of a Hindustani. In their native land, however, a Bengali tends to mock Hindustanis by nicknaming them as sattu[82], while a Hindustani mocks a Bengali as bhatu[83]. A Bengali can never expect such camaraderie from a Hindustani in Varanasi.

The turbans people use in Surat are quite different from the ones used in Ahmedabad. The Bhatuyas of Kutch and Mando wear yet another type of turban. The merchants of Kathiawar on the other hand wear another kind of turban. So, turban appears to be the identifying mark of one's native place in Gujarat. And the assumption of a tourist that the turban has both geographical and historical significance appears to be true in every way. We Bengali do not wear anything on our heads. This has proved advantageous for us here. People came to us and wanted to know our whereabouts. A curious onlooker came to me and asked, 'Is it true that Bengali men do not wear turbans, and Bengali women do not wear a bodice?' I do not know whether my answer convinced him. Gujarati women wear the sari in the Hindustani style, but their bodice is slightly different. The back remains open for all to view. Only a few threads keep the bodice in its place. The women seem to

82. Flour made of barley, pigeon pea, maize etc.

83. Derived from bhaat, which in Bengali means rice.

be fond of using pearl-studded hairpins. Even a poor woman wears hairpin studded with artificial pearls. Here women seem more hard working compared to the men. They perform hard tasks, like carrying heavy loads etc. However, they do not cover their heads. They colour their teeth with a red colour. The men shave off their hair and look quite hideous. The caps they use do not cover their heads. They also wear pearl earrings. The Vaishnavas anoint their foreheads with sandalwood paste and wear long chains.

The famous Swami Dayanand Saraswati was a Gujarati. His teacher was from Mathura and was born blind. Even he defied idol worship. When Dayanand tried to establish his point in Varanasi, two scholars, Vaman Acharya and Madhav Acharya, quoted the Vedas to prove that idol worship was there even during the Vedic age.

Bombay

(Mumbai)

On the 4th of Kartick, (sometime in middle of November), at 9 p.m., we left Baroda on a steam engine, and next morning reached a place full of coconut trees, palm trees, banana plantations, etc. We knew we had reached the district of Konkan. Leaving behind the village of Bandra and many others, we finally reached Charni Road railway station. A bullock cart took us to our destination. After lunch, we went to view the sea, and then took a tram and went from Colaba to Wiphala.

According to some historians, the name Mumbai was derived from a Portuguese word Buttan. In all likelihood, the name Mumbai was derived from the presiding deity Mumba Devi. I have been hearing a lot about the beauty of Bombay but today I found it to be city of thatched huts. Concrete houses are rare. And most of them are decorated with coloured glasses, presenting a garish sight. On entering one such house, we found small and narrow rooms, muddy floor, and wooden walls. The houses constructed by the government are, however, impressive. They are made of stones. There are very few open fields and fewer narrow parks in the city. Among all the cities of India only Bombay can be compared to Calcutta. But Calcutta is far better than Bombay.

Bombay is famous for its cleanliness, and that is correct. But the roadsides of the city are full of toilets and the night soils are carried in open cans by toilet cleaners. There is no drainage system like we have in Calcutta. The houses are not numbered, neither are the streets named properly. There are water taps here and there, but the water is not purified. There are gaslights on the streets, but their lights are not bright enough. Bombay is smaller than Calcutta but has a greater population density. Hence, most of the houses are extremely congested. The public conveyance system too is not as good as Calcutta. There are fewer buses and other vehicles. There is one shop called Amichandnama selling sweetmeats but only salty snacks, like namkeen, were available there. The rest of the shops were selling deep fried oily stuff. The Bombay port is not as active, commercially, as the one in Calcutta. Even their educational activities fall short of Calcutta's academic excellence.

There is very little longitudinal difference between Bombay and Calcutta. Consequently, the vegetations that grow in both these places are almost identical. For example, I have never found pineapple in any other state except Bengal. But here in Bombay I found pineapple being supplied locally. Other than pineapple, oranges and plantains grow here in profusion. The oranges, however, lack the expected flavour and taste. The plantains that grow here are better than the ones found in Bengal. A typical type of plantain that grows here turns yellow when ripened but is sweeter than the ones I have ever tasted before. They are called Konkani plantains. Then there is the red-coloured plantain. Coconuts of Mahim are extremely tasty. Nobody consumes green coconut. Dates also grow here in abundance, but the ones which come from Malta are better to taste.

Due to 15-degree longitudinal difference, the sun rises here an hour later than Calcutta. The people of the western side see the sun rising an hour later. Due to the obstructing Himalayas, the Indian Ocean is deprived of commercial trade winds. Instead, it is blessed with monsoon winds. From autumn to spring, the wind blows in the north-east direction, while from summer to autumn the wind blows in the south-west direction. The south-western wind is also known as the monsoon wind. And because monsoon is not a favoured season for trade, there is hardly any commercial vessel arriving or departing from Bombay in monsoon.

The most important site of Bombay is its harbour. It is an estuary of the sea. But the harbour is huge, and one cannot view the harbours in isolation. There are infinite number of harbours here. And each one trades in a different merchandise. There are several shops near some harbours dealing in those commodities which are available there. The most impressive and the most important of all these is the Prince's Dock. It is said that Rs 68 lakh was spent in constructing it. Thirty large vessels can simultaneously unload materials here. The total area is 90 bighas.

In 1884, one and half crore worth of merchandise was traded from this harbour. In the evening when the merchant navy crews assemble here both for evening stroll and for inhaling fresh sea air, band music is heard. English mail ships arrive at this harbour.

We boarded a ship from Karachi to visit the Elephanta Caves. The ship started vibrating and the boatsmen immediately set sail. It was my first sea voyage, hence, I was slightly nervous. Interestingly, ships sail smoothly in salty sea water, in comparison to fresh river water. And that is because sea water is loaded not only with salt but many other minerals, making it heavier than fresh river water. I have found the colour of the water of Bay of Bengal to be a mix of blue and green. But when it reaches the shore in the form of waves, the colour visibly becomes paler. However, the colour of the sea water here appears relatively fairer. But there are no high waves here. With receding of the sea during low tide, the Konkani fishermen use their harpoons to catch fish. Consequently, the sea being struck by the fishermen, strike back at their boats and this takes the boats forward.

On one side we beheld the sea, and on the other side there stood before us a range of mountains. In between stood desolate islands of Buchan, Hogg and Chinar Tikri. Bombay city, too, is an island so to say. There lie subterranean mountain range upon which pillars have been constructed to sustain the city. A lighthouse has been constructed for that purpose. It stands at the entry point of the harbour. The estuary spreads out to about nine miles. The lighthouse presented a wonderful sight with huge waves constantly dashing against it and cascades of water falling on each side. On reaching the top of the lighthouse, I looked ahead and remained awestruck. I said to the lights-man, 'Look I have managed to stand against the sky.' The highest floor of the lighthouse is a glass cage and inside it is a bright octagonal light-emitting machine, almost the height of a human being. Every ten seconds it keeps emitting a bright light and within eighty seconds the revolving lantern completes its circle. The entire structure is 150 feet high, inside it is about 12 feet wide. About Rs 6 lakh was spent in constructing the lighthouse. A British official resides here, with five attendants.

The distance between Apollo harbour to Gharapuri is about nine miles. However, sailing in the boat did not prove to be a tiring experience. I kept looking around at the ships that were anchored, and it appeared to me as if all of them were contemplating what they would do next. At a distance stood the boats from Kutch, and there was the Mandui harbour. Then there was a ship full of pilgrims on their journey to Mecca. A group of migrant workers were returning from a hilly terrain. Bombay is the marine yard for British warships. We found two warships there—one from Abyssinia and the other from Magdala. And one among them had gone to the Persian Gulf. The other one was anchored there. These warships are strange looking. There are four huge cannons installed in them—two in front of the ship and two at the rear part of the ship. They are placed on revolving platforms. There are rails beneath these platforms and the cannons keep revolving on their heavy iron wheels. There is a machine to move the platforms in whichever direction one wants. So, from whichever direction the enemy tries to attack, the revolving platform will rotate accordingly and attack the enemy.

The sewerage system comprising of tough iron pipes is found surrounding the body of the ship. In case water accumulates in all these pipes, the ship can submerge itself underwater with only the nozzles of the cannons and turret visible above the surface. And in case the enemy attacks them and sends volleys of bullets, the entire ship will remain intact. At the turret is a high podium meant for the captain to stand on. The turret is built of iron and is covered by wood, so is practically impenetrable. There are two small openings there to allow the captain to keep an eye on the enemies and to instruct his men.

Next, we sailed to Gharapuri bridge and on reaching the top, we had to pay a toll tax. A security personal accompanied us on our visit around. There is a large temple, carved out of a huge stone. The idols, too, are gigantic in size, almost 12 arms long in height. There is a large Shiva lingam in the central room. The walls are decorated with beautiful figures of Ardha Nariswar[84], the Trinity, Shiva and Parvati, marriage images of Shiva, Mother of Ganesh, Ravana's lifting of the Kailash

84. A deity of half woman and half man. It is supposed to be a composite figure of Shiva and Parvati.

Mountain, the chaos at Daksha yajna, Shiva's meditation and Bhairav. The headgears indicate that they were the handiworks of Dravidian sculptors. They were possibly built about thousand years ago. Since the origin of these works are not known, the locals attribute them to the Pandavas (of the *Mahabharata*). Several pillars and idols show signs of dilapidation and even the roofs are leaking in several places. Time is not afar when they will be destroyed completely. There is a statue of an elephant here, hence, the name Elephanta. But even that statue is damaged severely.

The sight of Chaupati and the estuary looks beautiful in twilight. The priest was ringing the bell and offering flowers while conducting the evening puja of the sea. Even a religious Parsi was offering his vespers, sometimes standing straight sometimes twisting himself while the Parsi ladies, clad in rainbow-coloured saris, were ambling about. The ice-cream vendor and other vendors were selling their multiple wares. The sight is undoubtedly beautiful, but I was reminded of the numerous people who lost their land when the harbour was being filled and converted into a visiting place. A British company had processed this valuable land, at the cost of local habitation.

Bandstand is a very narrow area where people keep jostling one another while walking. A crowd had gathered to view the soldiers who had returned from Sikkim. People were discussing about Egypt. The local people had vanished from the sight, allowing the Parsi community to continue their evening walk. The Parsi community seems to have lost its business interest. They are now happy with jobs which pay them a monthly salary of Rs 50-55. They seem to be happy just imitating the British ways of living.

There is a garden nearby, where there is a stone clock. It is worth seeing. We saw steam-driven trains of the Central Railways plying from Bombay to Baroda. Twenty trains ply from Bandra to Colaba, and vice versa. In order to have a proper view of the sea, we went from Balukeshwar to Mahalakshmi temple. Below the temple, we could hear the roaring sea striking the sea beach. A huge black stone was resting at the foot of the temple. We could see fishermen's boats sailing afar. The place had a solemn ambience. The magnanimous sight of the sea mesmerized us, and was unforgettable. The sun was setting for the day and we watched this ethereal sight to our hearts' content. A crimson hue coloured the horizon as the sun gradually set for the day. The sight was all the more spectacular when only half of the sun had submerged into the sea.

> Oh! sun have you really drowned,
> Into the dark waters of the sea?
> Proceed then, o God, proceed what can I say,
> Do not return to arise again.
> Is there any reason for you to return?
> O tell me, is there?
> India does not need illumination,
> One who is imprisoned for life.
> Illumination is the cause for her embarrassment.

From Malabar Hills, Bombay looks like a bow. And in one corner of the city is Colaba, while Malabar Hills is its other corner. On its east is the harbour. We looked at the panoramic view of the city and found rows of coconut trees dotting the landscape. It looked beautiful. At the topmost point of this hill stands the dakhma where dead bodies of people of the Parsi community are thrown. It consists of a well enclosed within a building, which is surrounded by high walls. There is a small door leading to the highrise wall and carcasses are hurled from here. Vultures, eagles, and crows feast on the carcasses and with time only the bones remain, which then find their way into the well.

The British township is set up here, upon this hill. But unlike Calcutta, there are not too many British citizens residing here in Bombay. Crawford Market, however, is worth visiting. The structured market boasts of variety of fruits, flowers, vegetables, fishes and meats. It also reflects our national affluence. At night it is illuminated by electric lights.

At the centre of Elphinstone Circle there is a small garden. The roads lying opposite to the garden has large mansions dotting it in a circle. Consequently, the entire place looks as if the mansions are guarding the garden on all sides. Interestingly, all the mansions are identically structured, both in terms of their heights and areas, thus presenting a beautiful sight. Externally, all these mansions are built of stones and it appears there is no provision to open them. Banks and other commercial offices are situated inside these mansions. It was during the war between Britain and America that Bombay, trading in cotton, made a tidy sum of money. This money was utilized in building these mansions.

On another day we went to visit both the Victoria Museum and garden. The beautiful museum, made of stone, was constructed by Khanderao Gaekwad. The beautiful architecture we had seen at Abuji could be compared to this museum. Engravings depicting minute details of dresses are to be found here. An amount of Rs 1,80,000. was spent in setting up this museum. The tower set up by Raichand Premchand is another interesting feature of the place.

Near our residence is Madhav Bagh. A merchant had set up an inn for pilgrims, a garden, and an auditorium here in the memory of his father. At the centre of the garden is a Lakshmi Narayan temple. The idols are made of white stone and decked in valuable jewels and ornaments. Decorating the idols with jewels and ornaments indicates the affluence of the local people.

Near it is a veterinary hospital. Next to it is a warehouse for merchants, and another temple of the goddess of the sea. There is a house here which serves as a banquet hall. In Bombay, due to scarcity of space, they often construct such banquet halls in different localities to entertain large numbers of guests. There is a temple of Bhuleshwar Shiva, where devotees keep streaming in. A signboard at the entrance of the temple says only Hindus are allowed to enter the temple. Plenty of beggars line up at the temple entrance, begging for their livelihood. When we visited the temple, we found the Shiva lingam capped with half maund of ghee. Possibly it was promised by some devotee. Among the three Vallabhachari temples in this locality, the temple of Jivanlal is the most important one. Interestingly, none of the temples here have pinnacles at the top. They are all flat-topped, like any residential building.

Free mixing among men and women surprised us. The men do not wear turbans. Neither do the Gujarati women care to pay much heed to men here. Seeing my inability to bypass the crowd to view the deity of Lord Krishna, a temple priest told me, 'When you have come to view the deity, don't bother about the crowd.' Goddess Mumba Devi previously resided in the fort, now she has shifted her base here. There are several Jain temples here. At one place I found an idol of Parasnath, covered with diamond. The radiating light of the diamonds keep illuminating the sanctum sanctorum.

There is a Parsi temple here known as Atash Behram. Men from other religions are not allowed inside it. Nearby, there are shops selling sandalwood and religious books. One day we went to view their prayer service. That day the prayer service was conducted in Hindi by a person from Orissa. His assistant sang an Oriya song, later followed by a Maharashtrian song. The foundation of the place was laid in 1872, by Sri Pratap Chandra Majumdar. Doctor Atmaram Pandarang is the leader of this community.[85] His son has adopted Christianity and his daughter has married a Britisher. A Bengali living here is presumably a jeweller. Nearly thirty per cent jewellers reside either at Colaba or at Devi Road. They have eight shops here and their wages vary from Rs 40 to Rs 120.

85. A physician and social reformer, Dr Pandarang founded the Prarthana Samaj, influenced by Keshab Chandra Sen, and was one of the two Indian co-founders of the Bombay Natural History Society. He also served briefly as the Sheriff of Bombay.

Since our residence was located at the side of the main thoroughfare, we were able to see plenty of different types of people. Early in the morning we would see multiple scenes and activities, for instance, Parsi men and women hurrying to their prayer halls, Hindustani milkmen on their way to supply milk to people, Gujarati brahmins with a plate full of worshipping materials going towards the sea to worship the sea god, a hawker collecting empty bottles, a lady selling spinach and a hawker selling salt, and many others. There was also a procession of people accompanied by a musical band carrying a corpse, there was a fruit seller and a sweetmeat (halwa) seller mounting the staircase of a house. Halwa seems to be the most popular sweet here in Bombay. There are three to four types of halwa found here in Bombay. Most of the halwa is made of semolina, in the Hindustani style.

Interestingly, even in summer the ladies of Bombay do not step out of the house without wrapping themselves with scarf. Right across our inn resides a royal employee. His wife from a second marriage is always preoccupied in decking up while her husband sits on a swing. A swing is a must for all living here, whether be it a Hindu Gujarati or a Muslim. Our neighbour is a Hindu Maharashtrian. The servants move about in the house wearing only their loin cloth and nobody seems to be embarrassed about it. Children, dressed formally in coats and trousers, go barefoot to school. In the afternoon arrive the hawkers selling clothes. And then come the flowersellers, selling garlands of different flowers like champak, juhi, rose etc. for the women. At the end of the day, they offer the unsold garlands to any temple they come across. Women here spend about ten to fifteen rupees per month to buy flowers. The hawker selling pistachios recited a lovely poem:

Salted broken headed pistachio.
Obtained from Surat,
If one gets a taste of it

There is another wanting to share it,
He goes in to fetch money.
One who tastes it remembers it lifelong.

There is also the groundnut seller selling his ware reciting, 'Do buy this warm oven roasted groundnuts.' The ice-cream vendor keeps calling out in tired voice, 'Ice, o ice'. Even at the dead of the night one hears the call of the ice-cream vendor. Mrs Mehta sent us different types of sweets one day, which she herself had prepared. Among them one was made of aromatic curd. For her both Hindustani and Bengali are of the same breed. One day she asked me, 'Why do your servants wear clothes that are tied from the waist? You don't seem to wear your clothes in that style?' In return I asked her, 'Why are the roofs of your houses made of tiles?' She seemed extremely surprised and asked in return, 'What else should we use instead of tiles?' Clearly, she had no idea of roofs made of cement, stone and sand.

A few merchants prefer consuming opium instead of alcohol. Barbers are scanty here in the city. Actually, a local barber is a walking encyclopedia of social gossip. But here the society does not approve of a person to thrive solely on trimming people's hair. In the villages of Gujarat, the barbers adopt multiple trades for sustenance, like small-scale surgeries, a lawyer for love birds, and also conducting marriages. A marriage cannot be held without the presence of a barber. Down the generations, barbers are the torchbearers of villages. Their wives are the midwives. Barbers universally keep mirrors with them, except in Bengal.

The house in which we have put up is large enough to accommodate 400 to 500 people. We have hired only two rooms at the rate of rupees seven per month. Even if you hire a room for a day, you have to pay a month's rent. But the municipal tax is lower than that of Calcutta. You have to pay 14 per cent of the rent that you earn.

There are five theater halls situated on Grant Road. Gujarati,

Maharashtrian and Hindustani plays are performed regularly there. We visited the Ripon theater. It is constructed in the style of British theaters and is illuminated by gas lights. There is a lounge in the middle of the theater where one can drink tea, coffee and sherbet. We could not procure a programme list. There was no opening orchestra. The dress-circle is divided into two parts—one for men and the other for women. But the women's portion was not covered. People had taken off their headgears, and as a result different shapes and sizes of heads were visible from afar.

The play *Shakuntala* was enacted in Marathi. The stage setup and acting were excellent. The only problem was of men playing the roles of female characters. The actors, when dressed up as girls, resembled brahmin girls with long hair tied in buns. On another day we went to see a Hindustani play. We paid for the seats of the first class, but when we went to occupy our seats, we were told there are no first-class seats. So, we argued with the theater owner and got a refund. The performance began with a mujra, and then after the mujra was over the play began. They had an actress who played the female role. But the garish paint that she had applied on herself looked terrible. We saw the fishermen's dance which was new to us. The audience comprised mainly of unruly Muslims who had to be constantly controlled by the security guards.

Parsis in general are serious and reserved people, like the British. They rarely go out of their way to talk to strangers. Except one or two old Parsi gentlemen, nobody cared to talk to us. The merchants, however, went out of their way to talk to us and get introduced. But overall, people seemed to be quite disillusioned about their culture and their heritage. A few who spoke to us enquired, 'What's so new about this place that has inspired you to come here all the way from Bengal?' They had all visited Calcutta.

We went to meet a Maharashtrian acquaintance of mine.

On the occasion of Deepavali, his house was decorated with different designs and colours. I insisted on sitting outside the house, but he requested me to walk in. 'Unlike your place we do not practice purdah system here.' While we were returning, he offered us betel leaf and betel nut. But because we had not finished our morning ablutions, we refused to accept them. He insisted that we accept it, as it is a matter of prestige for the house owner. Refusal meant disrespecting him.

A Maharashtrian shopkeeper called us and displayed an English matchbox and Indian perfume. Knives and scissors, manufactured abroad, and sold as arms in Bengal, are sold here as Indian products.

Since the High Court was not open, we went to a police court to see its workings. Gaekwad had recently lost a diamond pendant which had been broken into three pieces and sold. One of it was purchased by an ascetic living in Delhi (who was the chief accused) from a Hindustani devotee. The diamond piece was displayed to the judge.

Recently the court had witnessed a movement against a court ruling. Dadaji Vikaji had appealed to the court for attaining the marital rights over his wife Rukhma Bai (who incidentally was the adopted daughter of Dr Arjun Sakharam—she was biologically the daughter of her mother's first husband). Rukhma Bai was an educated lady and was married to Vikaji ten years ago, when she was only eleven years old. Now when she was an adult, she refused to go to Dadaji Vikaji. Her allegation against her husband was he was a patient suffering from respiratory problems, had tuberculosis and was incapable of providing for her. Moreover, when she was married she did not have the right to protest, hence, she was not legally bound to honour the marital vows. On hearing the plea of the lady, the Honorable Judge gave his verdict in favour of the lady and asked the gentleman to pay a hefty sum of money as damages. According to the judge, since the lady was not willing to stay with her husband it was not possible to drag her to his house like cattle. His judgement, he said, was based on equity. The verdict clearly went in favour of social reformers like Behramji Malabari who wanted the abolishment of child marriage.[86]

The commercial situation however, seemed similar as elsewhere—trade had increased but margins of profit had decreased. Introduction of telegraph and steam engines had somewhat equalized the cost of products. Only people selling and buying articles can expect a little profit. Bengal can sell rice, silk, and jute.

The import of cotton from Britain had virtually stopped after the war between England and America in 1861. India is the only country who is now legally assigned to export cotton. Consequently, Bombay has earned a revenue of eighty crores by selling cotton. And immediately after making such a huge profit, the business community of Bombay started a new business, that of moneylending. Several banks sprouted and many companies were established for filling the wetlands and constructing buildings in various parts of the city. The share price of Backbay Reclamation increased five times. It was at this time that the citizens of Bombay set up the Port Canning Shares in Calcutta.

In 1865, when the information of the end of the American War reached Bombay, the revenue of cotton dropped substantially. Along with it the share prices too dropped abysmally. This opened the eyes of the shareholders, who at once realized that their shares were no longer a means to earn money, rather they had turned into useless papers. Consequently, the companies engaged in landfilling became bankrupt. And banks which were financing them were liquidated. Fortunately, the general trade and commerce was not permanently affected because of it. The expected drop in the demand for cotton did not happen. When the citizens saw that the British were

86. Rukhma Bai was one of the first practicing woman doctors in colonial India and a feminist. She contributed to the Age of Consent Act in 1891.

exporting the local cotton to Manchester and weaving clothes out of them, and then bringing them back to India to sell at a higher price, they decided to set up cotton and textile mills themselves for manufacturing clothes locally. More and more people came forward to invest their capitals in setting up cotton and textile mills. And that became the general trend. After a time, production increased, but the scope for marketing them did not widen accordingly. Fortunately, because of the wide network of the British government (as the saying goes, the sun does not set on the British Empire) this gap between production and marketing was resolved with government assistance.

We visited a cotton mill of Manekji Patil, and saw the entire process of cloth manufacturing—right from husking the cotton seeds, producing threads, to weaving clothes and finally even folding them for marketing. The capital investment of the company for installing the machineries was Rs 40,50,000. Being divided into 4000 parts, the estimated cost per section comes to about Rs 1000. This amount was initially paid for installing the machines. Two engines are working at present whose capacity is approximately 700 horsepower each, i.e., fourteen hundred together. There are 61,248 spindles working nonstop. And for 1184 looms, 94,000 maunds of cotton are needed annually. 2800 men work here daily. Other than this there are forty-eight cotton and textile mills in the city.

We let off our guide and mounted a horse carriage to see a sawmill. After procuring permission from the authority, we entered the factory. There we found various kinds of steam-driven machines being used to hack and split different kinds of woods. We were extremely impressed at the sight. Last year, we had imported ten lakh maunds of sugar from both China and Mauritius. I had a tremendous urge to bring ghee from Bengal and start a business here, as there is high demand of ghee in Bombay. The dust produced at these sawmills is in high demand in the city.

Manikji Dinsha Petit, a Parsi, is considered to be the richest among the businessmen of Bombay.[87] As the saying goes, the valuation of his property is estimated to be Rs 2 crore. The family of Sarjam Seth Jiji Bai is at present not as rich as before. Having undertaken various charitable works in the past, it has now fallen into bad times. Previously they had a business of bottles with China and had grown exceedingly rich. The well-known Premchand Raichand, who had donated Rs 22 lakh to Bombay University has now grown quite poor, too. Premchand had worked hard and done a lot of charity. Among the Kapol merchants, the wealthiest one is Sir Mangaldas Nathu Bhai. But his arrogance born out of wealth has won him many enemies among his kinsmen. Consequently, another group of merchants, headed by Tribhuvan Das is growing increasingly powerful. Most of the merchants are Vallabhacharya Vaishnavs. Vaishnavs are generally considered to be extremely fierce Hindustani worshippers of Rama and Sita. But neither here nor in Bengal are Vaishnavs found to be fiercely fundamentalists. Wealthy and materialistic merchants here worship Lord Krishna and Sri Radha.

Bhatta Ballabhacharya of Telangana, in mid-fifteenth century, lived at Gokul. At first, he had adopted sannyasa but later after marrying and having a family, advised his followers not to observe fasts for worshipping God. One need not be frugal either about food or about clothing. Renouncing the world and going to the woods to practice asceticism was also not required. Eat well, dress well, enjoy material comforts and worship Lord Krishna, he said. Vanavyasa, a disciple of Ballabhacharya, had once prevented a young widow from

87. As broker to European firms, Manikji Dinsha Petit amassed a large fortune during the period of speculation in Bombay at the time of the American Civil War. He became a member of the Governor General's Legislative Council, and was criticized for playing a pro-colonial role by the nationalists. However, he devoted his wealth to significant philanthropic projects.

committing Sati. His argument was, 'Instead of offering your beautiful self to Lord Krishna, why are you offering yourself to a corpse.' So, requirement of physical beauty to worship Lord Krishna gradually became the cause of many disputes and violence among the followers. If beauty is essential for worshipping Lord Krishna, then why worship a repulsive deity—this became the cause of discontent. Vaishnavas consider worshipping Sri Radha as the highest form of worship. In fact, the Goswamis of Gokul address their servants as Radha. In Vrindavan, the security guards call out 'Radha, Radha' during their nocturnal rounds.

The present Guru of the Ballabhacharis is Avihit and he has about thirty or forty followers. His disciples consider him to be Lord Krishna incarnate. Both male and female disciples completely surrender themselves to him, both physically and materially. Consequently, he leads a luxurious life. Following him seems to be an expensive affair because frequently the disciples have to dole out hefty sums to serve their Guru. The charges are as follows: to meet the Guru they have to pay a sum of Rs 5; for touching him Rs 20; for washing his feet Rs 35; for rocking him on the swing Rs 40; for applying sandalwood paste Rs 42; for sharing seat with him Rs 60; for staying with him female disciples have to pay something between Rs 50 to 500; to get the touch of his assistant's feet Rs 11; to be hit by a lash Rs 13; for female disciples who intend to participate in Rasleela, the rate is Rs 150 to 200; and to participate in Rasleela with an assistant the rate is Rs 50 to 100. One who desires to lick the spit of the Guru has to pay Rs 17, and one who desires to drink the water that is leftover after washing the Guru's clothes has to pay Rs 19. The disciples and devotees have become so blind that they see nothing wrong in these practices. The Guru, in his turn, taking advantage of their blindness often encroaches upon the purity of ladies who come to him. But nobody seems to be bothered by it.

Karsandas Mulji,[88] a social reformer among the merchant community, had protested against this unethical practice. He even wrote several articles highlighting these. But the followers slapped a legal charge against him. When the charges were taken to the court, many scandalous incidents came to surface. Karsandas, however, is no longer alive. The baton is now carried on by another reformer, who possibly has not cared to take up the issue any further.

Jestha and Mula are two sun signs which are considered to be inauspicious. Whoever are born under these are named as Jethaji and Mulaji to counter the evil effect. Here both the Gujarati community and the Maharashtrians add their father's names before their family name. Many don't even use a surname but remain content with their father's name. A bride has to change her name after marriage, since addressing her by her maiden name is considered inappropriate. She is given a new name. When the bride arrives at her in-law's house, the couple is made to sit before the family deity. The mother-in-law writes a name which is kept in a container with a handful of rice, the girl then reads the name and whispers it in her husband's ear. For instance, if the name of the groom is Visveswar, (another name of Lord Shiva) the girl is called Annapurna (another name of Goddess Durga). If he is called Shankar, she is called Uma. If the groom is Krishna, the bride is renamed as Radha. And if the boy is called Vithova the bride is named as Rukmabai.

Among most castes, widows are allowed to remarry. Widow remarriage is known as natra. The dhoti of the groom is tied to the sari of the bride and the couple then mount a horse and proceed towards the groom's house. The accompanying crowd remains busy singing and dancing. There the priests worship the groom, and no other ritual is observed. The marriage can be annulled if both the boy and the girl mutually consent to

88. Karsandas Mulji was one of the pioneers among Indian social reformers, and worked for the cause of women's emancipation.

separate. If the girl is able to satisfy the monetary greed of her husband, she can easily get a release and go off to her loved one. Some fix marital alliances even before the birth of a child. But the proposal is annulled if the concerned mother gives birth to more than one child. Or else, the proposal stands good even if the child is born handicapped. If a mother dies when her son is a minor, that is eleven years old, her husband gets his ward married to a girl who may be either thirteen or fifteen years old! It serves two purposes at one stroke—being poor he is unable to remarry, so getting an older girl for his son assures a woman in the house, and the son needs to get married, so the future of the boy is assured in that manner. This practice, even though rare, does take place at times.

Here the practice of illegally declaring bankruptcy is rampant. Men of all religions—Hindu, Muslim and even Parsi—are adept at it. Some declare bankruptcy even five or six times at a stretch. The law that protects a bankrupt person often helps a poor person turn rich overnight. Such a crook donates large amounts of money either to his wife or to his mother to avoid detection. Some construct pilgrims' inn, some build new houses while some undertake new business ventures.

The brahmins among the Gujaratis are generally exceptionally good looking and are known as Nagarvan. Their original homeland is Mount Abu. When Muhammad of Ghazni had invaded Gujarat, the clan of brahmins who had assisted him are now demarcated as a separate clan. They are professionally either businessmen or writers and are known as Mehta. The other class, known as the Vikshu, is occupied in propagating the words of the scriptures. The *Sama Veda* is widely read and taught only among the Gujaratis.

There are many affluent people among the Khwaja and the Bora communities. Before someone's death, he or she has to procure a letter addressed to God's angel, Azrael. And to procure it, one has to pay a hefty sum to the mullah. The letter is placed in the grave with the corpse, expecting him/her to present it to the angel during last judgement. Azrael, on reading it, will plead his/her case to God and assure a seat in heaven for the departed soul.

Once a poor Gujarati Muslim had started selling English matches for the first time in the region. He earned one anna per day. Without spending his entire earning, he started saving some money. He spent two annas for his family and opened a shop. After some time, he found his savings increasing gradually. So, the lesson he learnt was whatever you earn must not be spent completely. Even though illiterate, he proved to be a wise man. He is cautious about spending money but is not a miser. He has learnt to value money and is now ready to spend money if he feels it necessary. He is not scared of poverty and neither is he inclined to inculcate the habits of luxuries. He is considered to be the wisest businessman of the locality, but otherwise he is a simple man by nature. He is not interested in politics and can go to any extent to retain his peace.

But in general, the Muslims of Bombay are not as peaceloving as this person. They are pretty rough and insist on their women rigidly following the burqa system. On reaching here I realized that the burqa is basically a system followed only by the Muslims, because the Hindu ladies move about with their faces exposed. Aristocratic ladies move about in carriages, entirely covered.

The Parsi script is found in *Avesta,* the Parsi scripture. They have three other scripts too. Some bear striking resemblance to modern Sanskrit. So, it can be surmised that the source language of the four scripts found in the *Avesta* is the same. At present two priests have been appointed at the Fire Temple to teach this language. The Parsi community comprises of two lakh members, most of whom stay in the city of Bombay. They are quite accomplished and work as doctors, lawyers, and also judges. If a person turns a pauper, there is the dharmshala for them to live in. A Parsi is never seen to beg for his living. Hence, there is no prostitution too among the Parsis. But the

Iranian Parsis are different from Gujarati Parsis. This maybe because of their marrying Hindu women. Now pure-blooded Parsis are rare to find. But most of them do not like to marry outside their community. There is a Parsi panchayat as well. It comprises of twelve senior Seths. The priest of the community performs multiple functions. He conducts nighttime prayers for a person who pays him. He also has to carry corpses. Right from negotiating marriages, a priest is expected even to break a marriage. Both Parsi men and women use muslins or other fine clothes known as sadbo to cover the upper parts of their bodies. And both wear woollen sacred thread on their waists which is known as kusti. Their holy text has in its twenty-second chapter, the specification of kusti—it should have twenty-two strings and every twelve years, twelve knots should be tied to it. A bare head is strictly prohibited for both male and female Parsis. They believe that bare head draws the evil eyes of Satan. Therefore, they use tall turbans for complete protection. The Parsi women cover their heads with a piece of white cloth. But recently the ladies are considering these headcovers to be rather immodest. Maybe in near future, the practice will completely vanish in the folds of the saris.

The Parsi ladies have a look of innocence on their faces, while Gujarati Hindu women are lovely to look at. At times, I keep recalling the radiating deity-like image of the Maharashtrian lady Sudevi. She is extremely somber in appearance. We found her sitting in a stately posture, with face turned towards the rising sun. Then letting down her cascade of hair she uttered the following words three times: 'Let the Devil be defeated'. These words, they believe, will prevent Satan from harming them in future.

The prayer book comprising of prayers written in Gujarati was read out in front of the fire. Wherever there is fire—kitchen, drawing room or in any other room—prayers must be offered in front of them. At other times, other natural agents like stars, moon, sea, trees, and even ponds have to be worshipped in the above manner. During the transition of the day, it is mandatory to pray at least five times. But because the prayers are all composed in an ancient language, most people are not able to follow them. Hence, every prayer service is concluded with an address in Gujarati.

The festival of Deepavali arrived. This is the major festival observed here. Apart from renovating their houses, the businessmen begin their transactions in a fresh account book. Other than these major items, there is the festivity of lights. The entire city of Bombay becomes illuminated. While crossing the cloth market, the Mathiyari market and the Parsi market, one forgets it's a new moon night as you are inundated with lights. It is not at all like the festival of light as found in Varanasi, where only glass lamps are lighted to mark the day. Following the ancient custom, lamps are floated on the sea, and their duration of illumination decides the fortune of the person who has floated it. Even though the following day is considered to be their new year, yet they start writing their accounts in new books on the last day of the year, unlike Bengal.

Sweets are sent to kinsmen and people wear new clothes and go out for social visits. The celebration is marked by streams of men and women both on the streets and houses. Before the sun arose, we headed towards the Bori Bandar railway station. This is the most expensive railway station in our country.

Maharashtra

Just as a human body comprises of bones and skeleton, similarly, the earth has the mountainous ranges. The Ghatkopar range that begins from Aurangabad extends up to Kanyakumari like a rocky wall, as if preventing the sea from inundating India. The northern part of this range is called Sahyadri. After crossing Badlapur, we started viewing the beauty of the mountain range.

While ascending the mountainous range at Bhorghat, our train switched on to a sturdier and heavier engine with a brake at the back of the train, so that while descending the train would not topple down. From there onwards till Lonavla our train kept on climbing for another 16 miles. We were to travel from the western side of the Ghatkopar range to its eastern side. There was a valley in between, named Bhorghat. The train penetrated through the rocky tunnels of the mountain ranges and kept moving. Its height was 2,000 feet above sea level.

There are several bridges all along for travelling from one mountain range to another. Mohakami bridge is 163 feet high. The scenic beauty was exceptional. The entire region was full of trees, flowers and other vegetations. But for us mountains meant snowy land, pine trees and snow-covered peaks. The threatening sight of a mountain impressed us more than this greenery. I have been to many places but have not found anything that equals the Himalayas. But Ghatkopar impressed me for another reason, I have never seen such railroads all along the side of the mountain ranges. This is really a remarkable sight in India. The train we were travelling in appeared like an airplane. The higher we went, the smaller grew the trees and houses of the plains. It was as if we were viewing the world up from the air. Tunnels have been dug at places where the rocky surface was not contiguous. There are about twenty tunnels in all. Travellers keep chanting loudly 'Vitthal Hari' all the way. On reaching Vivabh Singh station, we found that we had actually reached a dead end. So, we had to take a route that lay at a higher altitude. Much higher, we viewed the Khandawa bungalow. Finally, after a time we reached it. This is an ideal place for a hunter. There are plenty of deer and tigers prowling about. Here horned deer are to be found in plenty. At two in the afternoon, while strolling in the garden, we caught sight of the Ganesh Khind palace. We hired a brougham to travel to the capital of Maharashtra and ordered the driver to take us to Mr Seth's residence. On our way we came across a few grocery shops run by the Marwaris. Marwaris seem to be everywhere, none of us can do without them.

At first, we went to see the Parvati temple at the top the hill. It was built by Balaji Bajirao before the battle of Panipat. Then on being defeated at the battle, he came here heartbroken and breathed his last. Hargovind took us round the temple and when we reached a balcony, he started narrating the following in English: 'This is the place where the last Peshwa ruler in 1817, saw his 2800 soldiers being defeated by 1800 soldiers at a place called Khirki.' This palace of Bajirao was destroyed by lightning the year the British took possession of it. The priest who was taking us round, begged us to assist the poor homeless people residing at the temple premises. Next, we planned to see the garden that stood on the bank of river Mulamuta. Many people from the city of Pune visit this garden in the evening. A background score of English bands greeted us. The specialty of the garden is that the plants here are planted not on the soil but in flower tubs. A spring sprinkles water on all of them like an umbrella. The sight is beautiful. We stood mesmerized for quite some time. The gushing water of the spring flew all over the place. The droplets dazzled like bits of crystals. In the full-moon light, the sight seemed ethereal. Because of poor light the dam which channelized the water flow remained invisible, hence, all what we saw was a raging flow of energized water. It glittered and shimmered in the white incandescent light of the moon. It was marvelous.

The temple of the four-horned goddess stood at the top of a hill. On each step of the staircase that led to the temple sat strange-looking creatures playing cards and drinking wine, post lunch. It was a day of festivity for the goddess. The sanctum sanctorum reeked of alcohol. A string of betel leaves adorned the neckline of the deity. Rice, puffed puris, and wine are offered to the goddess. A lady in trance sat there answering in a few syllables questions that were put to her. We worshipped the deity and the priestess offered us a piece of coconut as prasad.

Down below the temple there is a large open space where animal sacrifices are performed. There are several figures carved all around and the place is known as Belbagh. Every morning Lord Narayan is worshipped through songs accompanied by the music of the mridangam and veena. Large number of people gather here on every Ekadashi afternoon. Today we found a large crowd sitting under a covered area and listening to the narration of a minstrel. The minstrel was standing and singing tales from the *Mahabharata*. His accompanists were sitting behind him with mridangam and cymbals. If the minstrel happens to be a brahmin, at the end of his recital, he selectively accepts hugs and lets the audience touch his feet. The audience finally departs after receiving the prasad of the goddess. In order to make his recital interesting, the minstrel at times recites 'abhangs' which are nothing but lines of poems. For instance, he talks about Tukaram's sacred deity Vithoba who resides at Pandarpur and is now being worshipped through massive celebrations.

The temple is structured like a royal throne and has several ornate pillars. Being very high, several miniature idols are placed on different levels of the temple. The process continues till the topmost point, which is invisible from below. In order to emphasize the sacredness of the temple, every day rangoli is drawn. They use small perforated metallic rollers which are filled with colours to make the rangolis. In the sanctum sanctorum there are the idols of Rama, Sita and Lakshman. But they are dressed in Maharashtrian outfits. The surrounding boundary wall is full of engravings of stories from the *Ramayana*, each bearing the names of the episodes and incidents depicted. Whoever sits under them feels blessed. There is a garden attached to the adjacent water body, ideal for spending some time.

Many important and eminent persons of Bombay reside here. The Governor's recreation palace is in Pune. The climate of this place is better than that of proper Bombay. The soldiers of Bombay reside here. Buildings in foreign styles have not been constructed here. But then this doesn't hold true for the British residential area. The community hall and the office of the health department are all made of glass. The dress of the local people has remained unchanged. A few among them wear English coats and pants. This makes it easy for us to discern our countrymen not inclined towards the British. The preachers here have shaved heads with a tuft of hair hanging behind their scalps. They wear wooden slippers and simple garments. The priests wear red garments waist down, and a scarf to cover the upper part of their body. A long flowing coat is normally worn on formal occasions. They wear high headgears. Ladies wear coloured saris whose ends are tucked into their waists. Even if allured by the stylish saris of the Parsi, no Maharashtrian woman wears these saris in public. Women are permitted to wear normal slippers. Unlike Bengal, the use of umbrella is not rampant here. It's only the poor farmers who use umbrellas when they have to undertake long journeys. The residents of Calcutta have a funny habit of carrying umbrellas even if there is no scorching sunshine or heavy rain.

There are separate wells for people of different castes. The wells are demarcated with writings like: brahmins' well, sudras' well etc. As we were entering the region, we heard loud sounds of washing clothes. It appears that brahmins are not the original inhabitants of this region or else why is there only two demarcated classes—brahmins and sudras. Possibly it was primarily the homeland of the Marathas, hence the name Maharashtra. Then why are the Marathas branded as sudras? We also visited the crematorium and found that corpses are burnt with dry cow dung cakes[89]. They offer chapattis and lentils to the departed souls as pindas[90].

---

89. Normally Hindus cremate their corpses by burning wood. This was a deviation which struck the author.

90. Food that are offered to ones parents after their death.

The Governor's Council Hall is huge and majestic. There are large oil paintings from Bengal adorning the walls. The pictures give an inkling of all the eminent people of our country. The paintings bear the names of the people depicted. There are pictures of Khan Bahadur Padamji Pestonji, Khan Bahadur Nasibwanji Prince of Travancore, Sir Mangaldass Nathu Bhai, Doctor Bhaudaji, King of Cochin, Sir Salarjung, Thakur of Bhavnagar, Thakur Mohabhir Thanderao, Gaekwad, Sir Trambak Madhav Rao and Sankar Seth. After viewing this hall, which reeked of opulence, a visit to the palace of the Peshwa is necessary to realize the variety of life.

We had put up at a place called Shanivarpet, which is very near to the palace of the late Peshwa. The premises of the palace is surrounded by a boundary wall. After procuring the permission of the security guard, when we entered, we were presented with a dismal sight. The place was in ruins. Ironically a place once highly protected by stone walls is now turned into a site of utter ruin. It was burnt down completely. It was here in 1795 on 25th October morning that the young Peshwa Madhura had jumped off the terrace of the palace and committed suicide. Chief Minister Nana Fadnavis had immediately assumed power. According to history, the king on seeing his minister arresting his brother, and himself being commanded by him, was so frustrated that he stopped attending the court. He went to the extent of not coming out of his bedroom. However, on Vijaya Dashami, unable to overcome the protocol, he did meet his soldiers and army chief along with the messengers. But mentally he was completely shattered. Two days after this incident he committed suicide. Having fallen upon a hard surface, his body was severely injured and two of his bones broke. He survived for two days in this state then finally died. Before he died, he put his head on the lap of his favourite Baba Rao Phadke and said that Bajirao, arch enemy of Nana Fadnavis, will ascend the throne.

And it was here in Junagadh, on 30 August 1773, that

Narayan Rao, only nineteen years old, having ruled for only nine months was slain by his personal security, Samar Singh. Narayan Rao had imprisoned his uncle Raghu Nath Rao in one corner of the palace. As a revenge and to escape confinement, Raghu Nath Rao had influenced two slayers and issued an order to capture Narayan Rao. Raghu Nath Rao's wife cleverly manipulated the order. When Narayan Rao read the order, he was only too happy to come and embrace his uncle. Despite contrary orders from the lady, Samar Singh stuck to the previous order and killed Narayan Rao.

Trying to drive out these gruesome reflections, I walked out of the palace. There is a market all around the palace, hence it is called mandi[91]. Right in front of the palace gate, I found vegetables, fruits and green chilies being sold in abundance. On another side, I found a potter selling his earthenwares. At another corner ovens for cooking were lined up. At the rear side of the palace dried meat was being sold. Limji's hotel is situated here. At night if one visits the hotel, one can see hilarious sights. Limji laughingly says that the hotel is meant for brahmins only and he does not serve wine and meat. But in the secrecy of the night, English-speaking modern vegetarian brahmins from Pune come here to consume both meat and wine. They do not consider it to be blasphemy on their part.

There are three theater halls in Pune. Tickets for these halls are available in the marketplace. We went to view *Karna Parva* with a Maharashtrian friend. Since the performance was delayed for some time, we sat outside the theater hall and were entertained by melodious music performed by a lady sitting next to us. The visuals of Bengal as portrayed in the theater were simply atrocious. There was a scene where Goddess Durga was seen killing the demon. The play began with ritual ringing of bell and the worship of Lord Ganesh. Then followed a ritual worship of Goddess Saraswati. She walked onto the stage with

---

91. Which means market in Hindi.

the swan tucked up to her dress and performed a wild dance. Another fellow dressed like a British then started flirting with Brahmi (another name for Saraswati). The goddess tried to stop him saying she is a goddess and people do not behave in this fashion with her. That formed the prelude or prologue of the play. Songs, though Maharashtrian, were sung in the Bengali kirtan style. The actors were acting with such vigour that they managed to kick and drop a lamp on the stage in the process. There were two female actors in the troupe. Here they do not observe purdah, hence, it is not disreputable for respectable ladies to perform on stage. Yet, the practice has not gained much popularity.

Social leaders in Bengal who are dead against women performing on stage may reflect on this practice of Maharashtra. In Calcutta women from the red light areas are often recruited in houses as domestic helps and gentle ladies interact with them with ease. So, the so-called ill-reputed ladies do have a social recognition. In that case these ladies may be allowed to perform on stage. Since male artists dressed up as girls perform atrociously, these ladies were included in the group. In Calcutta when male artists perform female roles, they look so repulsive.

As it was not possible for us to stay through the night, we got the doorman to open the gate and let us out.

Here, people from the backward section of the society prefer wrestling over plays. Hence, they do not go to theaters to view plays. Instead, they go to see wrestling competitions (held in the theater premises). In Bengal, the entry fee (for viewing a wrestling match) is either one anna or two annas. The organizer pays a little amount to the winner of the competition.

We stood at the gate of the theater hall for a long time. The place was full of people (who had come to see a wrestling match). A Sikh Punjabi was competing against a Maharashtrian wrestler. Finally, the latter won, and the teacher being elated, lifted the winner and twirled his moustache in pride. His kinsmen shook hands with him. A few dusted his body while another few fanned him. The winner seemed to be in the seventh heaven of delight while the loser did not know where to hide himself. On the wrestling ground, when the two had met to compete, there seemed to be no enmity between them. But after having won the game, the winner spat on him and dealt him several blows. This shows how a situation drives a person to evil unintentionally. The friends of the winner clad him in gorgeous dress and headgear and took him home, amidst cheer and the loud playing of a musical band. But no so-called gentleman was visible in the crowd. Ironically, these people would show off their skills when in Bengal. Next day, after viewing the wrestling competition, we visited a prayer service conducted by Honorable Babasaheb Mahagovinda Ranade. There, a Bengali Brahmo song was sung and being a Bengali, I basked in reflected glory.

Dadoba Pandurang, in order to do away with the evils of the caste system, had started a new organization with twelve of his students, which he named Paramhansa Sabha. After a prayer service, a debate regarding various social issues followed. It was mandatory to eat bread and drink water served by Muslims in this organization. With the remnants of this organization, the Prayer Sabha of Bombay was started. But many members feel that it is not right to tamper with social customs. If people are religious, educated, women become literate, and family commitments are strengthened, social vices like caste segregation, child marriage, rigours of widowhood etc. will be obliterated, they say. Recently, the ones who have returned from England have to go to Nasik and perform penitential services in order to return to the Hindu fold.

People had expected that Mahadev Ranade, after his wife's death, would not remarry a spinster. But due to social pressures he could not marry a widow.

Politically, Pune has now become extremely active. I had expected to find several Sanskrit scholars here pursuing their Vedic studies, and chanting Vedic hymns to purify the vicious

British ambience. I had also visualized it to be a place where the pious yajna fumes would be visible everywhere. But I realized that the British have been successful in obliterating this tradition completely. Vedotyajani Sabha has been founded to encourage students to learn the Vedas and they are rewarded for their efforts. At times scholars of the Vedas visit this Sabha to collect some money.

The rulers of this land are not brahmins but kayasthas. Consumption of meat, wine and chicken is allowed for them. They are learned and earn their livelihoods by being in employment. Even the Shenvi brahmins consume fish and meat. Two important brahmins of this category are Ramakrishna Gopal Bhandarkar and late Bhaudaji. Regarding the Chitpavan brahmins, Campbell has declared that they originally belonged to the Konkan race, who dwelt on the shores of rivers Sindhu and Saraswati before they merged into the sea. But the local people consider the Chitpavan brahmins as inferior brahmins. *Sajhadrikhanda*, the book which spoke derogatorily about the origin of Chitpavan brahmins, was destroyed by Bajirao. Chanakya, the chief minister of Chandragupta, belonged to Konkan district. He lived in a place named Kalyan.

The Maharashtrian brahmins are adept in politics. However powerful or valorous a king might be, but the rule of the land lies in the hands of the learned brahmins. At present most of the academic works in the state of Bombay are carried on by them. The head of the education department has declared that jobs now will not be distributed to the learned brahmin candidates only. Candidates from the lower strata of the society will also be considered as eligible. Civil society has strongly protested against this decision. The reply to this protest has been harsher. The director has condemned the brahmins for monopolizing learning and all academic works. The brahmins of Pune, in turn, have strongly voiced their protests in newspapers. Civil society of Pune too is crying hoarse about this decision.

A high school has been established here. All the teachers

right from class one to the school-leaving class are all graduates. They have vowed never to opt for government jobs. The profit earned from the school will be distributed among the teachers. Women, too, are encouraged to pursue a little learning from the very beginning. A girl belonging to a pundit's family learns a little bit of Sanskrit. An English-medium school for girls has been established a year ago. Recently a prize distribution ceremony was held in the school with lot of fanfare. Sayajirao Gaekwad had come to grace the occasion. And to welcome him an elaborate arrangement was made even at the railway station. He was welcomed with betel leaf and betel nut. The British officials could not accompany him for long. It was decided that the head of Maharashtra would chair the ceremony. The school inspector had inspected the program and invitations were widely distributed. The girl students had written down the (British) national anthem. The director for schools instructed everyone present to stand while singing the national anthem and show their respect for the Queen. The principal had informed the director that there was a possibility of the audience, comprising of many old men and women, would not comply with this ruling. And because it was very difficult for them to stand all the while it would be better that the cheering of Hail to the Queen be opted out. Reflecting on the practicality of the situation, the proposal was accepted and the national anthem part in the invitation letters, bore a cross sign. The director of education, on seeing this, got wild with rage and forced the girls to sing the anthem. He informed the government about his achievements too. Shankar Pandurang, the editor of *Vedanta Ratna*, (also the translator of the *Rig Veda*) responsible for striking off the anthem part from the invitation letters, was sacked from his government job. Leonard alleged that they had committed this offence in order to please the great Gaekwad. The Maharashtrians, however, emphasized that 'Jayshree Victoria' is not the correct translation of the national anthem. It was meant to be sung at the Durbar of Delhi; hence, it was not mandatory to stand while it was being sung. Even the Gujarati community professed that while singing 'Rani Jinay' it is not mandatory for everybody to stand up as mark of respect. However, amidst this growing confusion, the British national anthem was not sung. But despite all these debates and counter-debates, Shankar Pandurang never got back his job.

Following the tradition of Calcutta, we refrained from interacting with our neighbours. Neither were we interested to know anything about them. We had a feeling that it was not possible to find a Bengali-speaking person here. But one day we came across a Bengali-speaking gentleman. Here in exile, it was just not possible for us to follow the native Bengali etiquette of just looking at a person and walking away without uttering a word. Neither was it possible for us to merely smile at an acquaintance. Ten to twelve Bengalis reside here as they are employed in laying the railroads of south Maharashtra. We asked one of them about the novelty of this region. He spoke about the Maharashtrian style of wearing saris by the local ladies. Since my eyes were accustomed to seeing south Indian ladies in Varanasi wearing the sari in the said manner, I did not find the local style peculiar.

Here, like the south Indian women, the local women walk with uncovered faces in public, which I feel is a way to demonstrate women's liberation. Other than this there is not much of a difference with south Indian women and Maharashtrian women's sense of dressing. Even here women do not enjoy true freedom, like their counterparts throughout the world. It is perhaps nature's law that the weak will always be dominated by the strong. But human beings have minds of their own and so this kind of subjugation is not practically possible. Aren't Bengali women self-ruled—don't they compel their husbands to observe their superstitious rulings at home?

Maharashtrian married women use kumkum (vermillion) and bangles to indicate their marital status, even though spinsters can wear both these items. Widows are not allowed

Maharashtrian women in traditional attire

to view themselves in mirrors. They are also not allowed to participate in community feasts. They cannot accompany the bridegrooms' train while going to the wedding ceremony. But for a married woman it is an offence to walk out of her room without kumkum on her forehead. Right after she leaves her bed, she has to put on all the signs of a married woman and only then can she step out of her room. The fashionable ladies wear just a small dot of kumkum while the commoners wear large-sized dots on their foreheads.

A woman has to observe forty days of isolation after giving birth to a child and after that she is allowed to put on her bangles. It's called chuda after childbirth. A gift comprising of rice, betel leaf, betel nut, coconut, and few coins is offered to a bangle seller. The lady offers it to him with folded hands and the bangle seller in his turn blesses her with these words, 'remain married till death'. At other times she wears bangles bought from him and after paying him his dues, she folds her hands before him. After the death of one's husband, before his body is taken for cremation, the bangle seller comes to break the bangles of the widow and cut off her long tresses. The kumkum is rubbed off and the woman is forced into the confinement of a dark room. She is not allowed to even glance at anyone, for her glance is considered to be vicious. Only a widow can serve her food. And in case there is no widow around, a male member of the house serves her food. Neither a spinster nor a married woman is allowed into her room.

We could not trace Ganesh Vasudev Joshi who conducts the Lok Adalat[92]. Like it happened in Pabna in Bengal, just prior to the Revolt, there occurred a plundering of wholesale dealers here. During the weekly marketing days, the shops of both Maharashtrian and Marwari wholesale dealers were mercilessly plundered. Books, clothes and other articles were gathered and ignited. A commission was formed to detect the cause of such

92. Public court

violence. The members canvassed for implementing a special law of privilege for the deprived southern farmers under British rule. According to this law, a complainant before going to the court had to face a mediator. The mediator's job was to find a solution to the problem and in case that failed, the complainant was allowed to appeal to the court.

Implementation of a high rate of interest even if agreed upon was not legally allowed. A corrupt person's land, if not mortgaged, could not be sold for debt. A debtor could not be imprisoned. If a farmer's debt exceeded Rs 50, he could declare insolvency. Even though the government had formulated a lot of rules to protect the interest of the common citizens, it did not deem it necessary to convert them into effective laws.

Land revenue was temporary. Ownership was allowed for thirty years only. But men keep working hard in search of happiness. The effort they put in for their lands should legally give them a right of proprietorship. But that is not allowed. In case a person tries to grab proprietorship of someone else's land, then there is every chance for another person to come and grab his legally owned land. Consequently, no one is allowed to be happy and satisfied. It is the law of nature that a person tilling a piece of land will legally be its proprietor. The king earns his revenue both for protecting the life and land of his subjects. But the king in no way is the owner of the land tilled by his subjects. A person tilling a piece of land is actually its owner.

Like the other parts of ancient India, Maharashtra too was divided into many parts which were not related to one another. Grant Duff, a historian who wrote about Maharashtra, had presumed that on the banks of River Godavari the present city of Bhir was inhabited by a Rajput king whose name was Tagor. He was possibly killed by the Kuhumar race to establish their kingdom there with Mungi Paton as their capital city. Later it was shifted to Devagiri or Daulatabad in Maharashtra. When at the end of the thirteen century the Muslims reached

Maharashtra, they found that Devagiri was ruled by Yadav Ram Devrao. But unlike British rulers, the Muslims did not totally destroy the place. The lives of common people were spared, and they continued to lead a peaceful life as before. Only administration changed hands, and a Muslim became the ruler. He was happy as long as people acknowledged him as their king.

The lowest village employee is dhed or path indicator. He works as the village security guard, and also as a spy. He is also responsible for providing fodder to the horse of a traveller, and in case of emergency, he also has to carry the luggage of a traveller up to the boundaries of the village. The village headman is called makdam, Patel or Deshmukh. He looks after the village agriculture, settles local disputes, employs village security guards, etc. In case a dispute cannot be settled by a Patel, the parties are expected to approach the panchayat. For criminal cases, higher authorities are to be approached. But all these are to be initiated by the village headman. The village writer is called Kanungo, Deshpande or Kulkarni. The village writer, the headman and the security guard enjoy revenue-free land. Kulkarni maintains the annual accounts of the village. His account book contains a detailed account of the land, ownership, revenue etc. In all likelihood, both the village headman and the village writers previously were royal employees. The titles were hereditary and handed down the generations. There were however chances of these officials growing in power and rising up against the king and finally ousting him if he was weak.

By the 17th century, the Muslim rulers had weakened so much that the Marathas residing in the mountainous regions rose against them unitedly.

In 1627, Shivaji Bhonsle was born. Even though he was not able to sign his own name, he developed an outstanding skill in handling arms. He was skilled in archery. The stories of both the *Ramayana* and the *Mahabharata* inspired him. His father was employed with the Nizam of Bijapur. Shivaji went on to establish a kingdom of his own. To be an ideal king, it is necessary for the subjects to bestow the power of administration willingly to the king, and the king in his turn will execute his power in keeping with natural laws. But generally, this does not happen. When a subject kills another subject, he is punished severely but when a king kills thousands of men in the name of war he is not considered to be a criminal. This is because people believe that the king kills for the welfare of the country. In 1680, after completing a spiritual ritual, Shivaji died at Konkan in Raigad. He was fifty-three years old. A tomb was constructed to preserve his ashes. Modern educated Maratha youths now want to transfer these mortal remains to Pune. It is true that the grave of Napoleon Bonaparte was exhumed, and the coffin was taken to France. But that was because he lay buried in the soil of the enemies. But Shivaji lived in Raigad and all his valorous activities were performed there, so it is fully justified that his mortal remains should be preserved there itself. However, the followers of Shivaji feel Raigad, being geographically rather insignificant, the mortal remains should be shifted to Pune, a prominent city. Undoubtedly Shivaji was a valorous and extremely energetic person. And it was a fact that there was no other person around who could match these qualities of Shivaji. When Sambhaji met Emperor Aurangzeb, the Mughal king asked him to adopt Islam. When Sambhaji expressed contempt at the emperor's suggestion, he was ordered to be beheaded.

Maharashtra unfortunately did not see the rise of any other statesman like Shivaji or Balaji Viswanath Rao. Bajirao Peshwa Holkar sought British assistance to rule his kingdom. Consequently, after some time his power got subsumed within the larger imperial powers of the British. It was really tragic because Maharashtra as a kingdom survived for a very short period of time. In 1664 Shivaji became the ruler of Maharashtra, and by 1818, the state was taken over by the British. Maharashtra as a kingdom survived only for a period of 154 years. According to some, if the British had not arrived in India, there was every possibility of a Maharashtrian ruler taking over the empire of India from the Muslim rulers. And this was because the Muslim rulers had not succeeded in establishing their supremacy over the rulers of southern India. Shivaji took advantage of this and established his kingdom. Balaji Viswanath too added a little bit to Shivaji's expanding state.

The kings of the time did not have to sustain the soldiers and their chiefs. Instead, they were given land to fend for themselves. Consequently, with the dwindling powers of the king, the army chiefs could assume power over the land that was conferred to them. This is exactly what happened in Maharashtra. The moment the ruler became relatively weak, the state ownership fell into the hands of the British. But before this happened, the Peshwa had grown so autocratic that gentlemen of the kingdom feared to send their wives to his palace.

The history of the Maharashtrians, known as Bakhar, describes in detail the valour of the race in winning back the Singh fort, a place near Pune. After reading it I was compelled to visit it. There are plenty of forts situated in the region. Singhgarh is about 12 miles from Pune. After travelling 8 miles, we came across the lake of Khadakvasla. The entire water of Pune is supplied from here. A fast-flowing waterfall from a nearby mountain has been bound by a dam to create this lake. The lake is about a mile long. The mountain has been perforated in places beautifully to intensify the waterflow, making it look like a lacy waterwork. A Bengali engineer had once visited Khadakvasla just to view this beautiful sight.

After reaching the foothills of Singhgarh, we alighted from our vehicles to climb the steep cliff. The cliff is 4162 feet high from sea-level. But because the plain is about 1825 feet higher than the sea-level, we had to mount only 2337 feet. We had to cross two large gates. Now Singhgarh has been converted into a summer resort by the British. Since we were carrying our own food, we decided to finish our lunch and hence asked people where we could find sweet water source. People pointed us to a water cavity. The water was cold and crystal clear. We found fishes swimming inside the cavity. Two ancient temples stood nearby but there were no idols inside them. Ram Raja's temple was relatively in a better condition. The wooden slippers of Chhatrapati Shivaji stood near the Shiva lingam.

Grant Duff, referring to Bakhar, the historical document (in native tongue perhaps), quotes the story of the revolution. On a pitch-dark new moon night of January of 1670, Tanaji approached the Raigarh fort with a battalion of soldiers. He divided his soldiers into two divisions. One was posted at the foothill while the other group was posted near the fort. And to the rearmost part of the hill, which was practically inaccessible for any soldier, he sent a soldier to climb to the top and barricade it with a rope. The soldier then threw the rope down for the other soldiers to climb up. This was the strategy he adopted to send three hundred of his soldiers inside the fort And the moment all of them entered the fort, the Rajput soldiers who were on vigil, tried to see what was actually taking place. A sharp arrow silently answered his queries. And as the other soldiers guarding the fort heard the noise of weapons and were busy detecting the source, Tanaji seeing it to be an ideal moment, entered the fort with the rest of his men. The Maratha soldiers being greater in number and well prepared, won the battle even though their leader Tanaji was killed. Sensing the catastrophe, his brother Suryaji came forward and threatened the soldiers, 'whoever wants to see the corpses of their fathers being hurled down the hill, let them leave the battle'. (This is the worst form of ignominy that can befall a soldier because it was a custom to carry the dead soldiers from the battleground.) So, when this calamity struck the soldiers Suryaji tried this method of morale boosting. He instructed the leader to spread the word that a staircase had been burnt down and it was impossible to go down. Following the English custom of addressing the soldiers as my boys, he called out 'come my boys'. These words so inspired the soldiers that they fought tooth and nail shouting

'Har Har Mahadev' and established their victory. By the time the sun rose, about five hundred Rajput soldiers were slain, along with their chieftain Uday Nama Bodh. The few that survived surrendered. Hundreds of men unable to do otherwise tried descending the hill and were killed in the process. Shivaji however remained inconsolable and said, 'What is the use of all this, I have lost Tanaji. The lion is dead, and I have merely captured an empty cave.'

Jejuri, the nearest locality, is about 56 miles away Pune and we paid the horse carriage Rs 10 to reach there and return. The driver arrived early in the morning and promised to bring us back by eleven at night. Deccan horses are really strong and sturdy. Their movements look like a wave from afar. In these narrow hilly terrains, the roads too are steep and narrow. Without describing the entire journey, it is enough to say that it was quite comfortable. It was really refreshing to complete our morning ablutions in the open hilly terrains. In the afternoon we caught a glimpse of a temple at Parvati peak. Any place of pilgrimage is full of the pandas. While ascending the steps to reach the temple, we kept conversing with them. We found gateways and lamps constructed on various points approaching the temple. The lamps were meant for the pilgrims.

Khandwa, the presiding deity of Maharashtra, was a messenger of Lord Shiva. The Khandwa temple was constructed by the Holkars. Accordingly, he is worshipped in royal style. If a new moon happens to occur on a Monday, a fair is held to celebrate the occasion in the nearby village of Saswar, on the bank of river Kawat. Everyone, including the deity of Khandwa temple, visits the fair. A huge sword is preserved at the temple. There is a story behind it, which narrates how the sword was used by Lord Shiva to destroy a demon. I feebly enquired 'does a god really need a weapon to kill a demon?'

The girls are married to the sword following all the rituals like applying turmeric etc. And among the issueless couples of the Kunvi community, there is a practice of vowing to donate the first-born to Khandwa. The donated girl is then brought to the temple and married off to Mahadeva. She is made to wear a thread round her neck before she leaves for her home. She cannot marry any other person after that. When she comes of age, she is taken to the temple by her parents to serve the gods. Even a boy child is donated likewise and sent away from home. Girls who are donated in this manner are called Murli and the boys are known as Bakhiya. There are about 150 Murli in Jejuri. Some are sent away for begging. They are forced to take part in sex rackets. Otherwise, they make their living by dancing and singing. On enquiry, I came to know that at present this practice is on the wane. My friend told me that last time he had heard about a Murli was twelve years ago. How people are goaded to commit such horrible mistakes is to be seen here.

Our route lay through Saswar village. On reaching it we climbed down from the carriage to have a proper view of the place. Here both villages and cities are built almost identically. The houses of the cities are made of straws and so are the houses in the villages. Even though land is abundant in the village, the houses are clustered in one particular place making the pathway narrow. There are no vegetables or fruit trees around and hence there was hardly anything for us to see. The ancestral house of the Peshwas is situated here. During his stay here, Peshwa Purander had been gifted a fort. In 1749, he became the ruler. His house stands intact even today. In Pune all the properties of the Peshwa have been destroyed by fire. I was lucky enough to see just a tiny bit of his immense wealth preserved in this village. The walls of the house are made of stones. In Lucknow I had seen how the heritage buildings are being preserved. And here the palace walls of the Peshwa have been mutilated by the bullets fired by the British soldiers. The palace gate was covered by spiked mesh. Our tourist guide informed us that even elephants bearing the soldiers could not break open the gates because of these spikes. Daylight had waned, yet we climbed up the stairs, and the dwindling light there appeared to me as a symbol of the dwindling power of the Peshwa. Nobody lives in the house. It was a two-storied house, divided into four distinct parts. It badly needed a repair. How powerless we human beings are and how powerfully runs the wheel of time.

Since we had decided to see the Thal ghat early next morning, we began our journey from Pune by train. We reached our destination a little before sundown. At 10 p.m., we reached Nasik station and from there took a tonga and travelled six miles to reach Upadhayay's house. Nasik is supposed to be the Varanasi of southern India. It is said that Sri Ramachandra had torn the nose of Surpanakha here, hence the place is called Nasik. Here the Godavari river is called Ganga. About 16 miles from here there is Chakra tirtha where lies the origin of River Godavari. Then it travels through Maharashtra, the land of the Nizams and reaches the Bay of Bengal. It is 300 miles long. Just as the sewerage system keeps the house clean of all filth, similarly these river waters cleanse this earth.

Since this place is near the source, River Godavari is neither very broad nor deep here. So, for the purpose of bathing in the river, small water bodies and canals have been constructed. Due to variation of height of the flowing water, it looks very beautiful. On both sides of the river stand houses and temples. Since many kings from different states have constructed temples here, the architectures are quite different. We eagerly visited the Panchavati (where Sita of the *Ramayana* was confined) but was very disappointed. Five young banyan trees and a small, thatched hut resembling a cave stood there. The devotees still visualize the chariot that was brought here by Sri Rama to take Sita with him to reach Ayodhya. Except the banks of the River Godavari, there is nothing much in the city which is worth seeing. After having travelled around the country, I was of the opinion that the riverbank of Varanasi was the best. But the riverbank of Nasik too is very beautiful. In some places, it looked even better than Varanasi. At any time of the day if you visit the bank, you will see washerwomen washing clothes on the steps. The entire place resounds with the noise.

On one side of the bank, a mountain has been carved out to make steps. On a moonlit night, while sitting on those steps and watching the lighted lamps of Ramkund, I was reminded of Varanasi. On a full-moon night of autumn, Lord Shiva had killed Tripureswar, the demon. So, to celebrate the occasion, the entire riverbank was illuminated by lamps and ladies were bursting crackers.

At the Kapaleshwar temple, the idols of Rama, Lakshman and others were dressed magnificently. Many people were busy roaming about. Two horses were decorated and made to stand on two sides of the temple as if ready to provide service to Rama and Lakshman. The graves of the sages were cleaned, and disciples had placed lighted lamps on them. In Nasik we came across many such graves, but few living sannyasins. While on his way to England, the king of Kapurthala had died here. A marble slab has been erected at the place on the bank of Godavari where his body was actually cremated. A visit to the riverbank provided us an insight to the life of these people. The total population of the place is 22,436.

Pandulena is a place worth seeing. At first, I felt I would not be able to climb up the mountain. Despite wearing slippers, by the grace of Lord Buddha, I managed to climb it up. Out of all the temples carved out of the mountains, this temple seemed to me the most inaccessible one. There are many viharas constructed in it and inside are many idols of Lord Buddha. In one of the caves, we found elaborate writings in Pali. Ramakrishna Gopal[93] has explained these writings and also publicized them. The writings indicate that land was donated for the purpose, sometime between 118 to 120 BC. However,

93. Sir Ramakrishna Gopal was a scholar, Orientalist and social reformer, influenced by Keshab Chandra Sen.

according to a few foreign scholars, written scripts did not exist before the inscriptions of King Ashoka and these words have been derived from the Armenian alphabets. Are we to trust these people who thrive on pilfering the wealth of others, and claim that Indians learnt astrology from the Greeks and scripts from the Armenians—are we to trust to their words?

We proceeded to see Gangapura, a waterfall. Since it was coming down from a great height at great speed, the water was foaming up on which the sunlight was glittering. It appeares milk white from afar and is named as Dudhsthali (dudh stands for milk). Even if you are absolutely inert towards Nature, the sight of this waterfall is likely to impact you tremendously. The place where the water was accumulating drew me and I sat there for a long time enjoying the bliss and imprinting in my mind the beautiful sight. A fisherman was fishing there.

Trambak is 20 miles from Nasik. Local people believe that the Godavari originates from the top of the mountain and so they have named the place the doorway to Ganga. Accordingly other pilgrimages have been set up. But in reality, Gautami Ganga has not originated from there. Actually, the stream that originates from here gets mixed up with the sewerage and does not even soak the pebbles of the region. When I asked about this strange phenomenon, they said that River Ganga has hidden herself and hence, is not visible.

When we reached Trambak, the autumn festival was not over. Trambakeswar is considered to be a Jyotir Lingam. Only a brahmin wearing silken dress is allowed to visit the deity. Bajirao had set up this huge temple of Trambakeswar. We viewed it and many other temples that are there near the waterfall. Finally, we visited the goddess of epidemics and saw an animal sacrifice being performed. There are three thousand people dwelling in the village. A handful of rice had been collected from each house and cooked. A cow cart was filled with the cooked rice and the priests sprinkled some red colour upon it along with a stick of sugarcane and lighted torch for offering it to the goddess where the sacrifice had been performed. A coconut that was placed upon a pole was broken into two pieces and then with the beating of the drums, the cow cart started moving. After the cart had gone out of the village, the villagers were allowed to have their meals. We were to have our meal at Ganapati Panda Sankar Sukul's house. And because my companion would not have rice at a foreigner's house, he was offered puffed rice and sweetmeats instead. The women of the house served us our meal. At first one served two or three types of chutney, then another supplied us a small tub. Third one served rice. The amount of rice was so little that I was surprised. Maybe they consume little rice, I rationalized. But the lady continued serving rice till it took the shape of a ball. The small tub was then filled with ghee followed by various cooked curries. Only then did we start our meal. But whatever we ate tasted either bitter or sour. It was so spicy that I could hardly eat anything at all. Seeing my state, a lady asked me whether I needed more ghee. Since we are used to having ghee only at the beginning of our meal, I refused to accept it. Then we were served poli—a a chapati made of pulse and sugar and known as puran-cha-poli. You have to dip it into hot ghee and eat it. So next time when they offered ghee, I asked for a second helping and satisfied my hunger. The poli that was served was hot too. Now I realized since chapati is the staple food of the Maharashtrians they serve little rice at the beginning.

A tired girl came and sat in front of me. I asked her why she was not having her meal. She just replied, 'no'. A lady who was having her meal beside me replied, 'She is the younger brother's wife. Who is going to serve her first?'

Once we had the ill luck to eat a meal in Pune. The items that were served proved to be horrible in taste. They prepared green in pulses and that too was extremely spicy. We could not consume more than a bite or two. We tasted kadhi, which also was distasteful. Then we tasted another item called sar. It is supposed to be very nutritious. The cook told us that not everyone knows to cook sar properly. It is actually a Karnataka preparation. It has some medicinal values, especially when one is suffering from fever. But when I put it into my mouth I felt I had put liquid tamarind soaked in red chili and garnished with coriander leaves in my mouth. That day we were served rice and plain pulses and hence could fill up our hungry stomachs.

As a delicacy we were offered a chapati of jawar and chapati of wheat. The chapati of jawar looked rather dismal but it tasted better than the chapati made from wheat. The chapatis were soaked in ghee hence when we put it in the milk, the ghee started floating. Chapatis made from bajra comes third in the list of favourites. The farmers and other working-class people survive on them. Choudri is a vegetable found here and we had cooked its curry both in Pune and Bombay. Shrikhand is a famous dish made from yoghurt, sugar and other spices. The shrikhand we had tried did not taste good at all. Both in Bombay and other places there are tea and coffee shops.

At the door of Ganga in Trambak we mounted thirty-two steps and found Raghunath Bapu, a religious leader, sitting in his tea stall. Both Raghunath and his wife requested us to taste the tea and when we left his shop he invited us to visit his home and accept his betel leaf and betel nut.

Devagiri

In the afternoon we reached Nandgaon and went to the office of the mail contractor. He was a Parsi gentleman. When we were having our tiffin, they offered us a radiant yellow mango each. Aurangabad is 56 miles from here. We hired a tonga for Rs 50 and started our journey at eight in the evening. The driver kept changing horses at intervals and blowing a trumpet to warn everybody around, as we journeyed almost asleep. Since it was a mountainous terrain, we started feeling cold. And at times when we lifted our face cover, we glimpsed the moonlit surroundings. After travelling about 10 miles, we reached a village named Kasari. Crossing Kasari, we entered the kingdom of the Nizam. The boundaries of the kingdom were marked by heaps of round stones.

At about nine in the morning, we crossed Aurangabad and reached the bank of Gundanala. There was a Balaji temple within the campus of the British army, and we put up there. Britishers tend to put up their men wherever they find a friendly neighbour. And even if the region is ruled by a native ruler, they interfere in the workings of the state. We visited the tomb of the daughter of Emperor Aurangzeb, and also went to Panchakki. We then procured an entrance pass for Daulatabad fort from Mr Doyem, the talukdar of the region. And because it was late in the evening, we returned home.

Late the next morning we entered the Daulatabad fort. Even though it is surrounded by stone walls it was devastated inside. This was the historic site where Muhammad Bin Tughlaq (who introduced the silver coin) had forcibly changed the capital from Delhi and whipped the citizens to come and settle in Daulatabad. He had renamed the Devgarh (fort) to Daulatabad.

In Aurangabad I noticed something really strange—it was as if the entire Hindustani habitation had been lifted and brought here into the land of the Marathas. Everywhere there are cap and pajama-wearing Muslims whose mother tongue is Hindi. This feature made me deduce the above theory. Yesterday, while on our way to Aurangabad we had seen from afar a huge and magnificent palace at Devagiri fort. Today we saw it in front of us. As we entered the first part of the fort, we were told that the talukdar of Aurangabad had come to visit it. Today he would reside here to inspect the warring skills of the soldiers. The soldiers belonging to the Nizam were dressed in British style, and the arms they were carrying too were British. There was a small cannon at the entry point of the fort. The talukdar was a Parsi gentleman. He enquired about us, where we had come from etc., and the security personnel gave us a guard and torchbearer to show us the fort.

At a distance we viewed a minaret. It is said the first Muslim ruler who had conquered the place had set it up. Then we came across a wall with a door. The door was shut tight. But there was a small door within the large door, and we had to enter through it. The watchman at the door said, 'If anyone is carrying either a match box or any kind of arms, leave it here.' Since the path was steep, we had to mount several steps and then again descend. There was a pond upon which there was a small bridge. The actual Devgarh starts from here. The mountain-like structure is built of a single piece of stone and its shape resembles a Shiva lingam. The upper part is narrow and is 120 feet high. The entire structure was plainly chiseled. Precariously we climbed a few steps to the top by not touching its railings. We also bypassed a house on our way. Then to enter the interiors of the hill, we again had to climb further. The entrance door had a few stone carvings which denoted remnants of Hindu culture. With the help of a lighted torch, we walked into a tunnel and then crossing two houses we succeeded in reaching the top. The foothill of the mountain was carved out to build this tunnel and the houses. There is no other way to reach the top of the fort. If an enemy succeeds in traversing this dark path, then to check his advance an iron door is placed at the entry point of the tunnel and fire is ignited to stop him. The innumerable steps forced me to stop in between and rest. Gradually we reached the outer part of the tunnel and found ourselves in front of a large portico surrounded by several houses. This is the only point of shelter inside the fort. There was no plain land around as we climbed further to reach the top. There was a waterfall to supply water for the people living there. At the top were three different cannons placed at three different points, standing in full glory. One was called Kalapahar, the second was Meda. Opposite to the point where Meda had to be fed with ignitions, stood the figure of a sheep.

Hence, the name Meda. The third cannon was placed much higher, just below the flag of the Nizam. It was Balahissar. But in Maharashtrian it was written Durga. All the three cannons had Persian scripts written upon them.

Sri Durga or Balahissar had witnessed both Hindu and Muslim dynasty. Many had tried to take credit about the building of Balahissar, but the huge cannon had maintained its stoic silence. It is next to impossible to bring such a huge cannon to such a height. Hence, it is possible that it was cast here itself. That we could enter the closed door of the fort and come up so far indicated how lucky we were. Devgarh was the third mountain fort I had the fortune to view after Taragarh and Singhgarh. Undoubtedly, Devgarh appeared to be the best among all the three. The only method of defeating the inmates of Devgarh was to barricade it from all sides and stop the food supply. Then the inmates would be forced to surrender. Otherwise, it was impossible to attack the fort and conquer it. Previously when people used bows and arrows and swords to fight enemies, then constructing a fort was necessary. But now with the development of mountain battery, forts have become redundant.

When at the end of 13th century Allaudin Khilji had attacked King Ramdev Rao, the king was unable to protect his miracle city, and had escaped to this mountainous fort. And in order to win over the fort from the Muslim invaders, Harpal Dev and others had attacked the fort. But the emperor of Delhi had finally succeeded in killing Harpal Dev. In 1631, the sultan of Vijaypur, Adil Shah had attacked the fort.

Rouja is a city that has been destroyed. Here was the grave of Aurangzeb. We also saw a few stone chains of Aurangzeb's Guru. Strangely enough, the chains were carved out from a single stone. Both for our bath and afternoon meal we climbed down the mountain where the caves of Ellora are situated. We went to Virul, a nearby hamlet, and had to wait outside the village. We took shelter under a tree, where stood the Khandwa temple, constructed by Ahalyabai. A servant was sent to the hamlet to procure our food. Gajanan Shastri, a priest from the Agnihotri community, took us to see the deity of Gomeshwar and thereafter started reading out from *Rudri* (a scripture). He spoke highly about the broad outlook of the Nizam. The Nizam, we were informed, provided aid to the Hindus for worshipping their deities. In 1594, Shahji was born in this village. While sitting in the temple we came to know about a Guru who had named a pond according to different pilgrimages of different regions and thereby asked the pilgrims to bathe in it. Thanks to the blind faith of our people everyone would comply. We had soup and rice and by two o'clock when our meal was over, we started our journey towards Ellora, my dream destination.

Devagiri is actually crescent moon in shape. It is spread out both on the east and the west but is not very high. The arm of the cave seemed taller than the middle part. And most of the caves slide downwards. It is about two miles wide. This is undoubtedly one of the major wonders of India. Thirty-four caves have been carved out in the entire mountain range. None of them have been built from outside. Since the Prince of Wales had expressed his desire to see the caves, Sir Salar Jung had taken pains to clear the entire region and maintain it properly. Out of the thirty-four caves, twelve are Buddhist caves, seventeen are Hindu and five are Jain. Mr Jerez, for the convenience of the tourists had published a booklet, but it didn't give us any information about the time of the constructions of the caves, neither did it speak about the artists who spent their lives in these artistic creations. Only a local hearsay about King Illu gave us an inkling about these caves. The artists had probably expected their marvelous creation to live on for posterity and glorify their names by default. The creations have lived on undoubtedly, but nobody has any knowledge about the craftsmen. At one place we came across an engraving which depicted the places of worship, according to gradation, of Buddhist, Shaivite, and Jain religions.

How one religion gradually made way to another religious belief can be detected from these caves of Ellora. The carvings are different at different places. For instance, Gautam Buddha was born in 623 BC and attained nirvana eighty years later in 543 BC. From 7th century AD, his religion started declining. By 8th century AD it was gradually declining in popularity. In 9th century AD it had completely lost relevance in India. However, in certain places, like Varanasi, it was practiced even in 11th century AD. There are however Bengali Buddhists still to be found in Chittagong. Their language is Turonian or Mug. In Nepal there about 1400 Buddhist families. They are, however, non-Aryans. They have preserved both the Buddhist scriptures and the original language Buddhism could not take over entire India. Shaivites were strong at the time of Buddha.

Seeing an old infirm man, the son of Maya Devi had become indifferent towards the material world. The sight so disturbed and impacted him permanently that he became restless. He preached about the transiency of the material world and requested men to practice austerities to achieve nirvana. It is a very difficult advice but one who tries it will certainly be able to attain a state of desirelessness. The philosophy of Maya rests on this sermon of Buddha. Renunciation, liberation, and other hitherto unknown concepts, which Hindus ought to have mastered, was first preached by Buddha.

Siddhartha, who became Buddha, had once said that just as a seed gives birth to seedling yet does not realize that it is giving birth to a seedling, likewise a seedling too is not aware that it is born out of a seed. Therefore, even if both the seed and the seedling are not aware of their origins, it does not hamper their functional activities. Just as a limb is not conscious of its functions, similarly spiritual activities have no rational information about their sudden beginning. In other words, there is no particular person in this universe who generates consciousness. The activities of man's past life decides his joy and sorrow in this life. In order to avoid this cycle of

Ellora caves inscriptions, Kailash

birth and rebirth, man must aspire for nirvana. And in order to attain nirvana, one must practice meditation and yoga. The Buddhists monks practice both and lead a life of seclusion. And for the purpose, they built viharas in the mountain caves. Here we were now enjoying their wonderful efforts in sculpting out these caves. Had these spiritual feelings not guided men down the ages where would we find wonderful creations like Dilwara and Devagiri temples?

A tourist guide accompanied us. Local people have named the main temples themselves. We left Dhewra and went to Maharwara, Viswakarma, Dekhal and finally to Teenthal, a Buddhist Math. It is a three-storied cave—the first floor is known as Patal (underworld), the second floor is known as Martya (material world or earth), the third floor is known as Swarg (heaven). Hence, it is known as Teenthal or three worlds. In the sanctum sanctorum is the statue of Buddha sitting in a meditative posture. Throughout the enclosing walls there are the engravings of lotus-eyed ladies. At the entrance stands two huge statues of guards. The main deity on the first floor or the underworld is known as Nagraj. If you shut your umbrella inside the temple a strange sound is heard.

After that, we entered the arena of Kailash, which was built in 9th century AD. Among all the other buildings in Devagiri this is considered to be the best. I have seen Orissa's Khandgiri, Bombay's Gharapuri and Nasik's Pandulina but this has surpassed them all. It is majestic and astounding. Kailash had been built from the foothills of the mountain and rose up to the top of the mountain. It looks as if someone had just lifted a piece of stone from nowhere and placed it at the top. It is placed within a rectangle and at the centre stands the tall temple like the sun radiating a thousand rays. The courtyard is about 367 arms lengths wide. In front of it stands a beautiful entrance door, a theater hall, and the temple. On all the other three sides stand beautifully engraved pillars. And on the walls are pillar-like structures with long scratch marks which make them appear as if divided into rectangles. There were innumerable images of Brahma, Vishnu and Shiva. At one place there was the figure of demon Ravana beheading himself and offering his head to Lord Shiva. At another place we found Goddess Parvati worshipping Lord Shiva. Yet at another place there were Hara-Parvati sitting together and playing a game of dice while in front of them were Nag and Nandi. There were figures of Varaha Avatar, Narsimha Avatar, Krishna destroying the Kaliya, Batuk Bhairav, Kapal Bhairav, Navayogini Bhairav, and many others. Many stories both from the *Ramayana* and the *Mahabharata* along with the Puranas were engraved all over. One can guess the amount of time and labour that was employed in engraving these figures. The very thought baffled me. The wealth of the king who had undertaken these unparalleled constructions was beyond my imagination.

Crossing the stairways of the theater hall one came across the Nandi griha and another stairway. There was a huge portico there and in front of it was the entrance door. Beside the door stood a huge elephant and the engravings of a pond full of water, lotus flowers and a huge statue of Goddess Lakshmi. The craftsmanship of engraving the flowing water upon stone was spellbinding. On the petals of the lotus, one could see a few words. Just behind it was the Kailash Temple. It was a palatial temple, and stupendous in appearance. On all the four sides at the bottom were engravings of elephants and tigers, as if holding the temple upon their backs.

In the sanctum sanctorum was a huge Shiva lingam that was worshipped daily. A lighted lamp stood in front. The priest asked us to assist him in buying ghee for lighting the lamp. Inspecting the pedestal on which the Shiva lingam was placed, we knew it was older than the one found in Varanasi. Both the walls and ceilings were full of engravings of gods and goddesses. The ceiling was placed upon sixteen pillars and twenty half pillars. Right at the centre of the ceiling were the figures of Lakshmi and Narayana.

The building that stood north of Kailash temple was two-storied. In the sanctum sanctorum of this building was a Shiva lingam. It was filled with ancient figures of gods and goddesses. Dasa Avatar too was there among them. The pillars were so wide and numerous in number, that it was impossible to remember all of them. It reminded me of the pillars of Calcutta's Town Hall. The greatest defect of Hindu art and architecture is scarcity of light, according to the British. But here the saying did not hold good. There were numerous doors which were high and extremely wide. The pillars too were splendid pieces of art works. At present such stone pillars with engravings are rare. Now the stone pillars are differently designed.

We entered the caves of Rameswar, Neelkanth, Telikagan, Kumbharbada, and Janbasa. Then we went to see the Dumarlena—a huge temple. The statutes here were huge and comparable to the ones we saw at Gharapuri. At the base we found a beautiful engraving of Shiva marrying Parvati. Parvati's father was offering his daughter's hand to Shiva and a priest was chanting the mantras. Uma/Parvati was looking at Shiva. Since the figures were extremely large for a Bengali like me, unmarried Parvati appeared rather mature in her looks and size. Maybe because she belonged to the mountainous tribe she was rather well built compared to a Bengali girl.

Since the sun had set, we were in a hurry to leave. Consequently, we were not able to view the small Kailash, the courtroom of Indra, and the sabha of Lord Jagannath.

Jabalpur

While on our way to Jabalpur, we enjoyed the sights of our countryside as we travelled through the night and early morning. All round was barren land full of wild creepers. Next day at about 8 p.m., we reached Mahesh Chandra Bandyopadhyay's house.

Late in the morning we had a little tiffin and started our journey towards the river Narmada. Sweets are cheap here, possibly four annas per seer. Bhera Ghat is about 10 miles away. Our tonga travelled down the main road and all around we viewed the springs. Since it is at the border of southern states, the remnants of southern style were quite visible. We reached the Bhrigu land and in the clear water of the confluence of Van Ganga and Narmada we had a refreshing bath. The water was clear and our bodies while bathing were clearly visible underwater. We had no plans to bathe, but the crystal-clear water was so tempting that we couldn't but help taking a dip. Narmada was navigable at that point. But since it got deeper in the middle, we took a boat to reach the marble mountain range. We had to pay Rs 2 per head for our journey. The mountain range was sufficiently high. It appeared that Lord Indra had travelled here on elephant back and personally scooped out River Narmada. The sunrays reflected on the plain surface of the mountains sent glittering light all around. The river, reflecting the rays, further heightened the light. Our efforts to reach this place seemed worthwhile. It appeared that we were sailing on the heavenly river of Mandakini. And to us it seemed a land inaccessible to mortal men far away from the maddening crowd. We climbed some distance to get a view of the source of River Narmada. The torrential flowing water sent water bubbles while falling and below it looked like a flow of milk from heaven. Up above was the scorching sun fueling the milk that was falling incessantly on earth. Of all the waterfalls I had seen previously this seemed to surpass all in its beauty. The specialty of this waterfall was unlike the one at Verinag in Kashmir, or even the Dudhsthali in Nasik. The fine droplets of water of Dhuandhar waterfall drenched the people who were viewing it from below. The sunrays instantly converted the droplets into vapors, and one had a clear view of this process of conversion. In fact, the entire place appeared misty hence the name Dhuandhar (misty). Sitting on the bank of the river and

River Narmada flowing through the Marble Rocks, Vindhya range, Jabalpur

viewing the entire sight was indeed a wonderful experience for us.

On the upper part of the waterfall, water was not very deep, and pebbles scattered on its pathway were quite visible. There was an ashram of the Udasin school nearby. One of the ascetics saw us and chanted in a loud voice 'Har Har Mahadev'. The sound effect was tremendous, mixed with the sound of the waterfall. From there we went to see the Vanakund. There seemed to have emerged from the earth a Shiva lingam at the place. On the bank of the Narmada, there were fifty-two kunds. They are within the dense forest hence not visited by pilgrims. They were all situated adjacent to one another. All the kunds were full of white-coloured stones. During monsoon, all of them get inundated and the water finally mixes with the water of the Narmada. The one which had the Shiva lingam was called the Linga Kund. It remained full of water throughout the year.

The day was waning and our guide, a young boy had never been to that kund. Also the path was extremely dangerous, we had to tread carefully on stones which could slip and slide away any time. So, we could not reach the kund. There was a Gouri-Shankar temple at the top which had steps to climb. It was surrounded by trees on all sides and was beautiful to look at. Since I was reluctant to conclude the tour, we went into the temple. Inside the temple in the sanctum sanctorum were the idols of Hara Gauri. Outside the temple, but within the temple premise, there were numerous Dravidian sculptures of gods and goddesses. They were brought here from other places. But all were disfigured and broken.

South

Andhra

If you visit entire India, the experience is akin to visiting the world. In the plains you experience either extreme heat at some place or extreme cold in other places. Mountains, seas, delta, desert, snow, valley, sandy land, lowland and island—all are to be found here in our country, making it so beautiful. Even the flora and fauna of India is varied. Without going into a debate of heat and cold, let us agree there is no other place on earth like India.

Since there was no rail connectivity on the eastern banks to Chennapattanam, we had to travel to Barachura from Kalikakshetra by road. We bought our tickets from Jabalpur up to Khandwa. On each side were dense forests. Trickling down the pebbly path was a fast-flowing river and we saw a deer for a few seconds before it vanished. You hear a lot of about the thugs in this place. At a distance stood a dilapidated fort of the ancient thugs. On the fields were cotton trees full of blooming flowers hanging from the branches. Turban-clad farmers were busy tilling their lands. Their wives were assisting them by scattering wheat seeds upon the tilled land. A lady in red was wearing the sari in the Maharashtrian style—tucking it up like a dhoti. Their language was Nimadi. The court however used Hindi as the official language.

Like Jabalpur, here at Khandwa we put up at the railway retiring room. I can't recollect all that we saw when we went towards the central road. In my diary I had written that we saw a billboard which displayed the information about a pilgrim's resting place of Mahadev Rameshwar. Near Rameshwar was a kund. It had a steady water source tucked in somewhere, consequently a lot of water was flowing out of it. The water was supplied to the city through pipes. The encyclopedia speaks about many beautiful spots here worth visiting, but because we had not visited any one of them, my record doesn't talk about them.

Nimar, which is in central India, lies within Malwa. Ujjain is nearby but it belongs to another railway division. It is said that ancient Ujjain with all her glory had long been hidden under the earth. But the glory of King Vikramaditya and the talented Kalidas had not been buried with Ujjain. It has remained alive in Indian culture. Archeologists have excavated and discovered Greek, Baltic, Shak, and other ancient native coins. But before the dynasty of Vikramaditya there ruled many kings. Many scholars and authors had used the names of both Vikramaditya and Kalidas and composed their works. Now it is for the present scholars to decipher the writings found on the stones of ancient Ujjain and decide which are real and which writings are duplications. A lot of controversy too has risen in pinpointing the actual age of these ancient literary works. The poet has spoken highly about Vikramaditya, by comparing him with Dravidian axe etc. But whether Kalidas lived during the rule of Vikramaditya in first century BC or not is a debatable matter. However, that Kalidas's poetry has no equal is a fact.

Travellers on their pilgrimage to Avanti visit Saptapuri which is near ancient Ujjain. Sindhe Raihar of Maharashtra is the ruler here. The astronomers still consider this place as the equatorial region and calculate the longitudinal distances accordingly. At one point of time in Indian history, Vikramaditya had risen in central India and had spread his power like the overwhelming sun over the entire country. And like an associated heavenly body, Kalidas was his consort. But later when he lost his royal powers it was Kalidas who helped him reclaim his importance. So creative efforts finally outshone royal powers. As the saying goes, literary powers are permanent compared to the royal powers.

Tantia, the renowned Bhil thief was held captive in a nearby village. A brahmin girl had called him brother and during the full moon of monsoon season he would come to her for accepting her rakhi. The royal guards being aware of this annual visit came with hundred soldiers and surrounded the house. Seeing this Tantia called out to the leader and said, 'Don't worry, I will allow you to arrest me after I finish my meal. I will not flee.' The husband of the girl, out of greed for the reward, had informed the authorities about Tantia's arrival. The girl was not aware of it. It is said that Tantia would rob the rich and help the poor with the wealth he had robbed. And for survival he would have a simple meal of chapati of bajra, salt and chili. So, he hardly needed any money for himself.

The Bhil community lived in the nearby Khandesh forests. Their habitation extended from the Aravalli range to Sindh, Rajasthan deserts and Gujarat's mountainous range. Rajputana was under their control. At some places there was the custom of a Bhil minister anointing the king with sandalwood paste. Without this ceremony a king could not be coronated. They are the oldest of the tribes residing in our country. Professionally the Bhil tribe is employed in agriculture, hunting and also robbery. But to a person who seeks their help they are extremely generous, even sacrificing their lives for his welfare.

Here men dress in the Hindustani style and also speak in Hindustani. In fact, it is a kind of midway Hindi one can say. The language and customs are varied in the Dravidian land, but here the variation is not very marked. Up to Maharashtra the variation is of little consequence, but once you reach Karnataka, things change drastically.

After crossing a few railway stations, we reached Asirgarh. At the top of the hills there were a few houses and a mosque. There was a fort too and, by its side, a river was flowing. Gradually we saw the Satpura mountain range. The natural beauty of the place reminded us of Malwa. The soil of the place is dark in colour. The fields were full of little plants of sprouting jowar. The forests were full of well laid out paths, for what reason I could not understand. Later however, I realized they were not mere pathways but small outlets of the river. Since there was no water, they looked like pathways.

We reached Karnataka, the kingdom of the Nizam. There the cries of the hawkers told us that we had landed in a different world altogether. Before we alighted from the train, a railway guard came and inspected our washroom.

Raichur: We put up at a pilgrims' inn of a Gujarati merchant Khosaldas Khandas, who stayed at Chenapattan. We were unable to visit a famous fort of the king of Bijapur. The owner of the inn discouraged us saying, 'What is there to see? The residents of the place are so greedy that they have sold even the stones of the fort.' Adil Shahi Bijapur had declared its independence from 1489 to 1686 and finally being scared of Aurangzeb, had laid low. That helped Aurangzeb to curb the growing powers of Maharashtra. Asaf Jah became independent and became a part of the dynasty of the Nizam. Hyderabad was established by him. If one desires to see the remnants of the Mughal empire one must visit this place. Nizam is the foremost serf ruler in the British empire. His annual income is Rs 4 crore.

During our short trip to Karnataka, we saw a sight akin to Bengal. The residents were preparing sweet pies in earthenwares, like the ones Bengalis use to celebrate the arrival of winter. Isn't it an example of the Bengali influence upon the Dravidians?

In the railway station we saw Christians selling sweets to the Hindus. The sweets were prepared at Raichur by a businessman. But despite the touch of the Christian salesperson, the sweets were not considered to be untouchable. In the afternoon the train for Madras started its journey. After some time, we saw the wonderful sight of the Tungabhadra river and before long it grew dark.

According to rustic geography, the world is triangular. India undoubtedly is somewhat like that. And out of that its southern part is certainly triangular. The mountain ranges are all triangular. On the north is the Vindhya mountain range. On both the eastern and western sides are the Ghats and on the south is the Nilgiris which finally coincide and merge with the sea. The southern rivers divide the mountainous ranges and keep their flow uninterrupted. This had led to the mountains being named as ghats. In the mid-part of the southern region is a plateau which is about 600 miles in area.

The natural beauty keeps changing with geographical changes. Except the Nilgiris, the rest of southern India has moderate climate. Kerala, Dravid, Karnataka and Telangana, these four states are more or less similar. Their temples, dresses, language and customs are not very different. Dravidians in a mixed form are present throughout India.

Tirupati: Tirupati is situated at the far end of Telangana. In order to view Lord Venkateshwara many Hindu Vaishnavas visit Tirumala. Because of the difficulty in pronouncing the full name of the deity he is also addressed as Balaji. According to the scriptures it means Srinivas. Tirupati village and Tirupati hill are part of the Eastern Ghat. Now the mountain is also known as Sheshachal.

The house where we stayed in was owned by Venkat Rao. He helped us to go up the hill and visit the temple. We left our footwear behind and were informed that Muslims (yavana) are prohibited from visiting the temple. We climbed about a mile of steps and finally reached an exquisitely decorated entrance gate at the top. Looking below, the village of Tirupati was beautiful. I can't say more about it since I don't exactly remember how it looked. Litters were carrying people from one peak to another. A litter carrier got a sandalwood stick for us.

The entrance gate was so impressive that we took it to be the temple itself. The style was typically Dravidian as found in other parts of southern India. The temple is spread over a large area called Udraypuri. Three walls protect the temple.

The art and architecture of the gopurams amazed us. The word Karnattya explains the exquisiteness of the gate. The name of the state Karnataka had possibly been derived from it. Karna—is a twisted line, Attya—is high palatial building. The temple is rectangular and on top and there are several layers added to it. The first layer is built of black stone. It contains the message of the administrators—what to do and what not to do. The stone deity situated in the sanctum sanctorum is huge. On the northern arm is the chakra, while the other arm faces the earth. On the left arm is the conch shell and on the other is the lotus flower. The mobile idol is slightly different. It bears the Sheshnag on the head, and the hands carry the club, chakra, and the mudra of blessing. Worshipping the lord is rather expensive. We bought a rupee of camphor. Unlike Lord Shiva, Lord Srinivas is not readily accessible. Only half an hours' time is allotted for the general mass to worship him.

Thondaman Chakravarthy of the Chola dynasty had built this famous temple. It was built four hundred years ago. All those who had contributed to improve the temple are still remembered through prayer offerings. The annual income of the temple is Rs 21,000, and the annual expenditure is Rs 15,000. At the side of the temple stand thousand pillars which are exquisitely carved. Outside are huge statues carved out beautifully. Dried rice is sold as prasad. A Hindustani novitiate asked me to get him some rice and assured that there is no problem in touching rice here. In a cabin stood metallic statues of the king of Chandragiri, his two brothers and their wives. In another room Ramanuja Swami was being worshipped. The chief priest Bhagwan Das Mohant was accused of pilfering the excess money of the temple and was imprisoned. There was a dispute with him and the new boss of the temple.

For the temple of Lord Venkatesh, thousands of people reside at the mountain top. The kings of Travancore, Mysore, Kalahasti and Venkatgiri have constructed inns for pilgrims. We spent a night there and then got down to Telangana.

Kuchhi Venkat Rao guest house looked like a royal courtroom. His collection of ancient gold coins, golden statues of Hara Parvati and many other such precious items was amazing. He took them out and showed them to me. The coins were used in administration, and are extremely important for Indian archeologists. Had the coins of Nanda, Gupta, Pal, Nag and Moukhari not been discovered, a large chunk of our national history would remain unknown. The family title of Venkat Rao is Kuchhi. In this region the surname comes before the proper name. Before we left, we were presented the following articles—perfumed sandalwood, betel leaf, betel nut, and perfumes of different flowers.

Six miles away from Tirupati is western Chandragiri. The Cholas ruled the land from 11th century AD to 15th century AD. Later, a king belonging to another family became its ruler. The only temples of southern India that are worth viewing have been constructed by them.

Telangana is ancient Andhra. The kings of Andhra had been effective even before the Cholas though not much has been recorded about them. The head of the Tirupati temple has a huge number of stone edicts and copper edicts. A serious student of ancient history may derive much information from them. The Buddhists of Andhra were closely associated with the Buddhists of Magadh. The inhabitants of Andhra and Chola are referred to as kshatriyas in the Puranas. The king of the Chalukyas was the grandson (from daughter's side) of the Cholas. Since the Chalukyas were related to the Kadambas, Cholas and Pandyas they too can be called Dravidians. And the kings can also be called kshatriyas. If someone brands the Chalukyas as vaishyas it will not be really fair.

The founder of the Chalukya dynasty was Chulu Shaila. Pulakeshi Ballabh started ruling Gujjar in 489 AD. In 556 AD, Satyasraya Ballabh, son of Kirti Verma ruled the western part while Kubja Vishnu Vardhan ruled the eastern Chalukya regions. In Telangana the last king of the Kubja dynasty was second Kulutunga Chodeva who ruled in 1062 AD. For five hundred years southern India was ruled by kings whose accounts have not been maintained other than recording their time span of rule. The Chola empire continued for 1800 years. Despite ruling for such a long period their detailed account has not been recorded.

Much before the beginning of the Puranic age the Aryans had ventured into the southern part of our country. Apastambha and Boudhayana had been there three hundred years before the birth of Christ. Whatever these writers had written has only been preserved in the form of the sutras. Apastambha wrote *Kalpasutra* while Boudhayana wrote *Smartasutra*. According to him, the current practice of southern India was not to have meal with a person who has not been initiated. The couples had their meals together and maternal uncles could marry their niece.

Before the arrival of the Aryans the customs practiced here were rather flexible. Later with the arrival of the outsiders, in order to preserve their supremacy, they branded the practices of the intruders as unmanly. But customs keep changing and are formed according to the necessities. The edicts of Sage Manu were not widely followed. Even now the edicts formulated four hundred years ago are not in circulation.

For the good of a society and its people we ought to know which scripture to rely upon, and at what time. But it takes time to realize what is best. Hence, it is good to debate about the issues for some time. For instance, the founder of new India John Macaulay, while forming the rules of the judiciary, did not restrict himself only to the short-term benefits of the people. Rather, with the help of his foresight, he looked into the future and did what he felt would be good in the long run. After a long introspection the rules were laid out.

Apastya had written a sutra for all rules that are to be followed while conducting a yajna. In order to master Vedic literature, it is necessary to learn grammar, the ancient Vedic scriptures, rhetoric, prosody, astrology, ethics and the six scriptures. First Buddhism then Islam destroyed the Vedic culture and nurturing of the Vedic learning. But later when king Vikramaditya renounced Jainism and went back to the folds of Hinduism, the brahmins regained their lost status. But in southern India the ancient culture and learning continued to flourish, because theirs was an orthodox society. Ironically at present the northern Hindustanis are learning the Vedas from the South Indian brahmins and becoming Agnihotri. So, they preserved the Aryan culture in a non-Aryan land. *Sam Veda* is duly learnt and cultivated in the Gujjar region. But learning of the *Atharva Veda* is still rare. During the Basanti Puja in Varanasi, I found only two scholars who were well conversant in the *Atharva Veda*.

We follow the Vedas only in words, not in our actions. There are three thousand south Indians living in Varanasi. They have been preserving the Vedas as a legacy. But Vedic centres of learning are growing increasingly scarce. The persons practicing the art of the scriptures are miles away from the Vedic scholars. And because they are not dependent on people's munificence they do not appear in public. Furthermore, the legacy of Guru and disciple has grown feeble, consequently even those who are conversant in Vedic literature are rather inexperienced in terms of the worldly ways. You have to be a Vedic scholar to fathom the nuances and meaning of the Vedas. Efforts can help you to memorize but not to understand.

Telugu is the language spoken by the people of Andhra. Orissa is the state that divides Telangana and Bengal. The practice of using turmeric reached Bengal from Andhra via Orissa.

Karnataka

The main city of Karnataka is Bengaluru. Our neighbour Mr Senabdhani had given us a letter of introduction to one Mr Krishnamurti. The house which he had fixed for us, was according to him, worse than the pilgrims' inn. And even the lawyer had declared that showing us the inn would have been an insult to us. So, Mr Krishnamurti desisted from doing that.

This place is a plateau between two ghats and is slightly raised. It is about 2000 feet above sea level. It is relatively cool and humid. At night we felt quite cold. The British had posted a representative here with an army battalion. The court of Mysore state is situated here. The entire state of Mysore comprised of ninety-eight cities and 16,784 villages. The approximate area is 27,936 square miles. Here one does not have to pay tax through one's agricultural output. There are 1000 horsemen, 2000 artillery soldiers and 2000 guards employed to look after the security of the state. The king gets an annual allowance of Rs 13 lakh. Dewan Seshadri earns a monthly salary of Rs 4500. Even though he rules the state in the name of the king, his actual subservience lies with the British government. And it is the representative of the government who instructs him in matters of the state. The king of Mysore is different from the government of Mysore. If the king desires to spend something outside the usual expenditure or if he has to repair his fort, he has to inform the Indian government (read British).

We first visited the Lalbagh. The most attractive feature of a garden is its lush green carpet-like lawn followed by other accessories. This garden had them all. Hooked arcaria, magnolia, camelia and rotika trees are also to be found in it. Many of the vegetables that are sold in the market were not familiar to us. The apple of Kashmir that had been planted here was not sweet at all. It was quite sour. The only sweet that was available is the famous Mysore pak. Hence, it was easy for the Hindustani sweet dealers to sell their varied native wares here. In order to satisfy our tastes and at the same time fill our stomachs we had to put in a lot of effort. Recently, the way albumen and protein are being widely publicized, we felt that very soon artificial products will replace them all. But that will certainly not be as tasty as the natural ones. Consequently, satisfying hunger and taste will be difficult.

The fort contained the wooden seat used by Haider Ali's father. There was the garden museum of the king. The sandalwood trees from the king's garden are brought here and one particular trunk that was displayed was covered by a sheet of paper. These trunks are auctioned.

The book shop next to the Srinivas temple was interesting. If a temple is constructed with a donation room and a book shop, the general ambience of the place improves remarkably. The Seths of Mathura had donated Rs 30,000 for constructing this shop. Bengaluru city publishes two newspapers. We did not see any newspaper published in the native language. There was only the government gazette, whether original or translated I can't say, compensating our desire for information.

Halebidu's sculptures have been carved out magnificently in stones. But nothing could match what I saw at Mount Abu. I had desired to view Shiva Samudra and Kaitaveswar temples, and my desires were fulfilled.

The king's palace was recently constructed at the cost of Rs 30 lakh. After viewing the royal suites, I went to see the court room of the king. The prince and princess had different dressing and reading rooms. Near to the royal library was the billiard room. Inside the palace the ambience was quite rustic, full of foliage and other rustic accessories. The bed was made of crystal. I had seen this in the international exhibition in Calcutta. On it was a silken bed spread.

The king appeared gentle and modest. He normally does not interfere in the legalities of the state. He is either respectful or afraid of the brahmin employees. The representative stayed at

Palghat. The prominence of the brahmins has fueled discontent among the citizens of other castes.

The Kolar region of Mysore has many gold mines. Every month Rs 12 lakh worth gold is mined from there and sent to England to be sold. That India should not prosper in gold is the policy. A part of the mined gold goes to England while the king has the right to claim some too.

The court of royal representatives comprises of 340 common men. It discusses issues like the Europeans preaching their religion, business of coffee and the needs of the business community, and also the welfare of the subjects. The Dewan is present during these meetings. Only four days are assigned annually for general meeting. Mr Seshadri answers the questions put to him. Income and expenditure of the state too is discussed. However, the concept of quorum or approval of the representatives are not mandatory. The state has a population of 50 lakh. 1039 men had come to select the chief representatives of the state. The method of selection is clear from the number of members. The subjects, however, do not have the right to choose the council of ministers. In this limited capacity it is not possible for the subjects to develop political acumen.

The south-western sea winds weaken when they reach Mysore. And even the north-eastern winds have not favoured the state. Consequently, the agricultural lands have remained arid, the ponds have dried up, the animals are starving due to lack of grass and the people were suffering from famine. The king has temporarily stopped collecting royal taxes. Food grains are being brought from other regions. People would have died if there was no free business. Commerce is a complicated subject. Politics works in coalition with it. Here during autumn, the weather cools down a bit. At that time it is impossible for the rain clouds to accumulate in the sky. Only a few stormy showers occur. Unlike Andhra or Dravid, Mysore does not experience any cyclonic weather condition.

The climate of Mysore is somewhat like Scotland (quite

favourable for coffee plantation). One Muslim gentleman had once brought coffee seeds while returning from Mecca and had planted them here. Now the Scot merchants are producing a lot of coffee here. The European merchants are very pleased with the king. According to them the state is enjoying self-rule. In practice too this is an ideal state for the rest of the country. The farmers who are deep in debt and are unable to bear the expenses of the city courts go to the village courts for settling their disputes. For the development of the industries, practical advices in local languages are published in the papers. There is a proposal to provide allowances to the old and infirm people. Since business in silk and iron will not be viable here, the idea has been abandoned. The Dewan is trying to stop through the representatives' court, the practice of child marriages. The king of Karnataka had sent his Pandit, Ratnam Kasturi Rangachari, to attend a social meeting in Prayag where he was to argue about travelling across the seas and the irreligious practice of child marriage.

There are eight hundred temples in this state and for repairing the seventy inns the government was approached. The amount asked for the repair works was Rs 48,000. However only Rs 40,000 was sanctioned. The ponds of the temples would have to be cleaned too.

Mysore is the capital of the king of Karnataka. We put up at the inn of a feudal lord called Nasraj. Since a conference of all royal representatives of India had been arranged there, a jeweller called Gopinathan of Channapatna joined us at our residence. When he was not able to procure milk for consumption, I helped him to get milk. In return he sent a few cooked vegetables to me. He had cooked pulses with greens. It was so sour and spicy that even though we tried to drink it up like soup, we were unable to consume it.

Unable to satisfy our hunger we went out and ate some Dravidian fries. One person was extremely surprised to see us frying loochi. He remains satisfied with yoghurt, milk and rice. Except pulses no other protein is consumed by the local people.

Throughout the city flags were flying high to indicate the happiness of the people. The entire stretch of the main road was decorated with yellow-coloured cloths to convey good wishes. Victory flags decorated with flowers too were flying high. One among them in the shape of the state of Karnataka was decorated entirely with chrysanthemums. Banamali informed us that whenever he visited Karnataka in autumn, he found the entrance decorated with flowers. Governor General Lansdowne was seen coming in a carriage driven by four horses. He was accompanied by the mayor of the city and the king of Mysore. The carriage was escorted both in front and at the back by a troop of soldiers. In front was a silver drum and a decorated camel. The body guards were carrying silver sticks and umbrella to protect them against sun. In between moved a two-wheeled carriage bearing the Karnataka kings' bird-emblemed flag. The marketplace was full of beautiful girls wearing black garments with yellow borders and elaborate jewelleries. They stood with uncovered faces. It looked as if an exhibition was being held.

Gradually the crowd thinned. At the central road a stage was set up where a Roman Catholic priest stood with his students. He waved his hand and thrice welcomed the dignitary. I could see them from a distance. We made our way through the crowd and reached the Governor's House. In the huge courtyard stood the cavaliers in a long line. Then there was the ornately dressed spears men. Finally, came the infantry and the flag bearers. In places stood bearers carrying umbrellas and on the side a line of elephants. Electric lights illuminated the entire place. Similar elaborate decoration can be seen during the Vijaya Dashami celebrations. However, the king then dresses up elaborately in priceless ornaments and expensive dresses and sits on the royal throne made from ivory. Then follow gun salutes. The brahmins chant Vedic mantras by way of blessing the king and musicians play varied musical instruments. The soldiers cheered and hailed the king. The king in his turn after encircling the throne bowed before it and took his seat. That is, however, not relevant here. Different games began. Both the king and the Governor sat on a raised platform to observe them. I saw the dance of the natives of Coorg and left.

Next day was Deepavali. At the centre of Devaraj lake a boat was carrying a temple made of glass which was illuminated. It was moving and throwing rainbow colours all around. It was a magnificent sight. Upon the fort a glass container was illuminated, and it appeared like a dazzling ornament in the darkness of the night. I looked at the sight and walked past the theater to reach our inn. From there I looked back again at the sight, and it appeared even better than when I was near it. Jagmohan mansion's interior has exquisite historical pictures, which are wonderfully displayed.

We visited the Chamundi hills and its adjoining city. Then we climbed the hill to view the temple which stood at the top. The presiding deity of the kingdom is Goddess Chamundi. And it is said that after killing the demon Mahisashur she rested here for a while. The place where she had rested has been fenced with a stone wall, and a huge temple has been constructed. Near the temple are the residences of the priests. There are a few other guest houses named after the princes and princesses of the state. The idol is made of stone. The goddess has eight arms and is seen ridding upon a lion. Unlike the goddess of Bengal, she does not have ten arms. During Navaratri she is worshipped elaborately. The emotion with which we Bengalis worship the goddess along with Saraswati, Ganapati, Lakshmi, and Kartik is however not found here.

Srirangapattam: The teeming crowd that had gathered to welcome the Governor General now started moving and we had to reluctantly follow them. The natural beauty of the place is exquisite. The place comprises of mountainous terrains, valley, dense forest, lush green agricultural fields and fast flowing springs and waterfalls.

Alighting from the steam engine, we reached Appa's

house. The afternoon was spent in the garden with many local gentleman. Even though the deity, Ranganath, was seen lying on his bed, his face appeared extremely beautiful. I felt like looking at the deity again and again. It is useless travelling to places to view obscene figures.

We had our bath in the river Kaveri. Later we went round the dilapidated fort. At Lalbagh, there are the graves of Haider, Tipu and his mother. Our tourist guide said that Lalbagh is like Karbala, since Tipu became a martyr and was lain here. To become the sweeper of this place is also considered to be auspicious. The room where the three graves lie is made of black stones and surrounded by stone pillars. The black wooden door is studded with ivory artifacts. As a mark of respect, umbrellas are not allowed here. Recently, the king of Mysore spent Rs 30,000 to renovate Dariya Daulatbagh. It still bears in a glass case the permission of Lord Dalhousie. The letter says this place belonged to Haider and Tipu. It is sacred and worth seeing. Nobody should destroy it. The artistry found in Kashmir's mandi, or the coloured and golden works found in the Gurdwara of Amritsar is nothing compared with the ones found here. The place is worth seeing but indescribable. From outside we had felt that the place was nothing much.

The business of sandalwood is monopolized by the king. He makes a profit of Rs 10 lakh annually. Only after tearing the bark of the tree trunk does the sweet smell of sandalwood emanate. One ton of wood is sold at Rs 60.

We discussed with Mr Appa the history of Karnataka. In 1761, Haider Ali defeated Timal Rao and conquered his kingdom. But with the arrival of the British his power diminished. On the pretext of lack of supervision of such a large kingdom, in 1799 the British selected five-year-old Krishna Raj Wadiyar, the inheritor of a previous ruler, as the future ruler of the land. But the political power remained with them. Consequently, the Wadiyar family became subservient to the British rulers permanently. It is said that this cursed family has to adopt an heir every alternate generation. The present king, Chamrajendra Wadiyar, is the son of a farmer. He was adopted by the royal family in 1868. It was during his reign that irrigational tunnels and wells were dug, which resulted in the increase in agricultural output. Naturally the amount of taxes too increased with the increase in agricultural growth.

The ancient history of Karnataka, its boundaries etc. are lost. It is believed that Kishkindha, which is mentioned in the *Ramayana* belonged to this part of India. Relatively recent rules of the Cheras, Cholas, Chalukyas and Kadamviyas have been partly recorded. This record helps to identify their antecedents. When the king of Vijayanagar, who had defeated the Muslims lost his power, the leaders of the Paligar tried to gain freedom. Other leaders along with Wadiyar attacked and occupied the present dilapidated fort, destroying the rule of the king of Vijayanagar.

In the ancient history of southern India the three famous royal dynasties were the Chera, Chola, and Pandya. With time one among them became powerful and subjugated the other two. They were friendly with both Kalinga and Banga. The original name of the Ganga clan is Kengu. In Dravidian pronunciation Ganga has become Kanga. At one point of time Kerala was known as Kengu. The Cheras of Karnataka had extended their power to Kerala as well. The Cholas made headway in Bengal as well, and this has been recorded in the histories. In places, the Cheras and Cholas behave similarly.

Vijayanagar is a place worth seeing. But we could not go there. At present it is known as Hampi. It is totally destroyed now and has become a remote village. We travelled along the bank of River Tungabhadra to Hospet city which is several miles away from it. Kings appear like bubbles in the water of history, and there is really not much to say about them. But here was born an extraordinary king, somewhat like the mythical King Janaka. The rule of Vidyaranya Muni is really surprising.

The Chera Dynasty

Madhavacharya (Vidyaranya Muni) heard about the misrule of Vijayanagar after the death of King Jambukeshwar. He came to know about the Muslim invasion and also how they had overtaken the land and were destroying Hindu religion. He immediately left the seclusion of the Sringeri Math and like a falling meteor came rushing to the capital of the Vijayanagar kingdom. Utterly detached from all material cravings and worldly powers he assumed the responsibility of ruling the country. The country thereafter took the name of Vidyanagar after Vidyaranya Madhav.

After ruling for ten years and realizing the capacities of Bukarayalu, he gave up his throne to him and became his minister. Even while serving in the capacity of a minister he proved his selflessness. Vast portions of present Mysore were under Vidyanagar. King Buk with others defeated the sultan of Delhi once. By 1347, the Muslims were completely driven off from South India. King Buk continued his conquering spree and went up to Orissa and established himself as the emperor of South India. His successors continued serving the subjects irrespective of caste and creed. His rule is marked by enormous development of literature and art.

When the Muslims started conquering and destroying the Hindu temples, Vidyaranya was grief stricken. He personally went with a large battalion of soldiers and reclaimed the loss. This gave him peace. Madhav was an able politician, a committed ascetic and also a person dedicated to preserve his race and religion. Acharya Madhav compiled many books. A dexterous man like him, equipped to handle both the scriptures and arms with equal elan, is not found now.

We know little about his end. It is most likely that he renounced all material objects and led a life of a true ascetic.

Much later both Ramdas Swami and Shivaji had done something similar. But like Madhav and Buk all their efforts proved futile after a time as the Muslims did not leave our country. Many had felt that God Himself had arrived in the southern part of our nation to stabilize the Hindu kingdom. But being spiritually inclined they did not realize the necessity of preserving the trend through proper successions. They were rather indifferent towards the politics of war and society. Had the king educated his subjects, things would not have come to such a pass. Common people felt that a king would come and go, and a replacement would be found without making a difference in their lives. But you are responsible for your actions, if you do not fulfill your assigned actions you will be held responsible. You have no control over the end results. It is necessary to expand yourself to the world of others and that brings about the spirit of nationalism. Even though Hindus were divided by castes, languages, and races, it was not impossible for them to be united for a common cause. The urgency for being united was not there among them. Consequently, conquering the Hindus became an easy task for the Muslims.

In 1565, the brahmin who ruled Vijayanagar was easily destroyed by the Muslim invaders. The grandson (from the daughters' side) was then ruling another kingdom. And till date they are ruling the kingdom.

South Indians are divided into four categories—Smartya, Madhya, Srivaishnava, and Jangam. The merchant community largely belongs to the last category. Among the dualists and non-dualists, the ones following the middle path anoint their foreheads with a long tilak to indicate their orientation. The white tilak indicates they follow the middle path. The ones using the yellow tilak follow Goddess Lakshmi, and finally there are those without a tilak.

Shaivites do not allow women to take part in their rituals. They are averse to women. They are Smartya and those who are given to licentiousness are forced to practice rituals involving women so that they learn to control their base instincts.

Smartyas apply ash and they are marked by the symbols of trident and chakra. Their belief in non-dual philosophy is beyond the understanding of a common man, even though it has been acknowledged as a philosophy. Dravidian states have Shiva temples and near them stand Vishnu temples, establishing the rights of the Vaishnavas. Madhyas are in reality followers of the middle path. They worship both Shiva and Vishnu. They anoint the middle of their foreheads with ash.

Lingayats or Jangams are non-communal. Many of the social reformers of different regions were influenced by both Buddhism and Jainism.

Kerala

We crossed the southern plateau and travelled across the Malabar mountain range. To our left was the Western Ghat and we kept proceeding from one range to another. Dark clouds were visible in between the ranges. Once in a while a stony hillside could be seen. Had there been a divine architect, he would have carved out wonderful temples upon these ranges, making them magnificent sights. It was a region full of sandalwood. But unfortunately, we were yet to be blessed by the wonderful aroma of sandalwood. The trees that grow here are not sweet smelling. The sandalwoods that grow on the banks of River Kaveri in Karnataka are famous for their aroma. Our carriage kept penetrating the deep forests. There was no trace of human beings anywhere. Previously wild elephants and bison used to come and take shelter inside the railway waiting rooms. Gradually they started ravaging the bajra and ragi fields. But we found only tame elephants roaming free in the villages.

Yesterday we were in Karnataka and as night got over, we reached another Dravidian state—the state of Kerala. Nature is completely different here. It is a land of green foliage, flowers, and lush green gardens. Inside the tree-covered groves we caught glimpses of huts made of palm leaves, very much like Bengal. In the rice fields stood the women labourers.

Since it was the end of the winter festive season, we found many people had gathered there and were boarding our train. Two men, a woman and an adolescent girl boarded the second-class compartment we were in. The Malayali gentleman had a tuft of hair at the back of his head and the rest of his scalp was clean shaven like his beard and moustache. He wore a small earball and other than his loin cloth he was wearing a coat and a hat in the British style. The woman was dressed in manly attire. Her hair was tied in a top knot and the white cloth she used to cover the upper part of her body was drawn upward to cover her head as well. Her ear lobe had slackened downward, bearing the weight of a heavy golden earring. She was wearing a golden necklace, but her arms were bare.

We got down at Sornur station and took a cow-driven cart. Kochi is about 76 miles away from here. There is a bridge upon the river Soora. The other side of the river possibly is the beginning of Kochi. On our way to Trichur we crossed a stretch of dense forest. We found several forest nymphs walking freely in the forests. Even though we were embarrassed to look at them, they seemed totally unconcerned about our curious glances. There was a young lady carrying wood on her head, walking slowly. There were other girls moving about. They all appeared beautiful and perfectly made. Nakedness if not obscene is really pleasing to the eye. My companion was extremely surprised, and I had to explain to him that they are still untapped by the civilized ways of life. The action that is not considered to be repulsive, should not be considered embarrassing either. Previously, when the female singers of the royal court of Travancore covered their bosoms, it was considered sacrilegious and an insult to the king.

Malayalis moved about with palm leaves on their heads to protect them from the heat. Even the king of Kerala uses an umbrella made of palm leaves. They were carrying small knives tied around their waist, to cut open the soft unripe betel nuts for chewing with their betel leaves. On two sides of the central road were houses of the Christians and shops owned by them. That they all were inspired by the British ways was clear by the dresses they were wearing. Little girls were wearing hoops on their ear lobes.

Our carriage stopped at one a.m. in the morning when it was time for us to go to bed. The driver called out loudly 'Kokal, kokal'. We failed to understand what he was trying to do and so he went and called a young Muslim boy who knew a bit of Hindi. He came and told us that this place was known as Kokal and we had to board a raft to reach Kochi.

As the day dawned, we viewed more than a hundred covered rafts which carried goods to and from Kochi. The British regiment of both Kochi and Travancore reside in Trichur. Two of the boats owned by the regiment stood loaded with goods. When Tipu Sultan attacked, Jimin lost his entire regiment and left the country. But the king of Kochi admitted defeat and stayed back. Hence, he still bears his royal sceptre. It is not always advisable to sacrifice your life for freedom.

Since this is a country of rivers, many of the water bodies have not been specifically named. They are often referred to by the locality and banks they abut. We went to Kochi to get some rice and flattened rice. The only sweets we managed to collect were coconut balls. But they appeared to have been bought from the Christians and so we thought it wise to throw them away. Travelling along the backwaters, our raft started swinging violently. The natural beauty was really captivating, yet our hungry stomach did not allow us to enjoy the sights properly. Our only thought was to find land. Fortunately, in the meantime the wind was favourable, and our boatman released the sail. But we remained extremely disturbed and unhappy because here we were visiting a new place and the people who were accompanying us did not know our language. So other than sign language we could not communicate. Finally, we got down on a lowland and amidst a coconut plantation we decided to cook our meal.

Here nature looks similar to that of Bengal. During monsoon the lands are inundated and when the water recedes, they sow paddy here. Some ripen within three months while some ripen after four months. The stalk of the paddy which ripens after four months bears fourteen seeds while the one which ripens within three months bears seven seeds. So the land yields two crops annually.

After our meal we continued our journey and as we proceeded, we found more and more of coconut plantations. On both the banks of the small rivulet stood coconut trees which were overloaded with fruits and had bent down to almost reach the surface of the rivulet. Behind the coconut trees were rows of other trees and this combination added variety and richness to the scenic beauty. In between the tall coconut trees grew the short slim betel leaves, daintily nodding their heads. Then followed another row of banana plants, making the entire surroundings green. Compared to Bengal the greenery of Kerala appeared better. Suddenly my heart started beating to the tune 'Vande Mataram'. After Kashmir I had not seen such a beautiful and mesmerizing sight. I kept glancing thirstily and the more I looked at the greenery the more I loved it. It was simply enchanting.

The dry husks that fall from the coconut trees on the riverbanks are collected and used to demarcate and fence the houses. They look like pineapple stalks. And because the houses were constructed amidst the coconut groves, they were sheltered against the scorching sun rays and were relatively cool. In these groves girls were ambling about in their birthday suits like our ancestral mother Eve in the garden of Eden.

Since the entire grove was dark due to the long leaves, we prepared ourselves to go to sleep. The boatsmen however, did not sleep. As sun rose, we sent our servant in search of milk to prepare sweet dish of rice and milk. One or two oil shops were visible but there were shops which displayed golden yellow ripened bananas. At a few places the coconut fibers were being extracted with the help of machines, to prepare ropes with them. Few people were roaming about to grate the coconuts manually. A person had tied a rope round his ankles and was climbing up a coconut tree to pluck the ripened fruits. The householder stood guarding the tree below, against potential coconut thieves. A fruit that would eventually fall on the ground was carefully protected by a fence set up by the householder. The affluence of the state was totally dependent on the production of coconut.

As we advanced towards Belanagar, we saw more and more houses employed in either oil extraction or rope production. At a distance we saw a few large buildings and we were told that it was the Kochi harbour. The water behind these buildings appeared quite remote and on the water we found a few steamboats floating. The strait here was as wide as the sea.

Had a geologist been with us, I would have requested him to examine the sands over here and ascertain how old this island was. The height of a landmass within the sea grows by two and half feet by the turn of a century. Fifty years ago, the scholars had pronounced that human habitation on Earth had begun only six thousand years ago. But now scholars say human habitation began more than three lakh years ago. Mammoth hunters lived just a lakh years ago.

Kochi harbour is run by the Gujarati community from Bombay. It was a city full of Hindu Bhatias from Kutch and Mandui, Muslim eunuchs, Konkan brahmins and Jews from Cochin. The Bhatias plied till Africa and the eunuchs till Mauritius for business. A Bhatia merchant informed me that he had been to Africa seven times till date, to sell clothes. And on the way back he had brought back ivory with him. The forest-dwelling Africans however never learnt the art of cheating. They collected clothes on loan from the merchants of Bombay and repaid the loan after three months. Even European countries had now started commercial dealings with Africa and hence Indian business had declined a bit. The Vallabhacharya brahmins have apparently retained the purity of their class because they never consume food cooked by Muslims. In Bengal if people travelling to Europe could avoid consuming food cooked by other castes, they would never be outcasted. If our scriptures do not mention the ways of retaining the purity of castes, then mere outcasting someone will be a fruitless effort.

Ninety-four years ago, when Buchanan had come here, the price of coconut was Rs 13 for 1000 coconut, betel nut was 5 annas, black pepper Rs 125, cardamom (almost a maund) Rs 100.

	Transportation cost included from Cochin per maund	*Calcutta*
Coconut	Rs 7	Not known
Coconut oil	Rs 12	Rs 12
Coconut rope	Rs 3.50	Rs 4
Black pepper	Rs 16	Rs 15
Cardamom	Rs 69.50	Unknown

If the cost did not vary much between Kochi and Calcutta, then doing business with them would make no sense. Calcutta used to procure these items from elsewhere and Kochi used to send them to some other places. Hence, the price did not always become cost effective. If businessmen of Kochi send their wares to Calcutta and instead of taking money exchange them for items like rice and bags, then the tax levied on them would be reduced. And if they pre-pay for the items they want in return, then according to commercial rules they will purchase the items at a reduced price.

Many advise educated Bengali gentlemen to opt for business instead of vainly trying for a job. But only material profit without proper business acumen and deep reflective power is not enough to prosper in business. The power to speculate cannot be acquired by mere education. Not all are calculative either. You have to be pleasing to people and you should love what you are doing. Otherwise, you will never succeed. Since the cardamoms we find in Calcutta are taken from here by the Gujarati businessmen, we call them Gujarati cardamom. The Malayali cardamom is the property of the king. Like opium owned by the British government, it is sold at a high price.

Ambling about aimlessly we landed up at a strange-looking village. Extremely fair (as fair as the moonlight) Jewish ladies were seen waiting both at the doorsteps and inside the houses. Their fair complexion made their white garments look even brighter. The fair-complexioned Jews do not inter-marry with the dark-complexioned Jews. In the fourteenth century, the Jews had got a large piece of land from the brahmin king.

Both Islam and Christianity originated from the Jewish religion. Just as a language has an origin from which it grows and then deviates, similarly there is no religion on earth which does not have an origin from which it has grown and deviated. Monotheism, angels from heaven, divine scriptures, God's messenger, last day of judgement and God's order are the few concepts found in both the religions. Since Kerala lies on the coastal region, right from the ancient times, the adventure-loving Jews, Arabian Muslims and European Christians have been visiting Kerala.

On the other side of the city of Kochi we could see the royal church. We crossed the strait and journeyed towards our temporary home. The road was quiet and the soil being sandy had not turned slimy. Both Dravidian and Karnataka brahmins had set up their homes here to serve the king. Last night a minister had died and so we had to face some trouble. People were all busy conducting his funeral rites. Keralites cremate their dead bodies within the premise of their house. A part of their central land is set aside for the Nag god and another part is set aside as a cremation area. Dravidians claim that Shankaracharya was a Dravidian colonist and hence when his mother died there was no one to help him to carry his mother's dead body. He had to cremate her outside the village.

As is the custom of the place, the house where we stayed was inside a grove and its foundation was made of stone. The roof was made of wood from the jackfruit tree. On top of it lay layers of coconut leaves. The house was overshadowed by betel plants and coconut trees. And all around the place were fruit-bearing trees like banana, papaya, etc. The creeper of the black pepper looked healthy and strong as it wound itself up a tree. Even betel leaves were in the form of creepers here and they encircled any large tree. The portico was covered with crotons, basil leaves, pineapple, edible roots, and many others which had extended their leaves and made the place green. There was an external covering to prevent the sun rays directly entering the house. Consequently, the interior portion of the house remained moist throughout the year. The sewerage was not developed and consequently the outlets of the washroom remained clogged.

To worsen the situation, the outlets being hidden from the sunrays turned into breeding ground for various infectious diseases. Two scientific-minded youths had worked on twenty drops of the river water and seen that during sunset there are 160 vegetation borne bacteria in them. And because the water remained stagnant at night, the number of bacteria increased threefold. With the rise of the sun the number decreased appreciably. Elephantiasis is called pada in Cochin. My friend collected its bacteria. In the human body old membranes are replaced by new membranes which then predominate. Blood is the chief source of producing these membranes. If the blood becomes acidic and cannot revitalize itself then deformed membranes are formed. And consequently, after a few years the body will become prone to diseases. My friend living in rural Bengal had become disease prone. Now he was suffering from rheumatism.

Tripunithura was about eight miles from here. The king

lives there. At present a fortnight long festival is being held there. We drove in a three-wheeled elephant-driven carriage and reached the royal palace. The entire population and the palace are within a fort. Since we had no tilak on our forehead and had covered the upper part of our body, the security man thought us to be Christians and so stopped us from proceeding forward. I was introduced to a person in Varanasi who lives in Ernakulam. He lived beside our house there. And he too left our company there since people took us to be Christians. He was afraid of losing his reputation. We opened our vest and showed him our sacred thread, but the fellow was not convinced. Finally, when we conveyed our problem in English to a gentleman, he removed the poor fellow's doubts.

In the fort we had a newfound friend. According to him, if we do not find anyone who is familiar with our customs, we will not be able to enter the temple of the Trinity. In fact, the chief minister of the king of Kochi belongs to a lower caste and hence is not permitted to enter the temple of the Trinity. A Dravidian brahmin emerged and asked me, 'Don't you know the language of Kerala?' Since I replied in Sanskrit and continued our conversation in Sanskrit, he was convinced that I was a vaishya. Yet, he refused to accompany us. I hurriedly entered the temple after glancing at the door keeper. But he did not prevent me from entering.

It was a large, enclosed courtyard and in its centre stood a hexagonal Malayali-style temple. The structure was completely different from the Dravidian style of architecture. The entrance was more like a room and the entire external wall of the temple was decorated with lighted lamps like during Deepavali. On two sides of the entrance stood four oil-soaked doormen made of stones. We bravely found our way amidst the lighted lamps and straightaway reached the deity. Here sunlight is not allowed so infinite number of lamps are lit to illuminate the place. At the head of the deity, a large golden Seshnag is seen spreading its hood. In order to prevent free viewing of the deity, the door of the sanctum sanctorum is left slightly ajar. But I managed to finally complete my mission successfully.

When superstitious people combine scientific theories, they say that when a spiritual seeker ardently prays before a deity a spiritual power develops in the otherwise lifeless idol. Then that power emanates from the idol. So, what previously was either a clay or stone idol now becomes potent. But such arguments cannot really justify the worshippers of the Divine Mother. At Kamrup, the king of Cooch Behar Naranarayan had constructed the brick temple of Kamakshya Devi and had sacrificed 140 men. Then he had offered her these 140 heads on a copper plate. His nephew Raghudev in 1583 had reconstructed the Hara Gouri temple and along with donating land, sacrificed 700 men. The heads were then offered to the goddess on a copper plate. Does this kind of behaviour teach the spirit of self-sacrifice? Vaishnavas detest this form of sacrifice. Sombagh, the king of Kishengarh, used to conduct animal sacrifice. The enlightened Jains and the members of Arya Samaj collectively requested him to stop this practice. The idol of Gopala in the Kerala temple is similar to the idol of Narayana of Badri ashram. This may be because Shankaracharya was associated with both these places, hence the similarity.

Today was the third day of the festival. In the courtyard fifteen elephants decorated with golden tilak and gorgeous covers were seen waiting. Up above a canopy covered them. And upon the elephants sat an umbrella carrier, a fan bearer and also a flag bearer. The boy carrying the large umbrella kept extending his hand and touching the umbrella from time to time. The elephant in the middle was carrying a replica of Gopala on its head. A large number of people were playing drums, shehnai and other musical instruments. The temple was just adjacent to the royal palace. On the first floor of the palace the plump king of Kochi, Vir Keral Verma was seated in a cubicle and watching the celebration. But because the programme appeared slightly colourless to him, he was dozing. At a distance stood the gatekeeper with a golden stick in his hand. From the other parts of the palace the royal members were seen looking down at the courtyard where the celebrations were being held.

Malayalis are similar to Bengalis both in their complexion and physique. To the people of Madras, Malayalis are very beautiful. The members of the royal family had relatively fair complexion. They were all attired in white-coloured clothes. The temple authorities were wearing white clothes with black border down their waists, and on top they wore white clothes which had golden zari borders. In this land of gender equality, I saw many beautiful ladies using male clothes as shawls to cover the upper part of their body. They apply black tilak on their forehead and wear necklaces made of precious stones along with heavy earrings. But after a time, the ear lobes tear apart due to the weight of the earrings. Previously sudras were not allowed to wear either gold or silver ornaments. We saw a tall and beautiful young lady without any ornaments standing with her child at her bosom and looking wistfully at the festivities. As in Bengal, people here use coconut oil for their hair. And because it is not customary to tie one's hair tightly, one hardly comes across bald people here.

The royal family comprises of the daughter and her son. Even if the son touches his mother, the mother has to bathe in order to maintain her purity. The nephew of the king (sister's son) becomes the crown prince of the state. He then ascends the throne on the demise of his maternal uncle. The king does not marry but his sister gets married. A son from Kochi's royal family has to marry a brahmin girl from Travancore's royal family. But it is not necessary to spend more than three days in the marital relationship. This is a borrowed custom, but the progeny does not have a right to any kind of inheritance. Sankar Menon, in order to stop the practice of the nephew's inheritance, and initiate the practice of progeny's inheritance had appealed to the British. For the purpose he had sent an appeal to the Madras administration too. But his proposal was not accepted.

The Zamorin and Namboodri of Calicut had registered a strong protest. Widow re-marriage is widely practiced among the Namboodris and their sons can inherit the ancestral property. But other than the eldest son no one can marry. That's why to marry a girl from that clan is considered to be a difficult proposition. Throughout the country, flouting marital law is considered faithlessness but in Kerala to follow the marital rules is equivalent to faithlessness. If a girl marries a man lower in caste, she becomes a social outcaste.

Shankaracharya was of a Namboodri family, born in 775 BC in Kerala's Kalady. On the northern bank of River Kallai is Kalady village. When he was at Badri ashram he wrote an annotation of *Sharirak* and returned home only once. Then he departed from this earth at an early age of 32. Sri Chaitanya lived for 48 years while Christ was 29 years when he died. It is not necessary for an extraordinary person to live long.

Shankaracharaya firmly established the necessity and sanctity of Vedanta for the Hindus. And following his footsteps the Dandi school of Vedantic philosophers in India have kept the tradition alive. The maternal side of Shankararachrya still exists in a place called Palur. Since the Kallai is considered to be sacred, water is procured from it and consumed in the city of Kochi. It is brought by boats plying there. People also visit the river to bathe in it.

The representative of Chera royalties of Karnataka, Cheraman Perumal ruled over Kerala. Later he became independent. In 311 AD his son (or maybe his nephew) received the inheritance of the kingdom. The present annual income of Kochi is Rs 13 lakh. The treasury is protected by British guards. The state has 2000 soldiers but because the British government has not permitted the king to use his soldiers, he cannot unite them into a battalion. They pay an annual tax of Rs 2 lakh to the queen of England. The king is free to rule his subjects. The landed estate of the kingdom is 1361 square miles, and the population is 5,98,353. There is a long-standing rivalry between the king of Kochi and Travancore.

At the end of the day, we visited the seashore of Ernakulum and met two Bengali gentlemen. We accompanied them to a European guest house and conversed happily. During my last tour to Baroda, I had met the gentleman who had translated the *Mahabharata* into English. And this time I met another gentleman who had translated the *Ramayana* in English. They wanted to win the favour of the king and had succeeded in doing so. In front of the guest house was a large fair ground. And on the side of the road leading to the fair ground were shops lined up selling different products. In a few of those shops the Christians were selling rice pies roasted in bamboo sticks. Here the washermen and barbers are found in plenty. The washerman charges an anna for washing a garment while the barber charges one and half anna for shaving. Like the Cholamandala, the Malayali shore too is of moderate climate. At night a thick garment is enough to feel comfortable.

The spring wind that blows in Bengal is termed by the Bengali poets as Malayali wind. That possibly indicates the moderate climate of Kerala. Free love is allowed here, hence a person jilted in love easily finds another partner. But those who believe in child marriage and no love before marriage find it difficult to flow with the free love culture of this place.

Tastes or cultures vary from place to place. Accordingly, the concept of beauty too keeps varying. A thing that is considered to be beautiful in one place might be treated as ugly at another region. People beautify themselves to attract the opposite sex. But a person who is not beautiful finds it difficult to find a partner. Beauty is certainly not the only criteria for love, but it is definitely an incentive. And for that matter one is ready to renounce one's own happiness for the happiness of the other person. Without a positive attribute in one's personality, love cannot be permanent. Hence, hankering for physical beauty is termed as animal attraction. Beauty grows old but nobility keeps flowering with time. But that realization dawns rather late in life.

However, the rulings of the elders are not totally absent in this sea of love. Just as eating without care is harmful for one's health, likewise, sexual licentiousness has evil effects too. Society's purpose is to teach the members the art of self-control. It is for the good of people that society forms certain norms. A young girl is not given the freedom to choose whosoever she wants. It is up to the parents of both the boy and the girl to fix up a match.

At the Dravidian border there is a place called Palghat. The groom with his kinsmen arrives at the would-be bride's house for the pre-marital ceremony. The groom brings with him clothes and oil and on arrival, the bride's mother welcomes him with due ceremony. The moment the hostess accepts the gifts from the groom the negotiation is complete. In Kerala the match making is like this—nobody knows who the groom is and if the bride happens to find a brahmin groom she renounces all other offers. And the moment she follows one partner the other one is completely forgotten. If the groom belongs to the same caste, he accepts the dinner invitation at the would-be bride's house. And if possible, offers expensive ornaments as well. A brahmin groom carrying a stick and a Nair groom carrying a weapon indicate their intentions of protecting the house they are entering. This prevents other unwanted people from entering the house. But that practice is not followed at present. With civilization marriage has become a more religiously oriented ceremony.

Among the Toda tribes of the Nilgiri Hills and the Nairs of the Dravidian world polyandry was common. A Tibetan lady from Lhasa was surprised to hear about the practice of polygamy in India. When I asked her about the advantages of polyandry, she replied that all her husbands took good care of her, and she was the sole female in the house of many brothers. And because the youngest brother cannot inherit the ancestral property it is convenient for him to have one wife who is being looked after by all the other elder brothers. It also saves household expenditures. No wonder Royal Mother Kunti, in the *Mahabharata*, had advised her sons to share what Arjun had won, which happened to be Draupadi. In Bhutan, it is an accepted practice to have several husbands. When several brothers unitedly decide to marry, they go for marrying the same girl. In the valleys of Nepal, a girl is first married to wood apple and betel nut, then she is allowed to choose even five husbands. If one does not intend to select husbands, she has to immerse the wood apple in the water and lead the life of a widow. Previously they were allowed to have many husbands simultaneously. The practice is still there in the tribes of Khasi and Garo. Five hundred years ago the concept of marital fidelity was unheard of in Kamrup.

Just as polyandry was encouraged not without a cause, similarly polygamy too was encouraged for some solid reasons. When men are more in number, it is natural that one woman will be sexually enjoyed by several men. And no one will be able to stop that from happening. But men being physically stronger, the practice of having more than one wife is still prevalent in certain places. The headmen of the Vadiya tribe in Sri Lanka consider it a matter of prestige to have several wives.

In Kerala the pre-marriage ceremony of marrying by substitution is known as Taali-bandhan. The married women of Dravid wear silver toe rings and double-stringed neckwear known as taali. During the pre-marriage ceremony one string is given by the girl's father and the other by the groom. The Vaishnavas wear a small locket of Vishnu while the Shaivites a small locket of Shiva in the middle of the two strings. The lockets are generally made of gold. Taali therefore is an integral part of the pre-marriage ritual. The groom puts up at the girl's place for three nights and on the fourth day tears off his garments worn for the occasion and leaves the girl behind, indicating severing of ties.

In the olden times land ownership was very liberal in Kerala. Land was considered to be a social property. Assistance in animal husbandry too was prevalent. Society was created to help human beings. Affluence acquired either through one's capacity or inheritance or even by some other incident may prevail, but that does not mean one section of the society will roll in luxury while the other section will remain deprived of basic sustenance. Excess wealth should become public property.

When the brahmins first entered Kerala, they had established a martial rule there. A few villages were ruled by one leader called the Deshbali. And when they acquired many more villages, which they termed as Nad, the leader of Nad then came to be known as Nadbali or local ruler. He was however under the direct control of the king who was known as Kovilgam. Tax acquired from a land without inheritance, and also tax levied on goods and foreign articles were all collected by Kovilgam who then passed it on to the Chera emperor. This king was actually appointed by the society and was to an extent answerable to it. The rural society of the sudras was known as Torr. The natural ownership of rural land was under this society. The village elders comprised of the Torr. They used to be called for a meeting (Kutang) to discuss different duties. When the king was defeated, at one point of time the rural society lost its power to a large extent. At present the rural society functions as a large joint family where the rule of the members prevails. The rural structure that prevailed in Bengal previously like Mandal pati, Koshtha pal, and Pattya lekhak, were somewhat similar to the above-mentioned social structure.

Gradually the natural ownership of land in Kerala turned into village ownership and then finally it was controlled by the feudal lord, who controlled the usages. With time this ownership was converted into land taxes. The land that was donated to the gods and owned by the brahmins were however exempted from it. The farmers who tilled these lands also did not have to pay any tax. The profit from land was shared by the tax collectors and the ruler. The Nair community was then reduced to mere subjects, but they have remained owners of the land since then. As long as they can maintain the fertility of their land and pay due taxes, they could retain their ownership.

The portion of Kerala that is with the British came under the purview of the tax system similar to Bengal, since the turn of the century. But now realizing their mistake they are trying to increase the rights of their subjects. The subjects who cultivate the lands demand the price of cultivation and in lieu give the produce to the landowners, a practice that is called Verumpattam. It is the landowner who decides the price and demands one-third of it from the farmer. The subject deposits an amount of either the produce or money with the landowner and procures the ownership of the land for a maximum period of twelve years. This is known as Kanampattam. They cultivate the land and give the landowner half of the produce and get back the interest of the money they had deposited with the landowner. When the land is sold the upper class usually buys it. But the process being complicated, land cannot be bought and sold in British-ruled Kerala. When a land is gifted as salary or otherwise to a person, it remains with him and is passed on to his successors. But when there is no inheritor, the land goes back to the one who had gifted it. Previously the land that was donated to gods was looked after by the ruler of the land. But now it is maintained by the British government. Kochi does not belong to the British part of Kerala. Hence, the land rules are different.

We collected our ration which would sustain us for three days, and sailed on a raft towards Travancore. Then we sailed further from Ambudhi, and the water became less saline. And at the point where the canal water mixed with the water of the waterfall of the mountain ranges, the water sweetened remarkably. We gradually reached a large lake by the time the sun set. The sight turned extremely picturesque—the large expanse of water, the reflection of the coconut trees in them. It was as if we were floating in a meadow or were sailing through the waters of heaven. Even though the sea was not very far from there, we could not see it. Only a small strip of land lay between us and the sea. However, at night we could hear the roaring of the waves. The lighthouse of Travancore stood in the midst of the sea. We were checked to see whether we were carrying any alcohol or any other addictive materials.

In the morning we reached a newly set up plant for producing coconut fiber ropes, at the far end of Alapuzha city. On the wayside stood a few shops, but the doors were shut. Next day our boat reached Kollam city. At the very entrance stood steam propelled machines for producing coconut fiber rope and coconut oil. The merchants dealing with rice had large storehouses of black-coloured paddy crop of the rainy season. Small boats were seen plying constantly. Both a mother and her young daughter were seen plying their boats. Their bosoms remained uncovered while a long cloth covered their heads and fell upon their backs.

To procure rice our boatsmen anchored the raft at another place. Various tall trees stood on the banks which provided the required shelter. The entire place was covered with white and yellow flowers, and it looked like a flower bed. Having found an opportunity to amble about we climbed up to the bank and visited an ancient temple. The temple had heightened the attraction of the village. In order to enhance the beauty of a new habitation it is necessary to set up a temple there at the first opportunity. At times these temples also function as local dispensaries.

In the evening we reached a large pond where the sea with its raging waves was trying to enter. We could see a few sails of ships from afar. On the pond floated a boat that was about to set sail into the sea. Here wherever you wish to go you have to go by a boat. Have we once again reached Kashmir—I wondered. It was like paradise, beautiful natural setting and beautiful ladies plying their boats all around. My companion who was with me in Kashmir was not there and hence I could not share this experience with him. Young men were rowing their boats swiftly and singing mellifluously while leaving the village. At night we anchored near a tunnel. As we alighted from the boat, we found a light inside the tunnel. From the wall of the tunnel droplets of water were dripping constantly. This appeared like the abode of the rain god Varuna. In order to reduce the distance, many artificial channels and tunnels have been constructed to finally merge with the sea. As per the information in Mr Eastwick's travel guide, these tunnels are not natural.

When the day dawned, we once again viewed the coconut groves. The height of some of the trees is so short, that the fruits can be easily plucked while sitting under it. The fruits of these trees are also small in size. Some are red in colour. Sand has been spread out where the land is sticky and wet. Only professional climbers can climb the tall trees and a stepping ladder has been put up for them to climb.

In mid-April, the ritual of coconut plantation takes place. The ritual is called Parum and consists of the following activities: A small area of the plantation is selected. There at every ten arms length holes about one and half arms depth is dug. The holes are filled with salt. A coconut sapling is placed in them and the sides are covered with mud. Finally, a little water is sprinkled upon the mud. The holes are surrounded by thorny barbs and watered thrice a day for a period of twenty-one days. Thereafter for three years, the saplings are watered every alternate day. Every month ashes are poured at the roots of the saplings. After three years, during the month of Ashadh (mid-June to mid-July) i.e., during monsoon, another hole is dug at one and half arm length near each and every sapling to be filled with rainwater. After monsoon the land is tilled and made even. This process continues annually along with occasional application of ashes. And because the domestic animals are allowed to graze here, the land remains naturally fertile with their droppings.

The region where we went next had a different natural

setting. On both sides tall trees were lined up like guards of honour. The trees were full of fruits making the entire region look like a dense forest. There were flowering trees and pineapple plants. Since there was scarcity of salt our servant went to the riverbank and picked up a little salt along with a coin on the other hand. His indication was clear, we required salt and it had to be bought not with a coin. Local language proved useless for us. The businessman who was selling salt, looked at the coin we had offered and clearly indicated that money we were offering was not valid here. This is the first time I found someone who was refusing a coin which bore the emblem of the empress of Britain.

As we proceeded, the forest grew denser. Initially the trees and plants were small in size but as we proceeded, they grew larger and taller. Finally, we reached a sandy area full of plants, creepers, and sweet-smelling flowers. And when we finished our mid-day meal and lifted our eyes, we saw the huge mountain range in front of us. Once in a while we could catch glimpses of the forest dwellers and their huts from which thin trails of smoke were coming out. The water body that we saw was absolutely motionless, wide, straight, and went up a long distance like a blue mirror in front of us. There was no other traveller other than us. Both land and the river stood still and silent. Swarms of birds were fluttering about and twittering. The only sound that could be heard was the rowing of our boat. Since the boatman had rowed the entire night, after a hearty meal he had gone off to sleep. His son Miragunda had taken his place and was rowing the boat. They cook their meals in the boat itself. They procure red chili, turmeric and coconut kernels from outside and prepare a paste to make a curry of prawns which they eat with rice. And to recharge themselves they take a sip of local wine while rowing. In the evening we reached a canal which was known as the place of eternal sleep (Ananta sayanam)—the capital of Travancore, i.e., Trivandrum. It is here we alighted on the bank.

We sent off Venkat Rao and walked towards the royal palace. The palace looked beautiful, decorated with green foliage. It was a brahmin locality. We put up at the royal inn.

The Malayali community which resides here were originally outsiders too. Now they have formed a colony and have made it their homeland. The Poligars were the original inhabitants of the place. Professionally they were sudras and still are sudras. They have been serving the brahmins down the generations. There are Cherumar and other ancient races residing here who survive by rearing livestock. It was the Thiar community who first came here. Then followed the Nair community and finally the Namboodri community who came and colonized Kerala.

Kerala is the land of the Nairs. Nairs are matriarchal. They established a military rule and started enjoying the natural bounties of Kerala. Some of them became professional soldiers and have been thriving fine. While on our way to Thiruvananthapuram we had seen a procession of Nair soldiers playing a martial tune and marching with a flag. Looking at them I felt that if we had a separate kingdom in Bengal, even the fish-eating Bengalis would have been equally valorous as these soldiers.

The Namboodri clan is bound by sixty-four rules. If they touch a non-brahmin they are supposed to bathe to purify themselves. They are not allowed to greet brahmins of other orders. They cannot worship Lord Shiva and Lord Vishnu together. Water and rice touched by any other person cannot be consumed by them. They perform their eleventh-day shradh ceremony according to the constellations.

Namboodris get up early in the morning and before sunrise have their bath and enter a temple. They have to stay there till eleven o'clock and in the evening again after rubbing oil over their body take the second dip to enter the temple. At nine p.m., they leave the temple and go home. While in the temple they spend their time in worshipping the deity and reading the scriptures. Only the afternoon is assigned to them to fulfill their domestic responsibilities. In the afternoon they are also permitted to take a short nap.

A girl is not allowed to get married till she becomes an adult. And because not all the young boys are permitted to marry, the number of unmarried girls in the community is rather high. Unless the elder brother is issueless, the younger brother is not permitted to get married. And because the family property is owned by the state, it is wise for many of them to remain single. If anyone committed adultery or consumed prohibited food or killed someone, as punishment he would be banished from the state. The person then would adopt Islam as his religion to maintain his purity. Now they opt for Christianity as their path for redemption. Till date they have managed to retain the purity of their clan both by following and discussing the points raised in the scriptures. But because it is difficult for them to maintain their high standard of purity in cities, they prefer living in remote villages.

These fastidious puritans don't allow their deities to wear clothes which the washermen have washed. They wash the clothes again before putting them on the deities. If ever a Namboodri takes admission in an English medium school, it is considered to be a historic happening.

In this region whenever men and women come across either an aristocrat or the idol of a god, they are supposed to remove the coverings of the upper part of their body. Men remove it up to their waist. This practice is possibly because the country remains warm throughout the year.

Here violation of the rules in marriage is severely punishable. And if they are found guilty both men and women are thrown out of their castes. When the case remains unresolved, they have to bow before a lady ascetic and seek pardon. This seeking pardon is known as Kshmanamaskaram. This is followed by a purification meal. When the girl is unfaithful, the Namboodris resort to various means to make her confess her fault—she is not fed, she is tempted with large amounts of wealth, a year-long investigation follows, the kinsmen are called, the king's representative is summoned and entertained with meals to get rid of her. And when she confesses, a Nair male comes and gets to note down her confession amidst the cheering of the other males. Faithlessness in women is considered to be heinous compared to the men since it is their responsibility to give birth to children and carry on the wellbeing of the society.

In this country of enormous freedom marriage is considered to be 'kalyanam' or blessing. The groom ties a thread on his wrist and with a bamboo stick in his hand and a bodyguard reaches the bride's house. At the door a brahmin woman sudra welcomes the groom performing various rituals. After the bride and the groom finish their meals, the groom once again takes hold of the bamboo stick and the bride carries a mirror and an arrow with her. Then the bride's father washes the feet of the groom. And because of the strict purdah system the Namboodri mother of the bride is not allowed to meet the groom. So, a Nair woman representing the bride's mother once again performs the rituals for the groom. When the groom reaches the marriage hall, the girl offers flowers on the groom's feet and then places a garland round his neck. Then the groom and the bride are allowed to look at each other. Ululation of the women from inside follows. The bride's father offers her hand along with dowry to the groom. The couple then walk seven steps together and a yajna follows. The girl goes to her in-laws' place on that very day.

On the fourth day, a heap of unhusked rice, yellow garments, betel leaf, and betel nut is kept in a room. On the other side of the room a mat is laid out as the bed. The bed is decorated with a line of unhusked rice on all four sides. When the couple occupies the bed, a priest keeps chanting mantras for the wife to conceive. Then on the fifth day the groom unties the thread round his wrist and puts aside the bamboo stick. The ceremony of marriage is finally concluded.

Among the Namboodri of Payanoor village, because the

nephew is the legal owner of his maternal uncle's property, marrying between cousins is considered blasphemous.

As a part of marriage ritual of the brahmins who follow the strictures of the *Rig Veda*, the couple has to visit a pond and the girl has to catch a fish with a part of her clothes. This practice, according to some, represents Sage Parashuram's blessings. It is said that the sage had once accepted the fishing net from a fisherman and after taking out a thread from it given it back to him as a form of blessing. The fisherman, he said, would be blessed with many children, to increase the number of brahmins in their newly acquired colony.

It is believed that Dravidian brahmins who came to colonize the place had to retreat once because of the numerous snakes that were found here. I had met a brahmin in Srirangam with a tuft of hair at the top of his head, who possibly was a successor of these brahmins who retreated from here. A Hindustani had once heard that a king was forced to invite one lakh brahmins to live here. The king received them with due respect. That is how the clans of Taruri Panday and Machiya Panday came into existence. Similar was the case with the brahmins of Orissa. In Bengal there was a practice of marrying girls who came by boat and these brides were familiar as Bhaurar Meye.

The entire stretch of land from Goa to Kerala is known as the Konkan region.

In the ancient times men of both Poligar and Cherumar castes worked as slaves. Their progenies too were the properties of the owners. The owners would at times rent them out to others when requested. But with the arrival of the European priests these slaves converted to Christianity and became independent. Now they were earning a salary for their service. Even now when the brahmins die men from local sudra community is summoned. They cut down the mango tree from the owner's garden and on the northern side of the house cremate them, thus continuing their age-old profession.

The Thiar community collect the juice from sago, coconut

and palm trees and convert them into sugar candies which they sell. This is their chief livelihood. Now they have learnt the ways of the world. When the pundits of Thiar community convert to Christianity they can easily procure a job. The inferior status of lower castes is automatically nullified when they convert to Christianity or Islam. The brahmins who consider it a sin even to tread on the shadow of these men of lower castes, do not hesitate even a moment to greet them when they become Christians. Maybe it is for this reason that many living in the southern part of our country have become Christians, thus making up a sizable part of the population.

Just as among the Aryans, when there developed a scarcity of membership, many non-Aryans were graciously included in the Aryan group, likewise, during Muslim invasion, a tribe of fishermen converted to Islam. In many places of this region, a mixed population developed when foreign invaders interacted with the women. That is how Nazara and Mulappa communities came into being. Before the arrival of the Portuguese the Syrian Christians used to observe Hindu rites and rituals. They even stopped consuming beef. Hence, beef here was considered to be untouchable and unconsumable. But now after being exposed to the other foreigners they have adopted their ways and forgotten the old Hindu ways.

The Christians here are all traders. In Trichur if anybody dies on Sunday, it is impossible for them to buy any new clothes for the funeral. Both Christian and Muslim Moplas here are employed in agriculture. Their nephews are claimants to their properties. North Kerala Moplas follow the Muslim custom of inheritance. The Moplas are extremely short tempered and arrogant. In Punjab, Islam had instigated the rise of Sikhism and in Bengal Christianity had led to the development of Brahmo religion. But here no foreign religion has been able to influence the original ways of the local people.

Gandhar (present Afghanistan) now is not considered to be a part of the Aryan world. Likewise, Kerala too is no longer a land of the non-Aryans. Hindustan has shrunk on the northern side and extended on the southern side. Hindu religion too has changed its approach from materialism to spiritualism and has become more acceptable. Hindu religion had become extremely cumbersome due its rites and rituals and consequently lost its mass appeal. Then came Buddhism which negated all rituals. But with time men forgot the simplicity of Buddha's teachings and grew licentious. It was time for another change—to restrict religion according to one's orientations and capacities. This job was undertaken by Shankararacharya. He is not only well known here but much respected.

Kaladipalli

Among all the historical places of India, Kalady is very important as it's the birthplace of Shankaracharya. Even though the annotation of Vedanta was not done here, the person who annotated it grew up here. The ambience of the place was such that the scholarly work, even though undertaken later, was fueled by it. It will not be a diversion to mention here in this travelogue, the journey down this road to peace. In this material world man has to at times renounce the world of desire and follow the path of renunciation.

A person who desires to follow the path of renunciation has to realize what is permanent and what is temporal in this world. He should remain indifferent to joys and sorrows both in this world and the world thereafter. He should practice austerities. A person who lacks these qualities is not fit to realize Brahman nor will the philosophy of monotheism be of any use to him.

Realization of self is true consciousness. Consciousness of Brahman and consciousness of self are one and the same thing. The one who does not realize this will remain far from the truth. That I am one with the universe is consciousness. Consciousness actually means knowledge. Both these concepts, however, talk of spiritual enlightenment. But they are inseparable, just as the curl of the snake is inseparable from the snake. Consciousness and Brahman are one and the same thing, which again is manifested in the form of life on earth. Just as the spark of fire is not different from the fire, likewise, God and soul are one and the same thing.

My capacities are limited, yet, to me this world appears inert. Brahma and life, how can I conceive this world as a mass of consciousness. According to Shankar, where there is dualism, the Creator sees his creation and vice versa. But once the spiritual soul realizes this, he becomes inseparable with the Creator and does not see the world as an inert mass or a solid mass of consciousness.

One who is fully enlightened realizes that just as water and curd are not different from milk, similarly Brahma and I are one and the same thing. According to the later Vedantic scholars, the concept of differentiation, that is Brahma and the world, is born out of Maya, and is actually a delusion. One who treats his inner being as a different identity, is suffering from this delusion or Avidya. Since the world has been born out of Brahma, it is not possible that he is not present there.

According to Western philosophy, I am self-sufficient. The world is dependent on me. I enjoy its presence through my senses like touch, smell, sight etc. The feelings are a part of me, like a dream. The world is a collection of sensory perceptions. The soul is a world within. And soul too is a collection of feelings. Science is nothing but consciousness. The world outside me is a figment of my brain. I impose the world, even though nothing exists.

What is spiritual ecstasy, meditation etc. but just manifestation of dualism. If the soul is not a separate entity, then who will meditate and who will experience spiritual ecstasy? Then there will not be any need for spiritual efforts. If Brahma and I are one, then whom do I meditate upon? When a person is deeply concentrating on something, we know he can visualize it vividly as if it was there in front of him. This is how some perceive God. And if he is a Vedantic he will visualize God as projected in Vedanta. He loses his perception of the material world and even loses his personal identity.

Our soul accepts the sensory perceptions and experiences both material joy and sorrow. One who rises above it does not experience any of these feelings.

You have to raise yourself to a state of consciousness and only then will you be able to rise above all material qualities. According to the sayings of Sruti, a person who can elevate himself to that level of consciousness will succeed in realizing his true self. Hence, Sage Vyas says, the human soul will succeed in snapping all material ties and will merge with the super self. Shankararacharya writes, whatever is purely you will then appear before you. Nothing will obstruct your vision. This is called moksha. A person who has attained moksha will experience pure consciousness. He will no longer be tormented by sensory perceptions, and will not experience any material feelings of joy, sorrow or desire. Once liberated from the material world, non-dualism will automatically be accessible. A liberated human soul will merge with the divine soul. Since the world is created by Brahma, it is not a separate entity from Brahma. Only in that state can you declare Soham (I am He).

Philosophers and composers of scriptures have shown those aspects which help to understand the attributes of Brahma. I will talk about Brahma as revealed in Vedanta. Creation is eternal but it is necessary to point out the reactions to actions. According to the Western concept it is needless to conceptualize God without dwelling upon the attributes of the material world. World symbolizes the final knowledge.

All worldly elements are temporary, if one can develop this attitude then all worldly desires will be eliminated and he will realize the pathway to liberation. Yoga and other spiritual practices must be done repeatedly if one fails to achieve his goal at the first trial. Repeated practice increases concentration. Sit in a place and concentrate. This posture helps to increase mental concentration.

While meditating think how to acquire patience, non-attachment, a desireless state and indifference towards the material world. Once you succeed in concentrating in the correct manner you will achieve a state of bliss and happiness. This is called the realization of Brahman. Hence, Brahman is called Satchidananda (state of eternal bliss). I exist therefore I am real. I am experiencing supreme joy which is also real. Hence, I am Satchidananda. One who is not capable of meditating in this manner should meditate on an attributed form of the Supreme Being. Once he is able to master the art of concentration while meditating, he will be liberated.

Buddhist meditation talks about concentrating on the eternal void. This means total non-attachment. Even in the ancient scriptures this kind of meditation has been referred to.

One who has achieved a state of true knowledge need not worry about noble actions. Without action too he may attain moksha. When the ultimate aspiration is to attain this state, then it is not desirable to waste one's time in useless action that distorts the vision of the soul. As long as a liberated person has to complete his karma, he may do so with utter detachment. It may appear to the world that he is functioning as a materialistic person. And at times this proves to be beneficial. Once he realizes his true self, no sin in the past, present or future can affect him. A true Gyani can never commit a sin.

According to Buddhist philosophy, you have to implant the divine mind into your mind through the following three steps. First make your mind vacant. Then no external thought will enter your mind. Then your mind will be without any other aspiration. A weaker mind will at first have to proceed to that state through meditation of the mantra Om.

Both Patanjali and Vedanta define this state of ultimate liberation in these terms. When the mind realizes its true identity then liberation is achieved, which then becomes a permanent state. If you can free your mind from all attachments, then the only thing that is left in it is chaitanya or true knowledge. That becomes the natural state.

Patanjali has mentioned eight methods of yogic practice. Vedanta says, knowledge is part of spiritual practice and deciphering permanent and temporary objects through the four-fold path. But meditation and asanas are necessary even for that. Other than that, deep concentration should be practiced. There is no need for pranayama. Both of them are methods of looking within. Samskara both good and bad depends on the state of your mind. None of them is real. One who is completely non-attached is above both the holy and the unholy. The philosophy of Vedanta is far more intriguing than the philosophy of Patanjali.

Vedantic philosophy considers realization or chaitanya to be permanent. This varies according to states. Shankaracharya had actually, with his sharp intellect, interpreted Buddhist philosophy in a different way. While debating to establish his theory, he quoted arguments from dualism. But when he was propounding his philosophical theories, Buddhism was very much prevalent, and it is quite likely that he was to an extent influenced by it.

One who aspires for liberation should become a sannyasin. If a person stays within the space of the material world and attains the state of non-attachment, that's good. Even though the puranas strictly prohibit renouncement of the worldly life, the guru does not pay much heed to these restrictions. Willingly forgetting material sorrows can be achieved only through true renunciation. And that is the state we human beings should aspire for. Some say finish your karma, and only when your mind becomes pure and holy will you be qualified to know the Brahma. That principle, however, has been refuted. It is just not possible that a doer will be addressed by Brahman immediately after a religious ritual. Even before the development of the concept of Brahman, people following Vedanta had expressed a desire to know the Supreme. So, it is clear that with the development of a dispassionate mind, one will be able to realize Brahman. By remaining quiet you achieve knowledge and for a learned sannyasin this is an absolute necessity. Renounce feelings like anger, hatred, and such. Be like a child and have a pure mind, but that does not mean you have to accept all waywardness.

Shankaracharya was both a philosopher and an interpreter of the Puranas. He believed in all the ancient customs and hearsays. He never questioned the source of the original karma but accepted the concept of the karmic cycle. Nobody likes to end his life and desires to live even in the next life. But a Gyani does not believe in such superfluous things. Hence, a fully liberated soul is not reborn. He does not desire to extend his lifespan. According to Vedanta, people who worship God with attributes will go to Brahmalok (heaven). But those who worship God without attribute will be completely liberated. However, one who goes to heaven will return and work for moksha.

The later Vedantic schools have elaborated on the concept of consciousness. That had helped people who were suffering immensely in their material lives. This world is unreal, so what alternative is there to pacify the materialistically oriented people? It is Brahman—that is the clear answer. Trying to realize one's own self in the practical world means visualizing the form of God and fixing your mind there. This beautiful and practical approach of Vedanta has impressed readers and scholars alike. All thanks to the extraordinary scholarship of Shankararacharya.

You grow accustomed to a work you are performing regularly. Once you start practicing desirelessness, that will be a part of you and the very thought of desire will repel you. You can meditate for long. If you do not wish to see, hear, do, or even think of anything other than the Brahman, then why will your duration of meditation be snapped. If you meditate for a while and remain preoccupied with some other work, you will not attain samadhi. Whatever is done repeatedly will grow to be your instinct.

Kerala

(Conclusion)

We left the inn at Thiruvananthapuram and entered the fort. There was no pond inside. It was bound by mud walls on all the four sides. The walls of the northern and western sides were however, built of stones. Fifty thousand people live here attached to the royal palace. At Padma Tirtha there were women bathers who were standing at the footsteps with lotus flowers in their hands. After the daily ritual was over, we were allowed to enter the large open portico of the temple. Here brahmins have an open invitation for lunch and dinner. The gallery of the landowner Padmanava is not very big. In the sanctum sanctorum lies the huge black stone idol of Lord Narayana reclining. From the three doors hang three golden bells, and his huge idol is visible to the devotees. The interior portion is rather dark. A Namboodri priest with a smiling face offered prayer for us with a camphor lamp and showed us the deity. On the side of the extended portion of the temple stands a huge container meant for depositing donations. It is a brass pitcher. During the festivals the king deposits a large amount of golden coins in it.

Here stood Martand Varma with his courtiers and renounced his sword and other weapons before his successors and the entire kingdom and declared that 'I am offering everything to Lord Krishna'. Since then, the king of Travancore bears the emblem of Vishnu's conch shell as the royal insignia. For them religion means donation.

A view of Thiruvancode, Tamil Nadu

It was evening and a thousand metallic lamps were lit. The lamps were carried by women and the entire premise dazzled us. A bhajan was being sung, accompanied by mellifluous musical instruments, along with the evening worship. An ancient priest stood at the open portico and worshipped the Lord from head to foot, in circular motion. Then he deposited the lamp with five wicks with a lady attendant who stood there without her head covered. There was no one around to take the blessings from the lamp (a usual practice in Bengal). The idol of Padmanava is made of gold while Sri Devi's idol is that of a nude woman. Both the stone and brass idols looked bare.

It is not possible to view a temple within a day. So, every time we visited the temple through different doors as the doorkeepers kept questioning our whereabouts and preventing us from entering. The temple, which is as large as a village, has several rooms. The first room was hundred arms length long and thirty-three arms lengths wide, and made of stone carvings depicting the universe. This room is used by the priests for their meals. The mandap is made of multiple pillars. And inside each pillar there is a small square cavity where an idol of Ganapati is placed. At the foot of the large banyan tree are engraved the idols of eight armed Narayanas, and plenty of other gods and goddesses. The pillar tops are artistically decorated with different carvings. On top of all these is the ceiling which is decorated with floral designs and stories from the *Ramayana* and other sacred texts. Even the sewerage drains are constructed artistically. The wooden door of the dining room is aesthetically done. Other than Mount Abu, I have never seen such artistry anywhere else. The walls of the temple bear beautiful colourful engravings. The figures of elephants and others have erotic undertones.

There is a room where rests the idol of Varaha avatar anointed all over with sandalwood paste. Only his face is visible. On his lap rests Goddess Lakshmi. Such an idol is not to be found anywhere else in the country.

In the kitchen stands a brass pot where two maunds of rice can easily be cooked. There are several brass plates as well. The brahmins do not have to go home for their meals. Whatever be their numbers, they have two square meals a day and are paid some honorarium every month. If he is an outsider, he is doled out uncooked rice. Service is provided round the clock. The word 'no' is not heard here. That is the true spirit of the place. There are two hundred open kitchens and sixty temples in different parts of the state. One day I came across a Bengali Vaishnava. So, we were not the only outsiders who had come so far.

Dravidians follow the rules of new moon and full moon religiously. In order to please their ancestors, they fast on the last day. While telescopes and planetariums can now show the stars and the moon, people prefer the older ways of astronomy and calculating the movement of the stars.

As an impact of English learning, hospitals, dispensaries, art gallery, irrigation and water departments, forest department, mint and others which are the requirements of an ideal state have been constructed. And for propagating English learning further, they have built a school, whose entrance gate has an engraved figure of a book. Ram Varma, the nephew of the king, has completed his Bachelor of Arts. He is the inheritor of the kingdom. Hence the Hindi-speaking subjects call this state Ram Rajya.

The original king of the state was Perumal who lived in 4th century AD. He had refused to accept the Chera emperor. The present dynasty ruling here is known as Tirupat. After the coronation the king has to donate gold generously. The amount of gold that he has to donate is determined in the following manner—the priest of the state stands before him, and the amount of gold needed to cover his entire body is measured out from the exchequer and donated.

In 1729, Sri Padmanava Martand Varma became the king. He was a skillful soldier and great initiator in increasing the wealth of the kingdom. He grew friendly both towards the Dutch and the French. On 7 January 1750, Martand offered his entire kingdom to the presiding deity of the kingdom. His subjects had great regard for him. He had the fortune to have Ram Aiyar as his representative. He was such a dedicated minister that despite his high position in the kingdom, he could leave no property for posterity. At the age of fifty-three, on his birthday, he smeared sandalwood paste offered to the gods upon his eyes and head and died a peaceful death in his sleep. Before his death he called the crown prince and instructed the following: The property of Padmanava should never be divided; There should not be any family dispute for the ownership of the kingdom; Expenditure should not exceed income; The royal family should be maintained with the revenue earned through trade and commerce; Always maintain a friendly relationship with the East India Company.

Hyder Ali never interfered with other religions. But the brahmins of Karnataka did not trust Tipu Sultan. Since he was a Muslim, they did not trust him and fled from their native place to take shelter here. The king, scared of Muslim invasion, sought British help to protect his kingdom.

After two loyal British employees were killed in the kingdom, Colonel Macaulay had a tiff with the king. When there was an effort to dismantle the Nair troop of soldiers from here, the soldiers revolted. This forced the king to sign a friendship treaty with the British in 1805, to help prevent an internal insurrection. This reaffirmed the British control over the kingdom and also helped them to earn a tax from the king. The king had to bear the expense of more soldiers than was required for the kingdom. Everyone in the kingdom grew increasingly dissatisfied and the relationship between Macaulay and the king worsened. Macaulay tried to dethrone the king, which provoked him to try to kill the Resident. Needless to say, this stand of the king led to a battle. The victorious British captain collected a booty of sixteen elephants, hundreds of guns, and a large cannon. He sold them all and distributed the money among his soldiers. The king was not involved in all these happenings. He soon died.

The history of Kerala started 1500 years ago. Had it not been acquired by the British it would have been a Muslim empire. That would have been a great loss to the king and his inheritors. Lets see how the subjects have been benefitted. Even if there is a native king ruling a kingdom, one cannot term it to be free state. It is only when the subjects have a say in the workings of the state will it be truly independent. The king's role is to centralize the power to defend the sovereignty of his kingdom against neighbouring states. Without that a country's well being cannot be assured. And it is for this reason that trade should also be centralized.

We had to cross a long stretch of the seashore to visit the other regions of southern India. Labourers visit the sea shore, full of fine-leaved tamarisk trees, to enjoy the shade and relax after hard labour. They also come here to collect salt from the sea water with which they preserve green mangoes and other local fruits. We stood at the shore looking at the roaring sea and felt as insignificant as a straw. In front of us roared the infinite sea and on its other side lay countries like Africa and Arabia. Kanyakumari was nearby. The sea which merges with the Indian Ocean stretches up to the Polar region. It crosses the hot deserts of Arabia and flows as hot undercurrent via Persia up to the confluence of River Sindhu. Then travelling down all the way crossing several Asiatic countries and even Australia, by the time it reaches the border of China and enters Japan the water gets cool. That is how it integrates several countries on its path. While I was contemplating all these geographical features, I saw a wonderful rainbow.

On our way back we viewed the place of worship of goddess Bhadra Kali. She is worshipped by the Makua tribe. It is actually a tree trunk that they worship as the goddess. It was a large mango tree which was encircled by a betel leaf creeper.

Our carriage blared its horn and we proceeded towards Tinnavelli. We saw uncountable number of idols of snakes under a tree. As the day dawned, we found ourselves on the bank of a fast-flowing river. And before us was a bridge lit up beautifully. Now instead of coconut trees we saw rows of palm trees. The tall and slim palm trees, called the sister of the coconut tree, stood in line all along our path. Sugar is produced here from palm juice.

Gradually Kerala receded from our sight. Mother Earth now grew hard and red in colour. In several places we saw the earth had turned hard like stone. There were termite hills here and there. The colour of the termite hills was red. The sun grew fierce as the day advanced and then gradually prepared to sink. From that place onwards the Dravidian girls were seen dressed in red clothes. For some time, we saw them wearing two pieces of clothes, then as we proceeded, we found their garments being reduced to one piece. All of them had long holes in their ear lobes but the earrings they wore were quite different. Clearly here wearing ornaments was mandatory. They were people of extremely dark complexion. Instead of six-layer thatches on their huts like Kerala here people covered their houses with four layers. And instead of coconut leaves, here they use palm leaves. A clay idol of the village deity was seen in a small hut. It looked more like a demon than a god. At places we also saw clay crosses and the idol of Jesus, indicating the presence of Christians there. In front of the idol of Jesus was a lamp and a frankincense container.

Travancore ended at a place where the security personnel stopped us from proceeding further. This was because these border areas were notorious for robbers. Added to it there was tremendous famine going on in the Dravidian land at that point of time. This land is not as fertile as Kerala. In the evening we reached an inn. Even though it was late autumn, we found ripe mangoes in the shops. These had probably come from Sinhala. For the last fifty miles from Surnoor, we had not come across any railway tracks. Now after reaching here the sight of the railway tracks comforted us. Tuticorin is nearby. And if one desires to visit Lanka, it is here they have to cross the sea.

Dravid

It is not pleasant to travel along the same path regularly. Even if the new road is not very special it calls out to us. This reaction was born out of one's desire to explore more and know more of the world.

The pronunciation of words vary with each region. The musical notes of Hindustani classical music are straight while in Dravidian classical music the same notes are sung with a vibrato.

Madurai is the capital of the ancient Dravidian kingdom. Mr Narsingha Iyengar took us to Swami Naidu's inn, situated on the bank of a river. Our room was on the first floor of the inn. He fixed up a horse carriage for our use. I have often been blessed by many helpful people during my tour round the country. The way they took care of us can never be repaid. It can perhaps be repaid if we bestow similar favours to someone who comes to us asking for assistance.

The Tirumala House has now been converted into a court for the British. The architectural style is archaic. There are figures of gods and goddesses engraved on the pillars.

In the *Madhurasthala Purana*, this place is mentioned as Halsya Kshetra. Meenakshi the daughter of Pandya king Malayadhwaja and Sundar Pandya were supposed to be reincarnations of Shiva and Parvati. Malayadhwaja performed the Putreshti yajna[94] and after he had finished his offering, a

---

94. Performed for a son. It has a clear connotation to the *Ramayana* where King Dasharatha performed this yajna and became the father of four sons.

three-year-old girl with three bosoms appeared from the fire of the yajna and stood before him and said, 'O king seek a blessing'. The king accepted her as his daughter and named her Meenakshi. The three bosoms of the girl however made the king sad. He went to Kailash to fight a battle and met Mahadeva. It was then that one of the additional breasts of Meenakshi fell off. Mahadeva proposed marriage to Meenakshi, but her father said that to marry Meenakshi, Mahadeva would have to live at Madhurapuri. Mahadeva agreed and assumed the name of Sundar Pandya. That's how he is still known here.

This is the original land from where the practice of worshipping Lord Shiva started. Lord Shiva descends from here to the land of the Aryans. In Bengal if a brahmin worships Lord Shiva he is scandalized. Here, at the temple of Lord Shiva situated amidst the Bellal tribe, the priests are sudra by caste. They are all sannyasins wearing ochre clothes. The practice is handed down to all the disciples who follow the cult. To reduce the pain of others they surrender themselves to the higher power and practice austerities. Their success is marked by their offerings of lambs and horses to the goddess. The Jangam tribe do not depend on the workings of the brahmins.

The temple of Sundar Pandya is controlled by the Pindarang. Their dress code was decided by Shankaracharya. The priests of Varanasi and Badri ashram are Pindarang. The priests lie before the deity of Kumar Swami with lamps made of pasted rice placed upon their stomachs. When the lamps are ignited the other priests chant mantras in praise of the deity and wave brass wands which carry frankincense. Upadhyay, brahmins of Maharashtra, are against the Pindarang. They had once tied up the long tresses of their chief to a tree as a mark of their disapproval. Finally, it is they who manipulated the transfer of control of both Meenakshi and Rameswaram temples to the British.

In the eighth century, Kumaril Bhatt with the help of royal power, killed many Jains and Buddhists. But his great scholarship helped him to establish the brahminical system there. His power to debate and analyze has been recorded in many philosophical treatises. Hindu religion is undoubtedly indebted to him. After committing the heinous crime of killing the Jains and Buddhists he was repentant and was about to die. Shankaracharya met him at this point of time. The brutish treatment of the Muslims towards the Hindus is actually similar to the Hindu treatment of people of other religions.

From the 5th century AD to 13th century AD, the Pandya dynasty successfully ruled the Dravidians and then finally left the scene. It is said that in the *Mahabharata*, at Indraprastha, a Pandya king was refused entry to the Rajasuya Yajna, just because he was a non-Aryan. Even after the Muslim invasion the flames of the dynasty were ignited for the last time.

There is no other temple on earth which is as huge as the one found in Madurai. Like the Viswanath temple of Varanasi, it is constantly crowded with pilgrims and devotees. The Pandya king Naresh Sundar had set up the idol of Lord Shiva, after his name. His Tamil name was Tatataka. The last king of the dynasty was hunch backed.

Allaudin's general, Malik Kafur had destroyed the temple of Sundar Sekhar. He thought perhaps he was teaching the common people a lesson. The sanctum sanctorum somehow escaped the onslaught. The kings later reconstructed the broken parts of the temple. The construction work is still on and is yet to be completed. My companion went round the temple premise and said that it was about two miles. But the actual area is about one-third of a mile. It is like a complete village in itself. There is a garden, a pond, a market, vehicles for commuting, school, and a treasury. Other than thousand pillars, in the large premise there are several stone structures, models of airplanes, a golden flag at the top of the central temple and ten entrances.

Across the main road stands the Pandya king's daughter Meenakshi's temple. We crossed several iron spiked boundaries enclosing coconut trees and reached the Karnataka entrance.

The Meenakshi Temple at Madurai

There were coloured idols of several gods and goddesses and the place seemed rather narrow and had risen upwards in a circular manner. On the plain surface stood two tall figures of lion and a row of pitchers. In order to get inside there were steps made of stones. The chariot that was there in the courtyard was likewise of similar stature. The gopurams were carved with figures who wore head gears. All of them appeared to reside at the top of a high mountain. The enormous stature of the idols was however expected in the context of Girish (Lord Shiva) and his consort Parvati as they dwelt in the mountains. Here the Santhal deity of Merang Buru too is worshipped.

In the market various types of frankincense were available, along with sandalwood, Kasturi, coconut, fragrant flowers, banana and many other items.

Nearby was the Ashta Lakshmi mandapam. There was the idol of Maha Lakshmi and her mystical Sree Yantra.[95] On the western side was Venkatachalam. When his wish was fulfilled, a merchant had spent Rs 50,000 and had constructed this mandapam.

As we entered the second part, we found shops selling lumps of cooked rice. The entire stretch was decorated with lamps and there were idols of many deities in different dancing postures. We had reached the land of Lord Shiva. The devotees had their bath and rang the bell. In the Ganapati yard Vedic chanting was being performed. A person was reading the *Mahabharata* from a palm leaf manuscript. Another person sitting near him was explaining the stories.

For the benefit of the common people pictorial stories that are both historical and from the Puranas were presented. A few people were employed in producing oil by crushing the oil seeds in a machine. According to the Dravidian tradition, the

95. A mystical diagram consisting of nine interlocking triangles that surround a central point known as bindu. These triangles represent the cosmos and the human body.

king Sundareshwar had washed the feet of Meenakshi during his marriage. Their son Ugra Pandya was shown suffering from snake bite and nearby was an image of Nataraja destroying the demons. In the retiring room were the figures of the architect Arya Nayam Pillai, Aghor Veer Bhadra and a few dancers.

We were present during Kartik full moon night when the festival of lighting a lakh lamps was celebrated. An elephant carried water on its head for the deity to bathe. In the evening the place was crowded. More than a lakh lamps were lit across the entire stretch of the courtyard, and the entire place dazzled radiantly.

The third part was divided into two sections. The first part was the temple dedicated to Sundaresh and the second one dedicated to Meenakshi. The first one was decorated with a flag stand and adjacent to it in a room was a golden chariot, silver container, an umbrella stand etc., and there was also Lord Vishwanath's idol. The main temple had engravings of Tirumal. Stone dusts were used in engraving these idols. These figures however were not covered. The headgears of these deities were made of gold. There was a doorman at the entrance. Inside was the figure of the king Chidambaram and on both sides of him stood two of his sons—Subramaniam and Ganapati. But ironically the central deity, Sundaresh Shiva, to whom the temple was dedicated stood inside a dark room. His was the usual idol, found everywhere. In the second room where Goddess Meenakshi was placed, the entrance door had a string of paddy hanging from the top frame. In one of the mandaps we found the figures of a lion and an elephant, whose lower parts were more like human beings than animals. There was the idol of ten-armed Mahadeva dancing with Bhadra Kali. Since Mahadeva's clothes were falling off Devi seemed quite embarrassed and had stopped dancing. There was the fish-eyed deity whose one hand was postured in the form of giving strength and the other arm in the form of blessing.

It was time for evening prayers and musical instruments

started sounding all around. The chief of the temple, Pindar Swami Raj, came to perform the arati. He wore a silken garment around his waist and the upper part of his body was bare but smeared with ash. He was clean shaven and did not wear an earring. His hair was matted, and he wore a chain of round rudrakshas. He had a torch bearer in front of him, and a bodyguard behind him. He appeared to have just arrived from Shiva's Kailash mountain.

In 1623, King Tirumal after completing the construction of the temple had built a large mansion on the eastern side of the temple. Since it was constructed later it was called Pudu, or newly built mandapam. The place had a shopping centre where all the essential items his men required were sold. In the courtyard there were ten familiar figures from the epics and the Puranas. The figure of varaha avatar stood with an infant on his lap. Lord Vishnu was seen offering Gauri to Shiva and other such giant-sized figures decorated the place. There were three pillars carved out of large stones. In one place was Ravana lifting the Kailash mountain. There was also Lord Shiva feeding an elephant with grass and molasses, and next to him sat Uma. Her dress bore signs of intricate artistry. There was also Mahishasur Mardini's figure—she held a lion with one hand and with the other she controlled a boar. Lord Brahma too was there in the courtyard.

Other than a few variations, the architecture could not be typified. A major part of the work comprised of large pillars which varied with time of constructions. Actually, the pillars can be used to identify the time of constructions. The *Agastya Sambhita* and its messages were engraved all over the place. There was a clear reference to *Agastya Gita*. It seems the brahmins of the place considered him to be the founder of Brahminical practices.

The Shiva temple of Sundar Pandya however, could not be totally protected from destruction.

The princess of Vijayanagar had recently constructed a

multi-storied temple of Kedarnath in Varanasi in the style of Madurai. There is a pillar that is high and wide and holds up a mandapam. Before the pillar was constructed, Kumar Swami, the head of the Math, had removed the remnants of an old, dilapidated Shiva temple from the site. The debris was thrown into the Ganga. The body of the pillar being sixteen sided, could not be used for Shiva's temple. Compared to the architectural designs of Varanasi this is not very ornate. The queen had refused to bear the expenses of engraving flowers and other such ornate stuff on the pillar. Consequently, it is not an artistic piece to see and enjoy. But people come to such places, to appreciate the ancient artistry and architectural designs of walls, pillars, and idols. The pillar from that perspective is not worth noting.

Regarding Bengal we can say that there are hardly any ornate structures in her pilgrimages. But there is nothing to feel sad about it. Just as Bengali language is not eternal, similarly the Bengali race too cannot be eternal. Previously Magadh and Bengal were not split up, as it is now. If Rabindranath is able to accept the popular Bengali grammar as authentic, then even Bengal can be divided into two halves, east and west. Five hundred years ago, the language rustic people spoke in east Bengal, Mithila and Utkal were not only grammatically similar but also had similar sounding words. It is only when language started being written that their structures changed. When the original Vedic language kept changing, it assumed various forms and accordingly grammatical rules were framed to suit these changes. The language which was considered correct at that point of time assumed completely different form and Prakrit grammar came into existence.

The annual income of the Meenakshi Temple is Rs 60,000. The people of Madurai have selected five most reliable people to look after the workings of the temple. They work under the directions of the head, who is a Pindar. The deity possesses ornaments worth Rs 50,000, which is there within the temple premise.

One day we visited the People's Park. Standing upon the bridge I felt like verifying whether the sight I beheld was similar to the one described in the books.

While returning we found hens ambling about in a sudra locality. We saw persons with sacred threads on carrying a carpenter's tool, a sculptor's tool and a cockerel. A sudra is not allowed to visit a brahmin locality. Even in wayside inns they have a separate room to stay. If by chance they have to stay at the same place the brahmin covers his face. Ritual worship of a banyan tree was held on new moon nights on the ground floor of our place. No sudra was allowed to attend it. They had a separate tree to worship.

At night we saw a person whose head was shaved in the front and had a tuft of hair at the back. He was carrying a silver pitcher on his head and was wearing ornaments of flowers. A band of musicians followed him while he danced his way in the crowd.

The staple food for the people here is rice. Small bajra is called kombu here. Rice here costs one rupee for four seers. Ragi and kombu are made into a paste for cakes and chapatis. Cholam is somewhat like mustard and oil is produced from it. Chops of ragi are fried in cholam oil. Ragi is generally consumed by the poor people. It is heavier than rice.

Most of the south Indian males dress in a similar style. But women dress differently across regions and also to denote their castes. Marathi and Kannada women dress in similar fashion. Both tuck their saris up at the waists. They do not wear nose rings, instead put on a pearl on their noses. Usually, they wear stoned studded or diamond studded earrings. Gold necklaces or gold thread are used by them. The anklets of Telangana are similar to the ones found in Bengal. They have small bells attached to them. The women spread out the tucked-up part of their sari, while the Dravidian women let it hang out in frills. The part hung out keeps moving gracefully. They plait their hair and let the plaits hang down their shoulders at the back.

The sudra women of Dravid wear their hair like the Santhal women. They bring the hair at the back of their scalp and twist it before tying it up in a knot. The earrings are however quite ugly, as if meant to display the large holes in their earlobes. It is not considered inauspicious for married women to keep their arms empty of bangles. The front part of their sari is frilled and allowed to hang down their bosoms. They sudra are however not allowed to tuck up their saris like the women of upper castes. Since the Christian women were prevented from wearing the sari in the above manner, there was an internal rebellion at one point of time. And as protest houses were burnt and temples were destroyed. A white covering is used by Muslim women to cover their heads. Unlike women of Bengal, south Indian women do not cover their heads to show respect to the males.

There are twenty-seven alphabets in Tamil. Out of them twelve are vowels and fifteen are consonants. Unlike Bengali, vowels are not attached to the consonants. Consonants can be added to consonants. The alphabets used in south Indian languages are tilted towards the left.

Twisted alphabets have been introduced to write Sanskrit. There are quite a few long sounding words, which when pronounced by the scholars make the distinctions obvious. Hence, while writing, it is not possible to commit an error. While pronouncing the words when there is a gap of sound, a slight tremor is used to fill the gap. Since the written language's script is well defined there is no chance of getting it mixed up with the colloquial usage.

Brahmins often mix Sanskrit words in the Tamil language. This usage makes it appear like an ancient language.

Having journeyed across three major pilgrimages of our country, Badrinath, Dwarka, and Purushottam, we decided to visit Rameswaram to complete the fourth one. We travelled in a fast-moving horse carriage called topal to proceed towards Ramnad. On the way we found many Bengali widows travelling on foot, on their way to Varanasi. In between we had to stay at an inn. There we came across a female monk. There was also a rudraksha seller. This area is controlled by the Setupati. It is said that his throne was set here upon a stone by a group of monkeys. Hence, the king declares himself to be a descendent of the monkey clan. Previously both in Shiva Ganga and Ramnad the bull coin of Setupati was used. Far from the shore we saw a gigantic mandapam. To what purpose it was constructed and placed there we were not informed. I was reminded of the stories of Lord Rama.

Rameswaram Island: We crossed the Pamban channel to reach Rameswaram. According to poet Valmiki, the place was as remote as the sky, through which travelled the monkeys. We sailed across the sea. The bridge was not really very impressive. Yet, it has served its purpose for last several hundred years. We saw several rocky structures jutting out their heads above the surface of the sea. Three thousand four hundred years ago people used to travel from Pamban to Rameswaram and vice versa by crossing this bridge. But the English government decided to destroy the bridge, as their steamboats, plying at present, faced difficulties while sailing. At times however, the sands have to be removed for smooth sailing.

Every monsoon Muslim sailors carry boats full of various goods to Calcutta's Jagannath dock. We descended on to the shore to cross over easily. But now things appeared pretty tough. The snake island resembling a palm manifested a different aspect of the sea. But on the northern side the sea looked quite calm. The waves were slowly proceeding towards the shore that was full of snails, conches, and other sea creatures. It was a wide shore. However, things were not like that on the western side. It looked quite menacing. The sea waves were rising sky high and fishes were playfully jumping up and down with the waves. The flying fishes were rising up into the air and swiftly falling back into the water.

The coconut groves that dotted the shore were the dwelling place of the fishermen. There was the Adam bridge which went up to Mannar. Afar we could see the land of Lanka. The entire region resounded with the chirping of birds. Christian fishermen go up to Tuticorin in search of pearls. The rocky mountain that had emerged from the sea appeared full of coconut trees. They looked immaculately white from here.

By throwing a fishing net one can catch hold of various sea creatures. Some of them are as sticky as glue. While walking along the bank we too collected some sponge-like sea creatures and were quite thrilled. White corals looked so beautiful. They were ideal materials for home decors. They were so colourfully decorated by nature. No human hand could replicate the artistry. The fungus that grew all along looked like a bunch of flowers with stems and tied to one another. The corals embedded in the sand had the appearance of stones.

The shallow waters stretched up to the lighthouse and proceeded further beyond our vision. We could see only a bit of it here and there. In order to guide the steam ships and boats a sailor was sitting inside it. He is known as Nagalingam. He considers himself descendent of Ravana. He feels mortified at the depiction of his ancestor in the *Ramayana*. Both monkeys and the demons seem to be the original ancestors of us Indians. In Lanka however, Ravana was an extremely powerful king almost of the stature of a god.

There is a temple few furlongs away from the place where Ratnakar was redeemed. As we proceeded a few steps, an Upadhyay came forward and smeared me with sandalwood paste and put a garland of flowers round my neck. The majestic entrance of the Rameswaram temple was constructed by the queen of Sinhala. The entire area is decorated with bananas, coconut and chrysanthemum flowers woven into long garlands. Even Mahadeva standing in the sanctum sanctorum is decorated all over with flowers. A few snakes with their raised hoods stand guarding him. A three-armed mobile god visits the house of Parvati at night. On the walls are engraved figures of Rama with bow and arrow, Sita, figures of Satya (yuga) and Kali (yuga).

Srirangam: Deboarding the train in Trichinopoly, we reached an island. Srirangam is wonderfully described in the scriptures. It is said that in the 7th century AD, the Chola king had constructed this temple. The king of Vijayanagar had extended it. Being afraid of British soldiers, the French colonists had once taken shelter here. They had used it as a fort and later extended it further. It encloses a three-fold village. In the fourth fold lies the temple.

Since it was time for Vaikuntha festival I bypassed the sandalwood smeared priests who were hollering and climbed up to the highest mandap. A deity was being worshipped. There was a huge lamp lit and placed upon a silver pitcher. Amidst the pearl ornaments of the god shone a dazzling diamond pendant. I will remember it for a long time to come.

After the nocturnal ritual was over, a guard with high headgear dispersed the crowd. Narayan was proceeding towards his bedroom. We stood watching the scene like watchful neighbours. Puree made of lentils and fried in ghee and a sweet was the prasad we received, and it proved to be adequate for our supper. In the morning we woke at the musical sounds of the priests singing and playing mridangams.

The prince of England had contributed money to construct the gopurams. The gopurams were decorated with life-like engravings of various deities. A human touch was heightened by the application of bright colours. The god Maruti was decorated with flowers and before him was a flowery silhouette, which increased the grandeur of the image. Sweet rice and sweet balls made of semolina were being sold. On one side stood a stall selling sweet curd.

Arjuna mandap was decorated with banana trees and banana leaves. The metallic idols of Ramanuja and other gurus were carried by the priests on their shoulders and placed on their assigned thrones in a row. The festival will continue for twenty-two days. Rooms made of light materials were constructed for the visitors visiting the temple. At another part of the locality was the Jambukeshwar temple, which we went to see. Out of the five earthly elements this deity represents water. There are no other deities inside the temple. There is only one outlet from which water keeps pouring out.

Guru Ramanuja, like Muhammad escaping from Mecca, was afraid of the Chola king Krimikanta. He had fled from here and later established the Sri community in our country. Thereafter he had returned to his native land. He was born in 1017 in the village of Perambudur situated in Chengalpattu. Son of a renowned scholar Keshav Tripathi, the very talented Ramanuja spent his early life here in Srirangam. Right from his childhood Ramanuja was an ardent devotee of Lord Vishnu.

Lord Narayana stands on the north side of Ranganatha decorated with multiple precious stones. Ramanuja was able to impress many Buddhists and Jains alike. Many theories propounded by several Tirthankaras lost their relevance because of him. He died a natural death here. Seventy of his disciples have been conferred places of eminence. They formed two different schools of philosophy—the Vargala and the Pingala. Both the schools preached what they thought was best for man.

The Pingala school of philosophy was restricted to Kerala and some parts of the Dravidian land. The head of the school is known as Yoti. He dresses in white clothes and carries a stick. They are instructed to use a bunch, comprising of two to three sticks tied together.

The coffee field of the temple seems to be a very lucrative source of income. The devotees whose wishes have been fulfilled are supposed to bathe Lord Narayan with a drum full of oil. The oil is then used to cure patients suffering from skin diseases. The Hindustani Ramaiyat school of worshippers are disciples of this organization. Even though Chaitanya and

Srirangam, South India

Madhava were disciples of this school, the Bengali Vaishnavas are not much inclined either towards Sri community or the Shaivites. If one deducts divine love from devotion, then the depth of feeling is lost.

I met a member of this family, Nadadu Rangacharya, a multi-talented person. At one point of time, he could perform many activities, despite being a poet. Sports, calculation, and conversation flew simultaneously. If someone tried to interrupt him saying the house is on fire, he would remain unperturbed. I gave him five parts of different slokas, and he quoted them completely without a single mistake. I listened to him and realized that all his recitations could be threaded together to form one whole poem.

Devasthanam

There are many temples in entire south India. I have heard about the famous temples of Tanjore and Chidambaram. The latter one is famous for Lord Shiva, who is depicted as the universe. The sanctum sanctorum is empty and upon one of the pillars of the mandap hangs a strange looking chain made of stones. Like the temples of Mahabalipuram, where temples were constructed after scooping a part of the mountain, here too temples were constructed in the scooped-out portions of the mountain ranges. That Hindu gods could be without form pleased Tipu Sultan, and he donated a gold necklace worth a lakh of rupees.

We reached Kumbakonam and went to Belangiman village to meet Mr Govind Chetti. I had read about the occult powers of this demonologist in the journal *Tattyabiswasi*. We had a translator with us and managed to reach our destination. The person wrote out an answer and asked what relevance it had. I never ask questions which generally people tend to ask. I thought he would successfully answer my question what is my name? He could not answer.

I had been to another occultist elsewhere who had many elite disciples. He said, 'I have to utter many unpleasant truths in my profession. Yet, because you are an Indian like me, I will have to calculate your queries. Come tomorrow.' I never went back.

I have met people in Calcutta who can read the thoughts and feelings of others. Till I met these kind of people I neither believed nor disbelieved in such occult powers. Professor Gussi had helped Miss Rokay to stand on the stage and wove his hand before her eyes. Instantly her eyes started moving at a great speed. The professor then tied her eyes with a cloth. The lady in the blindfold took a few steps down the stairs and turned back. There was a piece of paper, where it was written what she had to profess. The gentleman who had mesmerized her sat among the audience. Later she went up to that particular person (whose thoughts she had to read) and performed the task she was assigned. One Englishman had suggested the following in an aside, 'Inside my garments there is a leather pouch which contains some coins. The coin should be given to him, (a person sitting quite some distance from him) and slapped.' The girl did exactly as she was instructed. The person who was controlling the girl called one person from the audience and said, 'You move along with her and keep thinking intensely what has to be done.' The result was satisfactory. I have heard that the ambience of California is such that these things can be easily performed without much practice. You do not need any external agent divine or demon for them. Human beings do possess such occult powers. Repeated practice can enhance it.

The stone temple of Kumbheswar looks like a chariot. Conch shells and a chakra carved out in stone have been added to the rear part of the temple. Many erotic imageries too were visible in places. The hermitage we stayed in had only a thatched roof. If we needed something we had to go to the temple premises to buy it. Whenever one sets up a new habitation or a temple, it is necessary to write its history and its importance. That is how the stories of the Puranas came about.

We had to visit Mahabalipuram. On our way down from Chengalpattu we found rows of coconut trees lining the sides of the road, providing shade and beauty. We marveled at the sight of small coconut trees hardly three or four arms length height, full of fruits. There was a dilapidated fort which is now used as a prison house for minors. That the imprisonment was not meant to punish the kids was clear from the ambience of this rectification home. Previously what was considered to be a crime by the king of a state is now considered to be unethical activity and nothing more than that. The prisoner is taught to make utensils, weave clothes and mould metals before he returns to the mainstream.

Pakshi Tirtha is done amidst scattered mountain ranges. In the afternoon only after a pair of vultures are fed are the pilgrims allowed to have their prasad. We had climbed the mountain range in the afternoon when the ritual was over. Birds are really useful creatures for human beings. They not only act as agents to scatter seeds in the fields but are also hunters of insects, which destroy crops. No one on earth migrates like them. In winter they migrate from Europe to the Gangetic plains. With a small body of four finger's length, they travel 3000 miles twice a year, just to retain the warmth of their bodies. This small creature serves human beings in infinite number of ways. We know bacteria are bad for human health, but they do contribute in their own way to enrich earth. The carcasses of animals are accepted by earth, and they help to enrich the soil needed for our agriculture. Curd is produced by conversion of milk with the help of bacteria.

After breakfast we sailed in a covered boat down the river and travelled to the eastern shore to reach Ambodi. I descended to the shore to view a temple town carved out of a mountain. A part of it, however, has been submerged in the sea due to an

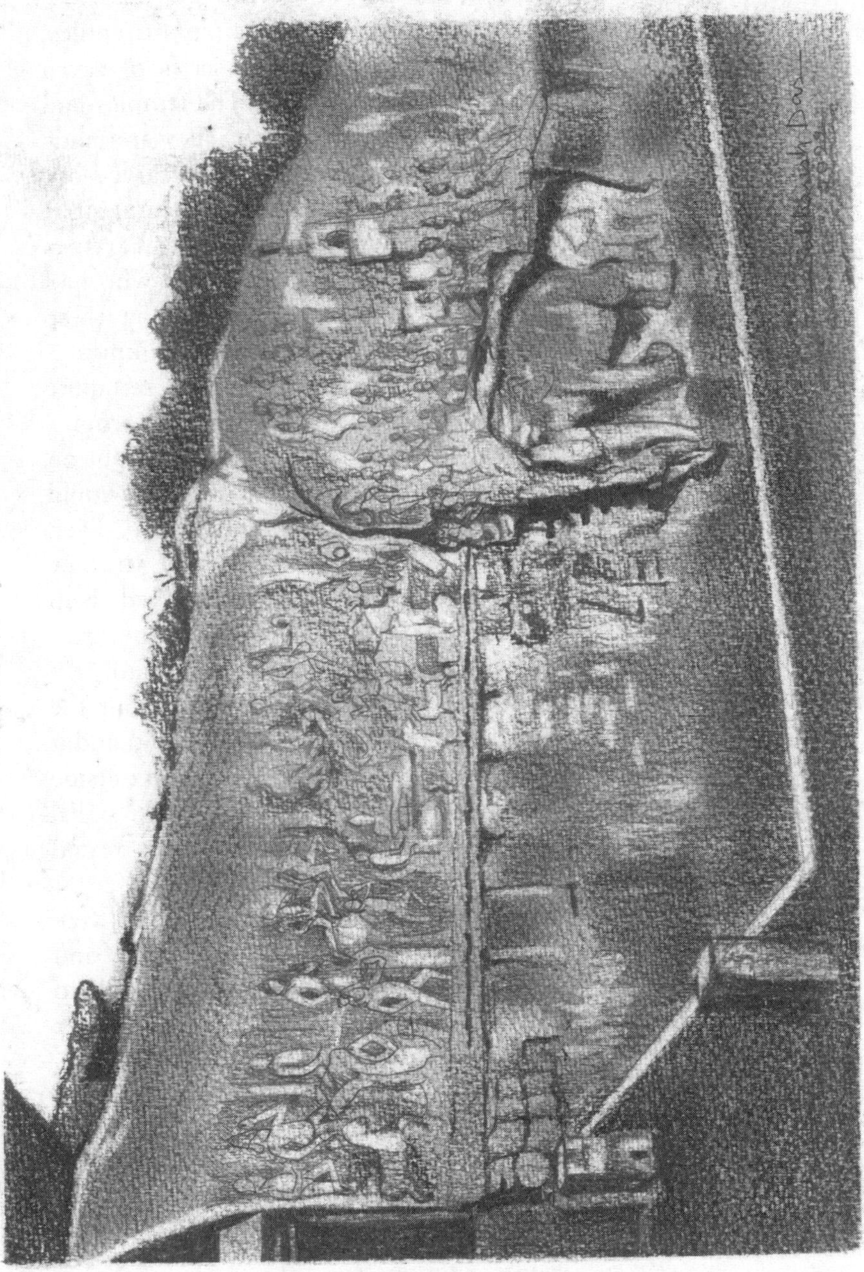

Wall carvings at Mahabalipuram

earthquake. This forest is probably full of a variety of reptiles. Sailors sailing in the sea get a glimpse of a series of seven temples. One among them is the Sun temple. The temples had been built at the top of the range by the kings. They are made of bricks. The interiors of these temples have been carved out of the mountain ranges. I don't think such architectural skills are to be found anywhere else in the world. The carvings indicate both Buddhist and Hindu influences. Those who had the capacity to utilize mica and granites in building these temples must have been extremely powerful Dravidian kings.

There are nine temples and thirteen caves, all set quite apart. There was the ten-armed goddess Mahishasur Mardini's battle scene, the playfulness of Lord Krishna all carved out on the temple walls. Due to the scorching heat of the sun, we could not view the temple built by Bali at the mountain top. Even though these temples were constructed in 7th century AD, they look like fresh constructions. The craftsman had carved them out with greatest care and had suddenly left the place never to return again. Their master too had departed centuries ago.

Some temples had the exteriors carved out fully, but the interiors remained unfinished. The place was a plain land and it seemed that large stone chunks were brought here from outside to build these gigantic rooms with figures of animals like bulls, elephants, lions and also idols of various deities. We rested there for quite some time.

The people of the land where such structures were constructed, must have been extremely intelligent and enlightened. Their present successors would certainly be able to retrieve the capacities of their ancestors. Their efforts will never fail. Despite being branded as worthless successors, I am sure they will regain their superiority in the future. Even if it's not in this birth, maybe after ten births. Their ambition and capacities can never be lost.

Kanchi: While travelling from Arakkonam in southern railways, I came across a different landscape. It was a land of lush green paddy fields flooded with rainwater. At frequent intervals palm and date trees stood guarding the paddy fields. The coloured gopurams were visible from the train.

Kanchi is divided in its worship of both Lord Shiva and Lord Vishnu. And that is clear from its name itself, Shiva Kanchi and Vishnu Kanchi. The Keshari dynasty which set up their rule in Bhubaneswar had marked influence here as well. In Shiva Kanchi the deity of Ekamranath is worshipped in the form of earth. However, unlike other places the traditional ritual of bathing of Lord Shiva is not observed here. In addition, there is the idol of Devi Kamakshi with a hen in her hand. In the courtyard there is a three-hundred-year-old mango tree. At its base is the idol of Goddess Parvati. She is found standing there, bearing the Shiva sign in her hand. There are Shiva temples all around. The tomb of Shankaracharya bears his statue. Tamil businessmen have decided to spend Rs 2 lakh to renovate the temple.

The way to Vishnu Kanchi is lined with coconut trees. The houses and the temples looked almost of the same height and shape. The gentleman whom we visited spoke to us in Sanskrit. In south India this place is famous for Sanskrit learning. Like Varanasi, many old people spend their last days here in search of moksha.

In the third room of the first floor of the temple there are both the static and movable idols of Varadaraja. We opened the lock and entered and viewed the deity in the camphor light.

In the 11th century, blessed by Lord Narayan, Ganga Gopal Rao had a son. So, a Shiva temple was destroyed, and a Vishnu temple was built in its place. Hence, the deity is known as Varadaraja (which means a carrier). The king of Vijayanagar Krishna Deva Raya constructed the main temple and for the worship of Varadaraja donated few villages whose annual revenue was thousand rupees. Even the government of Madras contributes Rs 9000 annually. The idol of the deity is adorned with precious stones, whose worth is perhaps few lakhs of rupees. Among the ornaments there is a necklace which Lord

Clive had gifted. The mandapam consists of sixty structures. One among them has been carved out from a stone. A stone chain hangs down from it. The stones were procured from distant places and the artists did not lack finesse in shaping them aesthetically. Students were seen studying there. At a distance a house was being built on the floor of the pond. It stood right in the middle.

Kanchi's importance cannot be overestimated. Here many Puranic and historical relics have been preserved side by side. At one point of time the Buddhist subjects of the king of Varanasi had been driven here by the Jains. They were then humiliated both by the Shaivites and the Vaishnavas. All the kings from different dynasties—Pandya, Chola, Pallava, Chalukya, Ballal et al have ruled here at different points of time. The memorable stories of Afghan and Maratha invasions and the tough resistance provided by the local rulers are still circulated among the local people.

Rajendra Chola invaded the Aryan lands with a host of other south Indian kings and increased his strength to a large extent. Another successor of his clan, Hemant Sen, had married a princess of King Sur, living in the plains. Ballal Sen was the son of Hemant Sen. In 1119 AD, he was coronated in Vikrampur. Ballal Sen belonged to the Kanchi royal family. Dravidian lands, along with Kannauj and Magadh, were considered to be the land of scholars.

Chennapattanam

(Chennai/Madras) (Origin)

Men always try to reduce the effort they have to put in to work. And opportunity provides them the required circumstances. Thanks to Mr Watt, in 1768, with the help of many more scientists he invented the steam engine. After fifty years, carriages could run with the help of these steam engines. In 1854, the English business association in India started running steam engines from Howrah to Hooghly. At present steam engines and railway carriages are running throughout the country. And it's with the help of Indian railways that we are able to undertake this journey across the country.

I wanted to visit Egmore, a place in New Madras city. I did not have to fret about how to reach it. After covering the western side of southern India, now we wanted to visit the coastal areas of the eastern part of South India. An important person seemed to be travelling with us in the train we had boarded. Hence, we found many aristocrats variously dressed being present at the station. People like the royal employee of Ramnad, Venkat Swami Naidu, King Sir Ramaswami Mudeli, Dewan Bahadur Raghunath Rao, J. Adam, Vijay Rang Mudeli, Itharazulu Chetti, Balwant Budhe, Shiva Ganga Mudeli, Aiyaswami Mudeli, Rai Bahadur Pandit Ranganathan Mudeli, Aiyappan Chetti, Ramaswami Naidu, Vir Raghav Chariya, Subramaniam Aiyar, Ramakrishna Aiyar, Kalyan Sundarang Chetti, Damodarang Pillai, Shiv Shankar Pandit, Subramaniam Chetti, Gopinath Takkar, Aiya Swami Pillai et al. Having seen them I felt my mission of visiting dignitaries was to a large extent fulfilled. The person whom all had come to meet belonged to the Marwar community. The community is notorious for all the misdeeds that occur in this part of the country. Initially, even though they did not enjoy the elevated status and powers of the Rajput community, now people are acknowledging their valour, which they say is equivalent to those of the Rajputs.

The moment we stepped inside the city I caught sight of a church. Seven years before the British conquered Bengal, they had taken possession of entire South India. And the first church in India was set up here. Last time, during my visit I had put up at Ranganath Thakur's large residence. It was the time for Deepavali celebrations of the Kathiawar Gujarati merchants.

Festivities were not over. But this time we arrived at the time of Christmas, and hence had to pay a higher rent.

Ranganath jeweler being a Gujarati, had the surname of Thakur which has been reduced to Takkar now. Their mother tongue is now Tamil. Gopinath's wife Padmavati wears yellow cotton saris, which are eighteen arms length long. They are woven out of fine cotton. She too tucks up her sari up to her waist. Her dress indicates her brahmin status.

In the morning, unlike the others who are addicted, I had perforce tasted a cup of tea. The headgear of the people here, has a special feature, very different from the ones used by the Gujaratis or even by the other Dravidians.

All the major cities are hygienically constructed in the European style for the Britishers. As per decorum a blind man should not be addressed as blind. Yet, the part of the city inhabited by the natives has been earmarked as 'black town'. There is scarcity of gas lights there. It has no drainage system either. Yet, it is better than Bombay since there are plenty of brick structures. Following the nomenclature of the chief of the place, Chenna Appa, Madras is addressed as Chennpattan by the old inhabitants. Mr Chenna, after having obtained King Chandragiri's permission, had allowed the British merchant association to construct a port here. Afraid of both Mughal and Maharashtrian conquests the black town was once surrounded by walls. The remnants of this wall are still visible. The entire town along the coastline encompasses an area of 26 square miles with a population of 4 lakhs.

Thirty-four years ago, Krishnananda Brahmachari without a penny in his pocket, and only God as his saviour, had come here walking all the way from Bengal. Writing his own experiences, he remarked that, 'The place where Saint George fort stands in Chennapattanam, is the actual Madras. There are eight to ten alms houses. There rice and flour are distributed. The water of the well is sweet and there are both thatched and concrete houses.'

There are no large lush green lawns here like the one found adjacent to the fort of Calcutta, or the one found in Prayag and elsewhere. But the city can boast of its large, wide and impressive roads. We were really impressed by them as we walked along. There were no jarring sound of the soldiers playing their drums here. The beautiful music that wafted from afar was so mellifluous. Here happy commoners and royalties can walk as equals. There is no hurry in inhaling the healthy sea breeze.

In the morning the playful activities of the fishermen on the sea are a sight to behold. The boats keep dancing with the rhythmic variation of the waves and when the fishermen throw their nets in the water, they seem to move to the beats of the waves. Unlike the ships and steamboats their rafts cannot overcome the reverse pull of the sea. As we had seen in Puri, the rafts are made of three broad pieces of wood tied together with a rope. There are no iron clamps to hold them. When not in use they lie idly on the shore. When the waves approach the shore, the fishermen throw their nets and wait patiently. Only when the waves recede, the fish get caught in the nets. A mother with a little boy came to the shore with a basket full of mashed potato and balls of rice paste for them to consume.

The forest of *tamarix gallica* that has grown on the sandy soil of the shore tempted us. But we bypassed it and proceeded towards a garden that lay beyond. Near the government palace was the chepak tree garden. The present nawab of Karnataka lives here. Its architecture is Sarcenic. There are also engraved figures of gods and goddesses on the walls of the rooms. According to the rulings of Muhammad, images of living creatures should never be drawn, instead flowers and leaves may be depicted in the pictures. The person who had ordered the construction of this mansion was possibly not aware of this ruling. At the top of the building is a golden pitcher with a moon. No sun rays are to be reflected on them. Here the revenue office of the British government is also located. The

Nawab of Karnataka having incurred heavy loans which he cannot repay has lost his political powers. One person from the family is residing at the Tiplicon locality and surviving on governmental doles.

The public library that is a part of the university had at its entrance gate the figure of Dasavatara. The metallic figure of the empress of India, a gift from the king of Vizagapatam is worth seeing. Everyday a person comes to decorate her with flower garland and another person anoints her with sandalwood paste. Even in Pudumandap of Madurai a similar ritual is observed for the statue of the empress of India.

The newly constructed High Court is a beautiful mansion. The mast of the building and the staircase is still etched in my memory. After ambling about for some time, I returned to my room. But before returning I caught sight of the courtroom, where a case was being filed. At the entrance of the courtroom stood the doorman, wearing a long coat and bearing a stick in his hand. Inside the room I espied an ancient judge, Sir Muthuswami Aiyar.[96] He is an independent minded scholar, much respected everywhere. His arguments are irrefutable. He was wearing a dhoti and a black gown but was bare footed. He had a white headgear whose golden tassels curved and joined in front. His forehead was anointed with ash drawn in the form of a full moon. In the middle of the moon shone a black dot.

Here both brahmins and sudras consume rice thrice a day. For the first meal they have baked rice with yogurt and pickle, followed by coffee. After meal they anoint their foreheads with ash dots which they wear throughout the day. In the evening they wash off the dot and apply fresh trident shaped ash paste. The black coloured dot indicates that they have had their meals at noon. The judge sitting there was a Waranama brahmin. His

96. Sir Muthuswami Aiyar was the first Indian to be appointed as judge of Madras High Court in 1877. He also acted as Chief Justice of Madras High Court in 1893.

bright clean-shaven face radiated the brightness of the entire Dravidian culture. The court case began. The complainant started reading his appeal. His argument was that his client had signed a blank sheet of paper. The judge laughed aloud. The complaint was refused. The lawyers then rose up.

The garden of the huge mansion of Mr Walnok was not open for the public. People's Park comprising of animals of various types was open for common people. However, I cannot recollect what I had seen there. And there is no record of it whatsoever.

There is a port in the eastern part of the river that encircles the Indian part. A large wall made of artificial stones surrounds the area. There the accumulated water looks like a large pond. All around goods of various sorts were being loaded and unloaded. The large storehouse meant for the sailors of the European ships and the treasury were located nearby. Mr Digby was trying to mount a carriage which was driven by electricity.

Compared to Calcutta and Bombay, the workers of Madras appeared less colourful to us. It is difficult to distinguish whether the men come from Andhra, Dravid or Karnataka. It's only in the women's attire that this distinction can be made. It is only through the spartan dresses of the Nair students that one can identify their place of habitation. They do not have long hair tied in a knot at the top of their heads. They have short hair like us and do not have tuft of hair hanging at the back of their scalps.

A businessman from Srirampur, dealing in silk clothes had once remarked, 'See the women here do not cover their faces with a hood, but the men here are fully covered. Often, they have to cover their heads with frilled cloth. The widows cover their heads. With the demise of their husbands, they have to remove the toe rings, and the sacred thread from their necks. These are then thrown either into water or milk. Other than the sudras, they do not have to shave off their hair. Instead of kumkum they then have to apply ash paste on their foreheads.

Every Thursday they are prohibited from applying oil and turmeric paste. That is their seriousness in observing the social rules. We can learn the art of self-control from them.'

On entering the Kotwal Cheri market we found a temple. Leaves of wood apple tree, chrysanthemums, white and yellow flowers, sweets, and basil leaves were being sold. Different types of oranges, dates, pomegranates, green and red colour ripened plantains, mangoes etc., banana leaves, eggplants, spinach, and various vegetables too were being sold. Here most of the vegetables are produced locally and are available round the year and are not seasonal. At one place fruit juice was being sold and tired businessmen came over for a sip. Fish, dosa (which are generally consumed with sambar and pickles) and many other prepared foods too were being sold. They looked really attractive as they were beautifully displayed for sale. But I do not know how they actually tasted. There were series of light snacks which were quite alluring. Looking at the large shops selling utensils for meals, we entered the courtyard. There again we came across a shop selling various colourful powders like turmeric, frankincense, fuller's earth et al. Outside the courtyard were small shopowners beckoning customers to buy articles like molasses, tamarind, betel nut, chili, groundnut, date etc., items that are essential for domestic use. There was however a separate shop for selling betel leaves, nuts and other ingredients. Can there be a dearth of goods in the capital city?

In order to celebrate the festival of Christmas, sugar candies moulded into the figures of Ganapati and Nataraja were being sold. Hindus however would not eat figures of gods and goddesses. In order to procure a cabbage, I had to visit a market which sold non-vegetarian food. They are not available at Kotwal Cheri. Cabbage is brought here from Bangalore, which is relatively cooler. The orthodox school does not approve of cabbage. They have also decried the use of round potato as foreign, little realizing that most of the flowers, fruits and vegetables sold in the market have foreign origin. They have entered their markets through both Muslim and Christian communities, like a few other food items.

A well-wisher of mine, one day invited us for a meal. I happened to know his father Bhim Shankar Sastri in Calcutta. They had prepared the food in Bengali style and not in their own style, hence, we had no reason to complain. While conversing Annaji remarked, 'I have spent many years in Bengal, but there are not many close associates there who are still in touch with me and enquire about my whereabouts.' People of Madras are hardworking, happy, simple, and satisfied with the present. That is the reason we found them to be poor but extremely cheerful.

Coffee and white cardamom are the items exported from here to different countries. While rice, musk, fan made of yak's tail and bags are imported from other places. Sastriji would carry ghee from Masulipatnam to Calcutta for business.[97] In Guntur, oil is extracted both from coconut and groundnut in large quantities and sent abroad for commercial purposes. The customers, however, are not concerned about the qualitative differences which occur from one place to another. Everything appears rather artificial. There's a kind of sugar produced in Nellikuppam called 'Palmyra' by Parry Company, which in Calcutta is known as Madrasi sugar.

The brahmins here are relatively affluent. They enjoy free land donated by the king and cultivate them with help of other people. That's how they make a living. Their land is known as 'Srotiyandar'. If that is not feasible, they undertake pilgrimages. The Cheri society of Natkot has constructed pilgrim's inns at an interval of hundred miles. There pilgrims can live for three days and avail beds and food. This is how the brahmins undertake pilgrimage twice a year. This serves two-fold purposes, visiting deities, and also spending their time. This is another aspect of the dark side of India.

---

97. The author was in the business of ghee, which his father had started. It is still flourishing after 170 years, headquartered in Kolkata.

The kshatriya practices (warfare) is not to be seen here. They might follow their customs in their personal lives but are not socially very relevant. After accepting the rule of the emperor of Vijayanagar, soldiers and scholars of Andhra, Dravid and Karnataka, have shifted their base to different regions. Caste distinction is not of much consequence in this matter.

Kshatriya

The Kamotis are all Vaishyas. They worship Goddess Kamakshi. But Kamotis are not ready to eat or socialize with men of other regions, even if they belong to the same caste. They have a few secret codes of conduct, which most of them know, hence they behave in that manner. They are prohibited to undertake agriculture or any form of art related works. Business is a must for them. In Sanskrit 'Chet' stands for slave. 'Satti' in Dravidian tongue stands for a rice container. That word has been modified to Chetti and now stands for anything that deals with business. Most of the rich people of this city belong to this community. I have seen many dark-complexioned men wearing white headgears sitting inside carriages and going to offices. There are about three lakh Chettis. The Seths living near the bridge of Natkot, have their hair shaved off. They are barefooted and do not wear any clothes to cover their upper part of the body. Wherever there is business, the Tamil Shaivites are present. They are ready to overcome any and every obstacle. They come and reside in Calcutta to meet the Marwaris, only to take loans. They never run out of money and that is because they transact crores of rupees through hundi. The converted gold is sent to Rangoon. An annual journey to Calcutta is undertaken by the Dravidian Koil made of silver, in the Tamil style. The preparation appears like undertaking a journey to the Parasnath hills. An umbrella, pomp, and accompanying music played aloud are all a part of this annual ritual. It appeared to me as if I were viewing a Chinese festival.

Here the farmers are constantly troubled by both divine interruptions and the king. The land is mountainous, hard, and uncultivable. There is no provision for irrigation other than rainwater. Rain is also sparse due to the mountain ranges. Madras is closer to the equatorial region compared to Calcutta and Bombay. Hence, it ought to be hotter than both the cities. But the presence of the sea acts as a saviour absorbing the hot winds and making it a place of moderate temperature. The highest temperature of Calcutta soars up to 85 and in Mumbai up to 80. But here in Madras the highest temperature is 79. At times however, it soars up to 90. It is difficult to say whether the heat here varies annually or on a monthly basis. Sometimes even in the months of December and January the temperature soars to such an extent, that programmes that are meant to be held in the afternoon are conducted in the morning itself. For the Europeans it is a land of eternal summer. Like Bombay, in Chenapattan, the trade winds blow twice a year.

More than half of the agricultural land is based on tenancy. A quarter of it belongs to the zamindar and just a little bit is gifted. The tax levied on the gifted land is very little. The portion that belongs to the zamindar is levied a tax which is renewed every thirty years. But neither the subject nor the zamindar can claim ownership. The Empress of India levies tax upon the subject, which is renewable every thirty years. And in case of too little rain or too much rain the tax is levied upon half the produce and not based on the area of the land that has been cultivated. If the land is well watered the tax levied is Rs 50 per bigha, and if the land is not well watered the tax levied is Rs 10 per bigha. The tax is levied upon the state of the land at that particular point of time and has to be paid for next thirty years. If the farmer happens to increase the fertility of the soil by personal hard labour, he has to pay a higher tax. This naturally leads to famine. In the last sixty years the state has witnessed famine six times.

Compared to Bengal the tax here is higher. In Madhya

Pradesh it is worse. Hence, famine occurs more frequently in Madhya Pradesh compared to the other parts of the country. Nowhere in Bengal the tax is higher than one-sixth of the produce. In the eastern region it is even less than that. In Madhya Pradesh they have levied useless charges and charge 72 per cent tax. The loans subjects take is the real cause of famine there. Even when there is good harvest, the farmers after paying taxes cannot save anything for themselves. In our scriptures, one-sixth of the earning is earmarked for taxes. If the British Government implements the same rule of taxes as that of Bengal, both Madras and the other states of our country will be benefitted. Previously famines occurred even in Bengal, but after the fixation of the tax rates, famines are not that frequent or that terrible. Here the government had promised not to increase the taxes, but in practice that did not happen.

Dr Buchanan[98] has written, 'According to the subjects, during the rule of Krishna Deva Raya, the king of Vijayanagar, they lived a happy life. Even Tipu Sultan did not flout the rules he had laid out. The rural society used to decide the workings of the people. The taluks were divided into havelis. A tehsildar owned land which paid an annual tax of rupees three thousand, and this is how a taluk was earmarked. A tehsildar had to be a brahmin. Each haveli had an assistant appointed by the king and was known as the amildar. Sikdar was generally a brahmin. He used to appoint a court in the village comprising of four village elders, who solved all land-related problems along with other personal and official problems. Without the approval of the amildar no person could be prosecuted. And the punishment too was light. The chief subject and farmer of a village was a Patel. He was a sudra and also the chief of the village. Right

98. Dr Buchanan was a surgeon, surveyor and botanist who served Bengal Medical Services from 1794 to 1815 and was the head of the Botanical Gardens in Calcutta. His survey work between 1800 and 1814 is one of the most detailed sources of social and cultural history of the early nineteenth century.

from collecting taxes, sorting out the village problems too were his responsibilities. He was however, guided by four village elders. In case a Patel could not sort out a problem, a written petition was sent to the amildar by the brahmin assistant. In case a subject was in financial stress, it was Patel's responsibility to help him through a loan. Other than that he also claimed a part of the agricultural produce. In such a system of hierarchy no one even dreams of misbehaving. These positions were all inherited. If anyone were able to collect more tax, in all likelihood the amildar would replace the existing Patel. The tax that was fixed during the rule of Krishna Deva Raya for non-irrigated land, was continued by the Muslim rulers. It was not raised at all. The subjects could not own the land it is true, but as long he paid his dues and taxes, no one could deprive him of the land he cultivated. If the farmer could not till the land the amildar would help him or relieve him of his farming job. Village servants were of four types. One, those who guarded the agriculture produce. Two, those who supplied water to the lands. Three, those who guarded the fields so that the farmers could not adopt malpractices. Four, the one who controlled everything. They all used to receive their salaries from the haveli.'

Had the British adopted the system of municipalities for the villages, it would have been really beneficial. Previously, the village cooperative used to collect food grains and store it in a place. And when famine struck, these were distributed. Western economics is applicable for affluent countries. A place without monetary resources and no fine arts cannot undertake independent business. Since the network of our railways is widespread, the agricultural products are now being sold at a higher rate and the profit is being spent on luxurious items. When need arises, they do not have either money or food grains left. Even if they have little amount of money, it is not enough to buy back the food grains at the rate it was sold.

During last famine rice was sold at Rs 2 per seer. It is

impossible to spend half anna daily and feed a family. The British government is unable to provide more than one and half anna to people who are there in the relief camps. Out of five crore people twelve and half lakh people die out of starvation. Most of the affluent Bengalis could do nothing other than reading indifferently this sorrowful plight of their own countrymen. Scarcity of food grains was the result of scarcity of monetary resource. Let the Empress of India stand before the Indians with a pleasant face and try to bless them. Let the government reduce the taxes.

I will conclude here with descriptions of Vaikuntha festival of Srirangam. All the deities of the temples of Chennpattan had been taken out of the temple premise the previous day, to visit the city. The procession was headed by a picture followed by musicians playing shehnai and mridangam. They reached a garden of chrysanthemums when the carriers stopped. Beneath the flower decorations, glimpses of ornaments made of precious stones were visible. Temple-dancers wearing saris and yellow-coloured pajamas underneath were singing and dancing. The music was soothing and extremely mellifluous. It sounded almost mournful but nowhere near our Bengali kirtans. Bengali tunes are both mournful and expressive of fear. The temple dancers were singing a soothing tune. Many social reformers are now trying to prevent the temple dancers from participating in any social or religious festivals. But like Maharashtra the Dravidian weavers support this custom of temple dancers. Even in ancient Europe this practice was rampant.

Mr Keshab Chandra Sen had established the Brahmo Samaj in southern India. Members of the Brahmo Samaj were accompanying the musicians with flags, which had Tamil words written upon them. They also had song books with them as they followed the idols from behind. Little boys and youth were singing with tanpura in their hands. At a little distance people were singing, either aloud or in soft tones. There are quite a few traditional followers of the customs of Sri Chaitanya and his disciples. I do not know whether they play the leather covered mridangam while singing bhajans or other devotional songs. Arya Samaj, Ramakrishna community and Radha-Krishna cult seem to satisfy the religious thirst of the local people. Hinduism is a tough nut to crack. If one tries to suppress it, its stature is reduced and if one tries to distort it, it assumes a different form. But both are too tedious to attempt. Since it is a mammoth effort if undertaken, people have allowed it to remain unchanged. Anything that has large volume, needs tremendous effort to change it radically.

Pachai Appa Chetti had donated his entire fortune in 1840 to set up a school. There is a large hall or auditorium in the school where all kinds of meetings are held. At its entrance I saw two oil paintings—one depicting Appa blessing a student by touching him on the head and promising financial assistance for his education. The student is seen expressing his gratitude with a smiling face. Behind both the figures a temple is visible. This shows that his donation for both Kanchi and Chidambaram are also unforgettable. Being informed by *The Hindu*, a English daily, about their seventieth meeting, we decided to return to this place.

Adyar

(Society for Theosophists)

Hindu religion includes the theories of all other religions like Buddhism, Jainism, Sikhism, Brahmo Samaj, Ramakrishna etc. But now the number of theorists have increased manifold. So, all hail the theorists. It helps people to express their own opinions.

In order to preserve the sanctity of history, it is necessary to expose the defects of either a society or a specific person.

The critics are annoyed at this practice. They do not desire to malign anyone, but express their opinions, thinking them to be the only correct alternative. If someone exposes their defects, they are annoyed, yet they remain fixed to their opinions. But if they come across any person who supports them, they are mighty pleased.

Every human being is a philosopher. We only accept what we think is right. We do not accept the basic truth that we may be wrong in our judgements. So, our actions remain committed to what we think are correct actions. All contrary opinions and customs appear extremely annoying to us. The world is full of egoists. Once we form an opinion, we tend to act according to it. We never try to deduce anything even after seeing the result of an action.

Madam Blavatsky was not afraid to manifest her occult powers and she was a good psychoanalyst too.

Dayanand Saraswati rejected idol worship and other Vedic gods, and instead propounded the concept of pure devotion. The English educated people found in him an ideal religious leader. But Hindu society could not get over the practice of caste distinction. And it was for this reason Colonel Olcott and his girlfriend had to adopt Buddhism. They refused to become the followers of Buddhism in public, rather preferred to follow the religion secretly. Human beings are nothing but a collection of different religious thoughts. None of these thoughts are permanent. And human life itself is transient and destructible. If there is no chance of rebirth then why not give way to greed, lust, and other vices. But human personalities are reborn. The karmic cycle does work.

Mr Olcott,[99] before starting the meeting of the society said, 'Due to the inattentiveness of the members, very few people

---

99. Colonel Henry Steel Olcott met Madam Blavatsky in the US and was the Founder-President of The Theosophical Society. In 1882 he bought a beautiful estate in Adyar, near Madras, where the headquarters of the Society was established.

have assembled here today.' One among the organizers started his speech. And this is what he said, 'It doesn't matter that people criticize us. Every year we will show the world what the representatives from different parts of the world have to say. Our Parsi judge has rightly said that by analyzing the theories we have been able to understand our subject better. The moment I reached India, I started corresponding (through letters) with the chairman of the Arya Samaj. But we do not endorse to their primary objective. He wants us to become the disciples of Arya Samaj and start exposing the loopholes of the Parsis and the Buddhists. We are secular. Let the Buddhists send their emissary to Europe to preach their religion. But Hindus will not be able to do that since Hinduism is based on caste distinctions. Yet, both these religions are tied to one another at the core. If one is publicized the other will automatically be known. We have to find a way of getting rid of the Christian missionaries. Both the temples of Tirupati and Bodh Gaya have been Hindu dominions for 750 years. How to restore them?'

When the Colonel is aware that Buddhism and Hinduism are similar at the core, then why was he instigating Dharmapal against the head priest of Bodh Gaya? This is because he wants to establish his supremacy among the Buddhists. But we Hindus also have to ensure that our brothers who visit Gaya for offering their homage to their ancestors, do not defile the idols and deities of other religions.

This meeting appeared to be a secular one, as far religion was concerned. Externally of course. Preaching universal brotherhood, retrieving ancient literatures, practicing the art of sacred and secret knowledge etc., are all fine. But those who consider the words of the disciples of sages like Kuthmi, Lal Singh, as sacred and real, then communalism is bound to creep in among them.

The rekra of Mumbai is known as jhatka here (both are names of carriages). I mounted one and proceeded towards Bengal. Another gentleman boarded the carriage, but he would

By the sea at Madras

not go up to Bengal. He listened to my interest in visiting the theosophical society and said, 'There are no more sages in the society.' Babu Sarat Chandra opines that the sages have fled from the world. Gradually travelling down the serpentine path of the Koyem river we crossed the confluence and reached the island. It was a beautiful place. Surrounded by the blue waves of the sea which flowed towards the river was a hermitage full of trees. The darkness had not yet receded from the trees. The place was ideal for practising mysterious knowledge. Without darkness deep knowledge cannot be pursued. Compared to Bombay, Madras seems more congenial for cultivating this secret knowledge.

I wanted to see everything for myself, so I walked in. The American colonel was celebrating his victory over our countrymen. Everywhere I could see lists of the branches of this secret society, with dates of their establishments. As a part of the room décor there was a figure of the universe, and the names of the sages who had practised this knowledge. The library contained manuscripts from Sinhala and India. There was a list of books, which were for sale.

There were books on theosophy, Buddhism, Hinduism, Zoroastrianism, Kabbalah, Christianity, and magic. There were books on spirits, psychology, oceanology and even the Vedas. Men come here and choose their books.

Other than members of their closed group, no one is allowed to enter the secret room. Inside the room hung pictures of two saints. Here, during a meeting of the society, a letter from one of the sages used to fall upon the forehead of any particular member. The thought and experiences of the Guru used to automatically flow into the consciousness of the disciple. Even in the absence of material presence, psychic power can always work. For instance, a devotee can experience the presence of God in his heart. And the experience is so vivid that the disciple feels it to be materially true. But it is very difficult to sieve out truth from falsehood in these experiences. And many crooks take advantage of such situations. For devotees with blind faith, these are all manifestations of spiritual advancement.

In Shanti Kunj established by Annie Besant, a Shiva temple has been set up by Upendra Babu. On the occasion, the brahmins of Varanasi were handsomely rewarded. It is said that he had once attended a Durga Puja in the house of Mr Mitra. Attired in silken garment, he had sat on a kusha (holy grass) asana (sitting mat) and chanted the tri syllabic Om mantra. In his last years, the Colonel had assumed the sacred thread. Ms Besant, unable to decide whom to support, had gone to Buddhist Sri Lanka and preached Hinduism.

Ms Besant had given her reason for preaching the Vedantic religion. According to her, Vedanta had provided her solutions to some questions for which science had no answer. Astral body, mental body, world of spirit, world of the gods, nirvana, karmic cycle, rebirth, and other terrestrial queries have been convincingly answered in the Vedanta. All of us know that it is impossible to understand theosophy without faith. In Vedanta God is defined as knowledge. And that knowledge is beyond human intellect. All debate ends with that. Science will always remain incomplete. Only faith can answer all questions.

Both Madam and Colonel had presumed that by renouncing atheism they will be looked down upon by the educated people. But there are different forms of atheism. Atheists believe in so many things. They are of the opinion that God is not the creator of the universe. Both Anne and Charles held the same opinion. Likewise, Bradley once wrote, 'I as an atheist believe in another consciousness. This consciousness is worldly consciousness. And it is known only by its attributes. I will believe only in those things which I can understand. The attributes that are conferred upon God is unbelievable. And I don't accept them.' Hence, he was an atheist. Whatever can be seen and experimented upon is bound by natural laws. He was not overwhelmed on seeing the natural phenomenon. He was not elated at the praises showered upon God. And that was because natural law cannot change or vary. Natural laws exist, but how they came into existence, no one can say. And to try to fathom them is a useless pursuit. Bradley admitted to the existence of natural laws. Men who believe in God depend upon Him. So, dependence is there on both sides, and that is what binds both believers and non-believers. Bradley was a person who believed in dependence. Bradley's philosophy however does not refute materialistic religion. In the world both animals and human beings are working towards an indefinite goal. That is the law or fate. Religion is just a part of it. No one has ever been able to circumvent fate. Religion varies from place to place. Whatever is considered to be religious in one place is treated as irreligious at some other place. So, religion too is dependent on place and time. I am a social being, existing everywhere. If I help the spirits, I will be benefitted, and if spirits torment me, I will suffer. The core of religion is based on the above assumption. It is not correct to mislead people through occult powers and force them to practice what is good and avoid what is evil. Superstition will prevent the natural tendencies of human beings. It is beneficial for human beings to believe and love religion. Particularly that religion which believes in humanism. Bradley was a humanist. He was famous for his love for truth. He had sacrificed his life for the benefit of his country and also of India. He wanted to protect those countries who were subjugated and were not free.

It is difficult to find a free thinker and an unbiased speaker now. Murugesh Mudeli's English weekly *Philosophical Questions*, published from Madras preached the ideologies of Bradley and other thinkers like him. In Bengal, Kedar Nath Basu, also tried to do the same. Both materialism and monotheism are based on reasoning and arguments, hence are acceptable. Free social thinkers have tried to put into practice their ideologies and that is what has made them unpopular.

Besant followed the path which people generally preferred. And theism was added as a décor to this secular philosophy. Hence, she did not think it wrong to discuss the state of

Bradley, in his afterlife. Sages do not like to pass opinions about the material world. After the demise of Olcott, it was by universal approval that she became the president of the International Theosophical Society. And ignoring the advice of the other members of the society she included a person as a member just because she was close to her. She was educated and well conversant with the workings of the human mind. She was well aware of human psychology. If you lose your identity, nothing remains. This universe is nothing but a collection of human sensory perceptions. Both joy and sorrow are elements which human beings experience within themselves. They are not external objects. I exist in the entire universe. That is what Miss Edgar and others had accepted and expressed through their theosophical society. They accepted those material objects which they thought should not be renounced and had independently arrived at the above conclusion. Endorsing their views, Roy Ishwari Prasad allowed the branch of the society of Varanasi to work from his residence. Besant had to balance everything and continue her works. She could not depend much upon Hinduism. It had become imperative by then to proclaim that Christ had manifested himself in the little boy Krishnamurti.

The Theosophical Society was helping Indian youths to inculcate within themselves the spirit of nationalism. Ms Besant has been a massive help to our country by setting up affordable educational institutions here. And for all these reasons she still deserves our gratitude and our reverence. Most of the religions have similar approaches. It is only through hostility that a society or a nation is harmed. Theosophy supports all human beings irrespective of their religions. This approach is indeed beneficial for us.

According to the members, it is not desirable for students to be involved in politics. It is also not good to play the role of judge while pursuing one's studies. Practice of both religion and politics should come after some knowledge in those fields.

There is no harm in following the footsteps of parents or other elders. One's faith depends on the place he is nurtured in, irrespective of his or her religious background

There are no enemies in theosophy. All are considered to be friends. Yet, why did the leaders renounce Christianity? Maybe people would not have sympathy for them had they not renounced Christianity.

A few subjects can be better understood in the light of theosophy. Ether is universally present. People residing in distant places can be unified as they are within the ether. A vibration produced in one person's brain can impact another person's thought process. But how is it possible to experience the feelings of another person? Ms Besant had explained it to me in the following manner—transmission of thought or feeling is done not through any material medium, but through the vibrations transmitted through ether.

To me Arya Samaj would be more beneficial than Theosophical Society. They stressed the age-old values and traditions. They were trying to purify both Christianity and Islam. According to Dayanand, violence is hatred, so no animal sacrifice. Non-vegetarians have accepted this argument while the vegetarians have remained alienated from them. While entering the Gurukul, a student had to accept the sacred thread, irrespective of his caste. A person one day had asked Dayanand, whose lord, are you? He had replied, 'I am the lord of my senses.' I thought he was referring to his sexual urges. But I had not grasped the true meaning. At another time he had advised, 'Our minds do become perturbed because of our sensory experiences, but we control these urges.'

Our age old tradition compels us to believe in Hindu religion. But when we come into contact with people of other religions, then we easily eat those food which Hindu religion prohibits. Ramakrishna community draws our attention to this point. Paramahansa (Ramakrishna) himself was illiterate, but he would talk of spiritual experiences in such lucid and colloquial terms. Since his approach was coupled with Bhakti yoga, common people presumed it to be a state of ecstasy. Catalepsy is a disease of the brain, and the symptoms are—the body remains immobile during the attack and one forgets one's own identity. Neither the pulse nor respiration stops, both continue to function as before. This disease is normally not harmful. But it generates anxiety. Whenever he used to be surcharged with bhakti, Ramakrishna used to experience that state. Maybe he was dancing to the tune of a bhajan, suddenly he would experience the state of ecstasy. He would continue to remain standing with his hands held upwards. He would lose external senses, yet would not fall. The viewers would marvel at the sight. This was the cause of his presumed greatness.

Vivekananda had said in his speech in America that human being is God's avatar. The entire audience was thunderstruck. The sannyasins of this organization have been oriented by Swamiji to become workers. They do not approve of the Theosophical Society. Don't hate the sinner, show your affection for him. Only then can he rectify himself. Everyone is part of God, no one is different. So, by relieving others of their pains, you are actually serving God. This is the real analysis of one's true identity. To unify knowledge, karma and bhakti and work unitedly is really praiseworthy. Working for others will lead you to the path of renunciation.

According to the Satsang association, it is not imperative to accept the Vedas. Only thing that one must unconditionally accept is the Guru and his words.

This school believes in worshipping sound as Brahma. Sit on a mat and undertake the Muktasana yogic posture. Close the nose on the left side and hear the sound through the right ear. Keep your mouth, nose and also your other ear shut. The sound that is audible in the right ear should be imagined to be the sound of the waves, thunder, conch shell, bell, and flute, which Lord Krishna used to play to inform Sri Radha of his presence. Concentrate deeply on that sound. One who develops a deep attachment for this kind of sound will never be tempted back to a materialistic life. He will be metamorphosed from within and ultimately surrender himself to this divine sound. Finally, no sound will be audible to him. It will be a world of total silence, the silence of Brahma. At one point of time, he will be able to sit inertly like a corpse. That is the ultimate state of achievement for a Hatha yogi. And that is his state of liberation.

Theosophy, however, does not instruct to follow Hatha Yoga. Various yogic mudras often adversely affect the human body. Raja Yoga helps to control the mind. And for Raja Yoga pranayama is not required. Some however claim that without Hatha Yoga, Raja Yoga cannot be practiced successfully. Yoga is divided into two categories—abhav yoga (practicing non-existence) and maha yoga (greater yoga). When one is able to conceptualize himself without attributes it is abhav yoga. And when one conceptualizes himself to be in unison with the Brahma, that state is known as maha yoga. For both of them withdrawal of physical senses is not required. In fact, activities of the senses often assist in reaching the goal.

According to the theosophists this material body through spiritual transformations can attain the ultimate knowledge. The transformations occur in the following stages: first is the material body or sthula sarira, then follows the subtle body or sukshma sarira which according to the Upanishads comprises of the following: a) Pranamaya kosha (vital breath or energy) b) Manomoya kosha (mind) c) Vijnanamaya kosha (intellect). Finally, the human soul reaches the Karana sarira which is the causal body bringing about the anandamaya kosha or bliss. Once the soul reaches the final stage it becomes aware of the ultimate knowledge and enjoys a state of eternal bliss. It is a state which cannot be defined. And a yogi reaching that stage is not attracted to any activities of the material world. He is unable to think anything on his own. Only his mind keeps enjoying the divine bliss. To the theosophists, that is more real than the state of physical awakening. His soul keeps working in the astral state (suksma sarira). It's only the elevated souls who have experienced the last stage that are a part of the closed group of the society and will be able to understand these different stages of the soul. One who was a member of the said group told me once, that it was not possible to explain everything without experiencing it. The middle order members were instructed by Besant through letters. One member had once asked, 'I see wild animals while I try to meditate. What is the remedy?' In primary section of the society, only the theory of the society is taught.

We treat the views of Brahma philosophy as whirlwind. Just as few opposite flowing winds gather together to form a whirlwind, and when it lands at a water surface a water pillar is formed, similar is the case with the Brahmo Samaj. The founders of Brahmo Samaj had semantically combined various thoughts to form a water pillar for us. However, their members were limited in number. A stormy wind sweeps off all the impurities of the world, similarly Brahmo Samaj had wiped out many impurities of Hindu religion. So, we are indebted to them. They are worshippers of truth and are well known for their courage. Even if heaven splits apart, they will stick to their principles and build a world of justice. The orthodox people ought to learn a lot from the members of Brahmo Samaj. In places however, Brahmo Samaj has split apart due to the uprise of the Sanatana Dharma. This has encouraged the rise of the Theosophical Society.

There had been social uprise (at that point of time) which led to the formation of many religious communities like Theosophical Society, the Arya Sama, Ramakrishna and Radhaswami. They all are relevant in the present times. A philosophy which is beneficial for the human race can be termed as the true religion for man. And that is the boundary line of Hinduism.

Chennapattanam

(Conclusion)

For several nights we spent a couple of hours watching plays. A team of Tamil artists had come to Mysore to perform. Their plays following the traditional format, had preludes, nandi and other such elements. Accordingly, the stage too was set up in the traditional style. *Chandi Kaushik* was the play that was performed with a Persian backdrop. It was musical play, and the music was heavenly without any melodic variation. Subba Rao Acharya's acting coupled with his flute recital was mesmerizing. The instrument by itself was interesting—it had two windpipes out of which only one was used to blow in the air. However, the stage seemed inferior compared to the European stage we find in Bengal. Aesthetically it was hardly impressive. Naturally we were not visually much enlightened. We didn't know the language, and except our auditory senses nothing much helped us to understand the play. In most cases these stages are built for commercial purposes and it has little to do with arts or human emotions. The stage to an extent influences the viewers emotionally. Most of the viewers empathize with the characters that are being played on stage.

In England a sailor had once tried to thrash a rogue who was insulting an actress. Drama as a form can be used for propagating the lessons of religion and ethics. There are three hundred theaters in London itself. And in small towns of England, there are three or four theaters. Poor English kids, instead of buying chocolates save their pennies to buy tickets to see plays.

It was still dark, and we hadn't left our beds. We could hear muffled sounds from the streets. No one was shouting. It sounded like the voice of female ghosts. It was barely audible. Here during Sankranti women get up in the wee hours of the morning and place small heaps of cow dung at the entrance of their homes. On the heaps are stuck a banana stalk. People buy those stalks to decorate their homes.

Here they calculate months according to the new moons but even Sankranti is observed. They follow the fortnightly sequences and perform their rituals accordingly. Their year begins in the month of Chaitra and their astrological calculations are based on the equinoxes. The cycle of a year is completed accordingly. They have distinct names for each year. This year is known Nandan.

They have an astrological centre in Madras. Astrologers from the entire country can assemble there and after deciding upon the location of the stars in the stellar system fix up the yearly almanac. To verify their data they do not need to consult the almanac followed by the sailors.

Almanacs are necessary in our lives for the following reasons—for maintaining our health, utilizing our time fruitfully, celebrating the birthdays of mythical persons, astrological calculations, and for ascertaining the exact dates for different rituals and pujas. All the gods we worship belong to the stellar system. Initially in the Vedas, gods were the stars in the stellar constitution. Gradually they were transformed into brahmins. And by the time they reached the Puranas they were attributed human qualities. It was after this change that gods were imagined to be like human beings. The question arises: why didn't they have children? The pole star is a prince. Sky is the galaxy and on earth flows River Ganga. On the northern side of the sun is the Devalok or abode of the gods. On the southern side lies the Pitralok, or abode of our ancestors. Agastya, the star of the galaxy, is considered to be a boat which carries human souls across the river Baitarini to reach paradise. The two stars of Punarvasu nakshatra[100], have been thought of as Yama and his sister. Orion has been visualized as Prajapati or Brahma.

---

100. The 7th nakshatra of the zodiac belt and it lies majorly in the sign of Gemini and partly in the sign of Cancer. The ruling deity of this nakshatra is Aditi, who is goddess of wealth and abundance.

Adra nakshatra is Rudra, and Sun is described as Vishnu. Eight thousand years before the birth of Christ, the Aryans while living in the polar region of eternal autumn had experienced six months cycle of day and night, and accordingly had sung the praise of gods in those terms. We are still continuing the tradition in our almanacs. So, to commit an error in the calculations of the almanacs will be very unfortunate.

In order to see horse racing and folk plays we proceeded forward. Just outside the city was a mountain, and there lay the racing field. Here is the country house of the ruler of Madras. After crossing many lanes and alleys we finally crossed Marmelong bridge. The racing field was quarter of a mile. Among the viewers were the kings of Vijayanagar and Ramnad, Gajapati and Bhashkar. All the horses carried their identities—names and numbers written on a card which hung round their necks. Four prizes were to be given out. The prize money for each was Rs 1000. People here, like their counterparts in Calcutta, were ready to gamble away their money on the racing horses. This tendency ultimately led to many vices.

It was time for us to return. Since the royalties were leaving the racing ground, the common people too started leaving. Within several minutes the place became relatively empty. A horse rider was seen galloping away with his long hair hidden under a round hat. Our jhatka would not move fast. We who were not afraid of the royalty, did not mind moving slowly. This would in fact give us time to observe everything minutely. The driver driving the brougham and his assistant standing at the back shouted 'hoy' to us. The drivers of brougham in Calcutta speak extremely harshly. When the brougham moved to the left the people who were walking, shifted to the right. This was because the hoofs of the horses aroused such quantities of dust that it was difficult for people to breathe.

For people interested in distilled spirit, all provisions were ready at hand. British people have promoted consumption of alcohol. Like our ancient sages they used to celebrate their festivals by drinking heavily. However, we have now realized the evil effects of alcohol and have stopped that practice in our daily lives.

Nungambakkan Lake was a huge water body. We bypassed it to visit a flower exhibition. Nearby was the Saidapet Agricultural School on the banks of the river. Half of the agricultural products of the state is acquired by the king. Naturally to increase the production of medicinal plants the king had set up this agriculture school where his employees would study and provide guidance to the farmers. But the farmers here consider it blasphemous to change the age-old agricultural appliances. They are also not conversant with the efficacy of using modern fertilizers to enhance production.

We left behind the sleeping outskirts and reached the busy city. Our abode was at Sowcarpet, and we were almost there. We had not seen the king Sir Shivali Ramaswami Mudeli. We had only seen the city lamps and the water tank where his name was written. Even though he had donated lakhs of rupees for different welfare schemes and built guest houses, the local people hardly took note of them. They deliberately ignored him. This was however due to sheer jealousy. Ramaswami was the agent of Arbuthnot. In his effort to become rich he had failed thrice to carry on any profitable business. At present he is employed in the company.

Near the railway waiting room Lord Wenlock had inaugurated a community kitchen. The wife of the Governor had planted a sapling with her own hands. The king had agreed to pay the amount needed to feed two hundred poor persons daily. Furthermore, he promised to repay the amount spent for setting up the kitchen. Within a span of two years, the money would be deposited to the treasury of the Empress of India, the king had assured. Recently he deposited Rs 20,000. The interest that will be generated on this amount will be used to meet the daily expenses. After two years, he would be given the charge of running the kitchen. The kitchen itself is a good and ornamental decoration for the city. The first room is reserved for the Mudeli, Naidu and Pillais. The second room is reserved for the brahmin cooks. The third room is open for all brahmins. The fourth room is reserved for the Marwaris and the Chettis. The last two rooms on the eastern side, are for the Muslims and Christians. The seventh room is reserved for the kinsmen or inheritors of the king. No Bengali gentleman could build such a community kitchen.

While ambling about we came across a marriage party returning home with the bride. They were accompanied by men carrying the gifts the groom had received from his in-laws. This practice to an extent has been able to remove the evil practice of child marriage.

There is no husking pedal here. In its place they use mortar for grinding. Suddenly we heard a musical sound and were wondering about its source. Just then we saw a corpse was being carried. Since the face of the corpse was uncovered, we knew it to be a woman. Her lips were crimson in colour and on her forehead was a kumkum bindi. She belonged to the Jangam community. Food was served in earthen vessels and kept near the grave with a belief that the spirit would come to eat it.

Near the army barrack of Pallavaram, we saw the graves of the royal families of the Pallava dynasty. The corpse of the males was placed in sitting postures while those of females were laid flat. A little above the ground was a stone slab which contained five-lined poetic epitaphs. The design reminded us of the ancient architecture of a house. When did this royal family extend their kingdom from Orissa to the mouth of River Pinakini. Here people of various religions lived peacefully—Buddhist monks, brahmins and men of other religions. The king was influenced both by the Buddhists and brahmins alike. In 11th century, AD, the Cholas drove off the Pallavas from Kanchi. The last leader of the Pallava dynasty was Aniruddha Ther who wrote many books in Pali and Sanskrit. Ther stands for a caste in Bengal. For me Ther is actually Thiyar. At present they enjoy a very low status in the society. And they have no access to education also.

In Buddhism a socially inferior person could attain a respectable position, hence the socially inferior people appreciated Buddhism. Three boxes have been found, which contain stories narrated by Lord Buddha. In one of the stories, we are told Lord Buddha had stated, 'I do not consider a person to be brahmin just by his birth. If he is full of all vices like anger, even if he calls himself a brahmin he will not be one. A person pure at heart, innocent and dispassionate is a true brahmin.' (Dhammapada)

A true friend is never afar. Even though the place where we had put up in Chenapattan, was far away from the sea, yet we were constantly allured by it. We loved watching the sea everyday encroaching the shore. We never grew tired of watching the sky. The lighthouse seemed to us the brightest lamp on earth. Situated on top of twenty-one stairs, it is a lamp made of hundred metals. Nine sides of it are transparent, and three sides opaque. The blinding light shines for a moment and then again withdraws into darkness.

Muslim boatmen known as labboy fearlessly row their wooden rafts which are called masula. Their parentage is native mother and either Persian or Arabian sailors. The women of this community wear red saris designed with yellow colour and white-coloured, thin but large scarves. The American preachers finally set up schools for these marginalized Muslim women. The Muslims talk in Hindi, but their Hindi is very distorted.

Recently, the king of Vijayanagar built a townhall in Varanasi. So, it is hardly surprising that he will build a palace for common people here as well. He personally had laid its foundation stone. The artistry of the first floor is worth enjoying. In Mylapore the king resides in the Admiralty building. Old Rai Bahadur Raghunath Rao, the Dewan from Calcutta has been appointed a member of the municipality here. Ranganatham Mudeli has been appointed the sheriff of the city.

From 8th century onwards Buddhism reached Japan from India and became deep rooted. It did not remain a mere religion, but permeated into the national culture, art, literature and even politics. Then in 16th century when the Christian missionaries started preaching, they reached Japan too. They acted as eye openers for the Japanese population. The result was revolution. For the last twenty-three years, the emperor has been ruling Japan and helping the nation to progress. The emperor belongs to the ancient royal family.

Since our king is an outsider, he can retain his secular approach. This approach of the English king in the long run will help us to enhance our work efficiency at the national level and alter our previous attitudes. We will also reach a state of maturity. New India has retained the essence of our ancient religion but has modified itself to suit the contemporary times. Both in art and literature we see the influence of Western culture. Even in politics Western influence is perceptible. Even though our interests do not match with that of England, yet there is a similarity at the core. Progress of one will also lead the other to the path of progress. Most people do not realize this. Consequently, we as a nation are liable to suffer. Hindus are very strong mentally. Due to various factors like increasing population, excess expenditure etc., our national psyche is now highly inflammable. Previously Hindus were sympathetic towards the Christians and so were the Christians. But now they are trying hard to increase the foothold of their religion.

The non-brahmins have sent a petition to Lord Wenlock that the brahmins have monopolized various royal services and this is very unfair. There is a committee at the national level, which is known as the Mahasamiti, (Great Committee) whose members are trying to protect the interests of the brahmins.

The government is trying to educate the Pariya community. And according to Dewan Bahadur Srinivas Iyengar if the entire community of Pariya is converted into Christianity their condition will improve rapidly. *The Hindu* has suggested the conversion of all the lower caste people of the society into Christianity. To discuss the issue a large meeting is to be held soon. One social worker however has remarked, 'Their backward state is due to their poor economic condition. After converting them, will the Christians give them all their own wealth?' During the rule of Emperor Aurangzeb all the weavers of Varanasi became Muslims. But their poverty was never alleviated. The Christians too have class distinctions which are different from ours. Aristocrats do not socialize with non-aristocrats, neither do they allow their children to marry anyone who does not belong to their class.

At present the upper caste Hindus are interested in rectifying the evils inherent in their society. And for the purpose they have sought the advice of Jagat Guru of Sringeri Math. Here the Maharashtrian brahmins are permitting their wards to marry Karnataka brahmins. What is the harm in allowing marriage between different castes, different states, and different people as such?

If you examine Vidyasagar carefully you will realize that his part of the brain which contained love and affection for others was larger in size, compared to other human beings. Practice helps man to achieve many things, it is true. However, it is his brain that makes him good or bad. People might be angry with him for that. It is for this reason Vidyasagar was also known as the Sea of Kindness. He used to suffer when he saw women suffering. He wrote boldly, a father can get his widowed daughter remarried. And for that matter the widow has to be her own guardian. Let the practice of bequeathing one's daughter end. Unlike land or other fixed assets, woman is not a commodity of a man. However, for an abstainer like Vidyasagar, marriage was not an important happening in one's life. People used to marvel at his self-control. The marriage negotiators of Bellal community first visit the bride's home and family to enquire about her whereabouts. Most marriages are held during the day. Only after the marriage date is finalized, they buy turmeric. Then on an auspicious date they order the ornaments and other accessories. The mandap has a rectangular podium in the middle and this is mandatory. It is known as 'manovari'. Branches of wild fig tree is fixed on the north-western side of the podium. The podium is covered at the top. Betel nut is collected from the temples of Shiva and Vishnu for distributing among their kinsmen. The bride's family brings home the groom for marriage. Then when the groom arrives, married women perform camphor aarti before him and takes him inside the house. Once inside he is made to sit upon a bed. Next the groom is offered a refreshment of banana and milk. After that he proceeds towards the mandap and sits on the podium facing eastward. There he inserts a branch of a mango tree which is smeared with turmeric paste. After completing the task, he again enters the bride's house for a shave and bath. The barber before shaving the groom offers banana and coconut to Lord Pillai. The bride on the other hand is accompanied by many other ladies for completing her premarital bath in a pond or lake.

The priest sits on one side of the 'manovari'. A lamp is lit. An idol of Lord Pillai is created out of cowdung, who is then offered rice, banana, and coconut. In the meantime, the maternal uncles are gifted their presents. Then after receiving the permission of the brahmin, the fully dressed groom comes out and sits upon the podium. Next the bride is brought to the mandap. Her friends deck her up with auspicious garments, flowers, and ornaments. She then goes to the kitchen and on a newly bought pitcher draws three lines with turmeric paste and places three betel leaves upon them. A swastika is drawn at the edge of the pitcher with vermilion. The pitcher is then filled with water and placed upon an oven. The girl walks out with her entourage. The couple interacts with the guests who are present and seeks their blessings. Either their Guru or the priest utters mantras for purifying the neckpiece (mangalsutra) that is required for the 'taali' ceremony. All those who are present bless the couple. The barber blows the conch shell and musicians start playing the drums. The brahmin offers the purified neckpiece to the groom. This he slowly puts round the neck of the bride. It is up to the groom's sister to tighten the neckpiece. She takes the flower garland from her brother's neck and puts it around the bride's neck. Then the couple exchange the flower garlands with one another. That concludes the marriage. The priest puts two turmeric smeared iron bangles on the wrists of the bride and the groom. The bride's father addresses the groom's father and says, 'I have given my daughter in marriage to your son.' The couple goes round the podium hand in hand three times. It is only after a star is visible in the sky that they are allowed to walk into the house. The guests are then treated to a marriage feast.

As in Bengal turmeric occupies an important place in Dravidian marriages. The iron bangle is a must for both the bride and the groom.

The astrological signs that are considered for marriage are totally unscientific. Whatever one learns and believes from childhood is impossible to forget or override. The world is controlled by the stellar system and human fate depends on the workings of the material world. But things do happen which cannot be explained by the activities of the material world alone. So, a different kind of astrological calculation is required to explain the inexplicable. Till date no such calculation has been possible.

Among the Tamil sudras, Bellals are considered the highest. Their total population is 25 lakhs and are divided into four categories. Their surnames are Pillai, Naidu and Mudeli. Professionally they are involved in agriculture, commerce and academics. Pallava, Chola, Pandya and Kangu are the four different categories of Bellal community. And this division is based on the regions they come from. During Kangu and Bellal marriages the ascetic Pandarangs or their disciples are employed to perform the marriage ceremony. No brahmin is required to conduct the marriage. Even for conducting the funeral rites, Pandarangs are employed by all castes of people. At that time however, the chief priest or Upadhyay wears the sacred thread. Consuming alcohol is strictly prohibited among them. And if instructed they have to renounce non-vegetarian foods as well. They are not allowed to consume rice and food served by any other castes, except the brahmins. Different castes, however, have different rules regarding food consumptions. But in marriage these laxities are not allowed. People of lower castes often try to upgrade themselves to become Bellals. The Malayali Nair is of that category. The Nayaks of Madurai's royal family are actually Nair.

Hindu religion is constrained by rites and rituals. The concept of good and bad deeds keeps varying regionally. At present the caste system is not within the purview of the English king. Madras is more orthodox in this respect. A brahmin becomes impure by even glancing at a person who eats meat. He is not even allowed to touch a person who eats non-vegetarian food. Like the brahmins of Bengal, here people of all other castes avoid eating certain non-vegetarian items, drink prohibited drinks or allow their widows to remarry.

There is a dearth of Ayurvedic treatment in Chenapattan. But it is expected that the method which has been so popular in Bengal will soon be adopted here as well. At present allopathic treatment is at its infancy. The allopathic doctors have just managed to discover the roles played by bacteria and other natural sickness causing agents. It is just like the recent discovery that sun vaporizes the water from earth and sends it back in the form of rain. The vaporized water is invisible like the bacteria and others microscopic creatures but becomes visible when they accumulate in the form of dark clouds. Similarly, these microscopic agents are invisible to human eye but become palpable when a person falls sick.

Finally, we visited the art gallery. At first, we saw a statue of Buddha and then the Tanjore wood craft of Maharashtrian courtroom and a temple. We also saw the old weapons. There were brass utensils engraved with silver and copper filigree works. They were exquisite pieces. We wanted to buy a few things from there. There were small artistic pieces displayed in glass cases which shone brightly in the gallery. In the dark section of the gallery, we saw woods required for yajna and also the paintings of idols of second century. Looking at them we felt we had walked few centuries ahead of our times.

It is good they have not displayed the valuable minerals and diamonds of Godavari, the silver of Madurai and the iron of Raipur. Instead of increasing the greed of foreign merchants, it is better to hide our national wealth.

The Sea

At the end of the day, we bid farewell to Chenapattan and proceeded towards the dock, with an intention to continue our journey back home. The waiting ship was belching out huge amounts of smoke as if expressing its power. In the ship there were hawkers selling peacock tail fans, embroidered silken clothes, long necklaces of rudraksha and toys. There was a magician too. Most of the people from Madras had come to see the ship. The Europeans who had not disembarked could well see and understand the psyche of our people.

The first-class cabin was full of household articles for sale. And all of them were for Rs 75. Upstairs there were rooms for common people. The base of the ship was engraved. There was a huge carpet laid out at the entrance hall, which had beautiful floral designs upon it. Several chairs and reading tables were placed upon it. On one side of it stood a grand piano. Next to the hall were the quarters of the senior crew of the ship and also a chart room. Above these rooms was the captain's cabin. The ship had come from Liverpool.

There were hundred crew members on board. The attendants were all Muslims from Bengal and Bihar. The captain declared that the ship would sail at five in the evening. The entire ship was four-storied and full of cargo. So, by the time the entire cargo was dispatched to the port it was well past seven p.m. The ship had become lighter. Because of the tidal movements, initially the ship was oscillating a bit and then it started moving forward. At the port we could see the red headgears of the Tamil luggage carriers. Gradually the Cholam shore vanished from our vision.

The chief attendant had taken me to a cabin which had a mirror, a tap, a washbasin, bed, and electric lamp. Once I put on the switch, the cabin was flooded with light. There was a life jacket hanging on the wall. If needed the bed would prove helpful for floating in the water. It was four days of sailing and

I tasted lovely sweet, thick milk along with seasickness.

In the morning, clutching the brass railings of the ship I went up. My first journey across the country had begun with a sea voyage to Puri. Now, the conclusion too involved another sea voyage. I was reminded of my previous experiences. A vast expanse of water lay before me, but I was not able to see much ahead. The horizon and the merging point of the sky and the sea were only visible. The wonderful interplay of colours of the clouds were engrossing. The depth of the water was nowhere more than four and half miles.

According to geologists, centuries ago large glaciers of the north pole had reached the Shivalik range. Otherwise, why are ancient fossils of sea creatures found there? Later the entire region comprising of lowlands, valleys and other higher regions were submerged into the sea and had disappeared. But those places had been lying there, unchanged. Gradually with the receding sea water they have come to surface. And now people are predicting that even the land is undergoing certain changes. Some of them are disappearing into the sea while some are raising up their heads above the sea. Bengal however is gradually sinking. The shore of Madras is rising. That sea never crosses its limits even though the river waters keep falling into it. The excess water is converted into water vapour and the balance of the sea is retained thereby.

Our village-like ship was gradually sailing all alone in the sea. The white foams of the blue water were giving rise to many illusory images. Each wave that was approaching us appeared different from the previous one. The more I looked the newer they appeared. Here were waves full of foams. While the very next moment there came waves, which had no trace of foam. Where do they (the foams) disappear? Here the water was deeper than the water near the shore. And the colour too was deeper. Due to interplay of light and shade the colour kept varying. Just as salt and the presence of insects changes the colour of the river water, similarly the presence of sea animals and salinity kept changing the colour of the sea.

An old man was sitting near me. His name was Harichand Chintaman. He was returning from London. He teaches Marathi and Gujrati in Indian Institute. A Maharashtrian lady asked me, 'Are the Bengali ladies still prevented from coming out in the open?' She was an adolescent girl, and her name was Jhuntha Bai. She was very fluent in English and was excellent in conversation. She was spending her time reading a new novel. Her father was wearing a Turkish headgear, her mother was clad in sari, and she was wearing a gown. So, it was combination of three countries within one family.

In the evening when I was busy glancing at a blue-eyed beauty, a fish suddenly dashed upon the deck of our ship. Its color was that of topshe[101] fish but its shape resembled a 'Bata'[102] fish. It tried to escape but landed in the hands of a bigger enemy. Since it was more used to flying and swimming, all its efforts to escape proved futile. Non-vegetarians believe that fish are created for their consumptions.

The sharks look like fishes. They move with as much speed as that of a ship. Swordfishes are dangerous, as their sword-like mouths can perforate the bottom of a ship. Carnivorous fishes have this dangerous quality. The body goes limp if one touches a torpedo fish. They can transmit electrical shocks. There is a type of fish whose head resembles a frog, and the rest of its body looks like a monkey. The scales of some fish are ground into powders and artificial pearls are made from these powders. Both male and female gold and silver fishes are to be found. Star fish have a smooth body and are without scales. The oysters which carry pearls inside them turn unconscious when they come into contact with the secretion of a starfish.

Other than fish there are thousands of sea animals, which bear marked resemblance to land animals. And they are named accordingly. The animals which resemble horses are known as

101. Bengali name of typical type of fish, which is soft and practically boneless.

102. Another name of a different type of fish

seahorses. Fish which have tusks like elephants are known as sea elephants. Crocodiles are not found here. They rarely visit the Indian Ocean.

Different gods and Yakshas live in the sea. Shaligram Shila that is worshipped as Lord Narayan, is basically the fossil of ammonite shells. It is composed of many cells. It is believed that various gods and goddesses live in each of these cells.

Fish which have heads resembling human beings are six feet long. The upper part of its body resembles a monkey while the lower part is that of a fish. Red Sea is supposed to be its favourite hunting ground. They cannot be trapped easily as they are able to remove the nets with their hands. It is reported that once at night at the confluence of Bay of Bengal one such creature was spotted. It was busy catching fish with its hand and eating them at the seashore. The sound it was creating drew the attention of the people who were passing in a boat nearby. To them it appeared like someone conversing. They thought it was a sea-god.

There is another fish which has two hands and two ears. It uses one of its ears like a harpoon. The way it uses its two limbs to swim, it looks like a boat sailing with its sail raised high. Maybe it is from these fish that men have learnt the art of sailing. The tail of the fish looks like the nozzle of a boat.

While going out of my cabin I met the captain of the ship and wished him 'good morning'. For passing on various information to the passengers, a notice board has been hung at the top of the staircase. On it was written, 'Since yesterday afternoon the ship has sailed a distance of 310 miles.' In all we will have to travel a distance of 500 miles.

Every day with help of the crescent-shaped sextant, the latitude and longitude of the ship are detected. Thereafter looking into the geographical map, the crews decide how far north or how far south they were to travel. The leading is used to measure the depth of the water level and that in a way help them to access the distance they can travel in an hour.

The sun was gradually sinking into the sea. It seemed to

have cooled down a bit after coming in contact with the water. It was not difficult now to look at him. But why was he in such a hurry? Do wait for some time. Let us look at you to our heart's content. No wonder the sages have composed beautiful lines in your praise.

At night a pilot came from the Hooghly river to take charge of the ship. Right now, the ship is immobile. An employee from the tax department came over to the ship on a boat. He wanted to find out whether anyone among us was carrying any arms. The captain, who so long was steering the ship so well had now to take the help of another person.

At times, submerged hills raise their heads and put ships into grave trouble. Those sailors are worthy of their jobs who can carefully navigate their ships from these terrible dangers. After some time, the colour of the water changed completely. It had turned muddy due to silt deposits. A buoy was floated in the water for us to climb down. A red-coloured small ship awaited us at the port of Calcutta. On the eastern side we saw two ships waiting to set sail.

Now I started feeling cold. In southern India we did not need to take out our warm clothes. On the left we could see the land. This is the confluence of Gangasagar—the land of Kapil Muni. He had propounded the theories of modern logic; he was also the founder of Tantra. No wonder he is considered to be the confluence of the Vaishnavas and the Nayikas. This is the right place for the liberation of our ancestors. The place which was termed as Chatak by the sages of *Rig Veda* is actually Bengal, the true land of the Aryans. Here instead of muscle power intellect rules. It is here that Jagadish Chandra Bose had discovered that the so-called inanimate things too have life. And discovered the wireless telegraph, much before Marconi had done.

Today is Makar Sankranti. But there was nobody around for a holy dip. This is a canal which had been dug out later. This is not the Bhagirathi. For a holy dip in the Ganga, it is necessary to go to Calcutta. After many days it was sheer bliss to be back in my motherland.